THE LANGUAGE
OF ARGUMENT

The ideal American citizen?

It's hard to be a good citizen without good information. Without it, we all might as well be sheep.

Yet we're routinely denied information. Crucial information.

We aren't told about risks to our health. People with ideas our government doesn't like are turned away at the border. Federal employees are muzzled, for life.

As we have since 1980, we're fighting back. We're People For the American Way, the 250,000 member constitutional liberties organization.

We don't want the government deciding what we should hear, see, read or think. That's censorship.

We want Americans to be as informed as possible. That's why we prepared a special publication called *Government Secrecy*. It's free.

It's important. It's available only through People For the American Way.

Don't be sheepish. Write today.

Dear People For:

Please send me your complimentary publication, *Government Secrecy*.

☐ Enclosed is a contribution of $ _____ to support your work.

Name (please print)

Address

City _____ State _____ Zip

Clip and return to: People For the American Way Action Fund 1424 16th St. N.W., Washington, DC 20036

///⭐ People For The American Way

What we don't know can hurt us.

THE LANGUAGE

OF ARGUMENT **Sixth Edition**

DANIEL McDONALD   University of South Alabama

HARPER & ROW, PUBLISHERS, New York
Cambridge, Philadelphia, San Francisco,
London, Mexico City, São Paulo, Singapore, Sydney

Sponsoring Editor: Lucy Rosendahl
Project Editor: Vivian Koenig
Text Design: Grafica
Cover Design: A Good Thing Inc.
Production Manager: Jeanie Berke
Production Assistant: Paula Roppolo
Compositor: ComCom Division of Haddon Craftsmen, Inc.
Printer and Binder: R. R. Donnelley & Sons Co.
Cover Printer: NEBC

The Language of Argument, *Sixth Edition*

Library of Congress Cataloging-in-Publication Data

McDonald, Daniel Lamont.
  The language of argument / Daniel McDonald.—6th ed.
    p. cm.
  Includes index.
  ISBN 0-06-044352-9
  1. College readers. 2. Persuasion (Rhetoric) 3. English
language—Rhetoric. I. Title.
PE1417.M43 1989   88-22812
808'.0427—dc19   CIP

88 89 90 91 9 8 7 6 5 4 3 2 1

For Mike and Nancy Hanna

CONTENTS

Frontispiece: "The Ideal American Citizen?"   ii
Subjects Treated in This Book   xvii
Preface   xxiii

PART ONE Forms of Argument   1

Logic and Composition   3

WIN YOUR AUDIENCE   3
DEFINE THE ISSUE   4
MAKE YOUR CASE   6
EXERCISES   6

"Concerning Abortion: An Attempt at a Rational View"
    Charles Hartshorne   7

"Help Me Fight the National Rifle Association"
    Mrs. James Brady   13

"AB-1 and Homosexuality"
    Thaddeus E. Shoemaker   15

"Order Your Mint-Perfect Statue of Liberty 'Double Eagle'
    Commemorative"   18

"Psychometry"
    David St. Clair   20

Induction   26

IS THE SAMPLE KNOWN?   27
IS THE SAMPLE SUFFICIENT?   27
IS THE SAMPLE REPRESENTATIVE?   28
POLLING   29
OCCAM'S RAZOR   30
EXERCISES   31
ESSAY ASSIGNMENTS   32

"Elvis Is Alive"
    Patrick Cotter   33

"It's a Perfectly Safe Investment If Nothing Goes Wrong"
American Bankers Association   36

"Coaches Are Rare, Deserve Higher Pay"
Charles Gilman   38

"Smoking Is Very Glamorous"
American Cancer Society   40

"John Hinckley: Wrong Reasons Won't Yield Right Answers"
Robert Gillmore   42

Deduction   44

ARE THE PREMISES TRUE?   45
IS THE LANGUAGE UNAMBIGUOUS?   45
IS THE SYLLOGISM VALID?   46
INDUCTION OR DEDUCTION?   47
EXERCISES   48
ESSAY ASSIGNMENTS   49

"PRO/CON: Birth-Control Clinics in Schools?"
Laurie Zabin and Bishop Leo Maher   50

"When You Live a Cutty Above"
Cutty Sark   53

"End the Hypocrisy and Pay the Players"
Jeff Riggenbach   55

"John Saad Is Pro-Life"   57

"Aid and Comfort to Our Avowed Enemy"
C. B. Williams   59

Argument by Authority   61

EXPERT TESTIMONY   61
    RELIGIOUS AUTHORITY   62
    MASS AUTHORITY   63
    DIVIDED AUTHORITY   63
    CRITICAL AUTHORITY   64
BIASED TESTIMONY   64
    REWARDED OPINIONS   64
    PREDICTABLE JUDGMENTS   65
DISTORTING QUOTATIONS   66
    AUDIOTAPED AND VIDEOTAPED EVIDENCE   67
    LIES   68
EXERCISES   68
ESSAY ASSIGNMENTS   69

"Vitamin E in the Hands of Creative Physicians"
Ruth Adams and Frank Murray   70

"Future Generations Must Be Inheritors. . .Not Just Survivors"
Rolex 76

"Government Document Reveals Crash of Three 'Flying Saucers' "
Jane Hulse 78

Headlines (December 22, 1987, issue)
Weekly World News 81

"The Bible and the Death Penalty"
John Lofton 83

Semantic Argument 86

SNARL AND PURR WORDS 86
    NAMES 88
INDIRECT STATEMENT 88
PERSUASIVE STYLE 89
EXERCISES 90
ESSAY ASSIGNMENTS 92

"Ban Surrogate Births; Selling Babies Is Wrong"
Diane Culbertson 93

"Introductory Psychology 101"
Young Americans for Freedom 95

"Heinous Ruling Gets an 'Apology' "
Mike Royko 97

"Bill Hays: A Citizen's Approach to County Government" 99

"It's Time to Get Out of Bed and Kick Jap Butt!"
Ed Anger 101

Fallacies 103

FALSE ANALOGY 103
PRESUMED CAUSE-EFFECT 104
    ARGUMENT IN A CIRCLE 104
    POST HOC ERGO PROPTER HOC 105
    NON SEQUITUR 106
BEGGING THE QUESTION 106
IGNORING THE QUESTION 107
    AD HOMINEM ARGUMENT 107
    EXTENSION 107
    EITHER-OR 107
FALLACIES IN OTHER FORMS 108
EXERCISES 108
ESSAY ASSIGNMENTS 109

"Diary of an Unborn Child" 110

"Proposed Federal Cigarette Ad Ban: The 'Slippery Slope'"
Tobacco Observer   112

"A G.I. Bill for Mothers"
Ellen Goodman   114

"Well, There They Go! . . .Violating Our Civil Rights
Again!"
Bob Gorrell   116

"Meet George Crockett, Esquire"
William F. Buckley, Jr.   117

Statistics   120

AVERAGES   120
QUESTIONABLE FIGURES   120
IRRELEVANT NUMBERS   121
HOMEMADE STATISTICS   123
ENHANCING A STATISTIC   124
EXERCISES   125
ESSAY ASSIGNMENTS   126

"The Federal Deficit"
Fred Shaw   127

"God Bless America"
Handgun Control   135

"The Baldness Experiment"
George Deleon   137

"In the U.S., Crime Pays Because Criminals Don't!"
National Rifle Association   141

"The Trail of 666"
Southwest Radio Church   143

PART TWO Argument for Analysis   145

"We Consider Ourselves Practicing Catholics"
Steve Kelly   147

"The Hundredth Monkey Phenomenon"
Ron Amundson   148

"No More Killing, No More Lies"
Witness for Peace   155

"Varsity Racism?"
Kenneth S. Kantzer   156

"Holding Human Health Hostage"
Michael E. DeBakey, M.D.   159

"A Recent Graduate of the Bernhard Goetz School of
Self-Defense"
  H. Clay Bennett   163

"Answers to the Most Asked Questions About Cigarettes"
  Tobacco Institute   164

"Why Spanish Translations?"
  Mauricio Molina   166

"If They're Old Enough to Get Pregnant, They're Old
Enough Not To"
  Planned Parenthood   168

"*Time* Resorts to Hokum"
  James J. Kilpatrick   169

"Union Solidarity"
  John Claude Bru   171

"Never Met a Scoundrel I Didn't Like"
  Revlon   172

"Evolution as Fact and Theory"
  Stephen Jay Gould   173

"Cocaine Doesn't Make You Sexy—It Makes You Dead"
  Glenbeigh of Tampa   180

"Porn Doesn't Cause Violence, But a Fear of New Ideas
Does"
  Ruth McGaffey   181

"Left-Handers (Those Sickos) Got No Reason to Live!"
  Roger L. Guffey   183

"An All-Electric Home? I Think I'll Pass!"
  Louisiana Gas Service Company   184

"The Little Red School House"
  Edward Patterson   185

"Is This That Old-Time Religion?"
  The Philadelphia Inquirer   187

"You Don't Have to Be a Man to Appreciate a Great Beer"
  Coors   188

"For the Birds"
  Lillian R. Jackson   189

"Should U.S. Women Go Mini Again?"
  Alan Millstein   190

"Do You Have the Right Name?"
  Krishna Ram-Davi   192

"Access to Public Lands: A National Necessity"
  Cynthia Riggs   193

"What Jesus Said About Homosexuality"
Dignity/USA   198

"South Africa Pullout Is Unprincipled"
Cal Thomas   199

"Marriage and Catholic Doctrine"
James Council   200

"A Simple Yes or No Will Be Sufficient, Colonel"
Don Addis   202

"The Episcopal Church Meets the Sexual Revolution"
Raymond J. Lawrence   203

"Only a Tough Law Can Fix Trade Problems"
Lane Kirkland   205

"When They Tell You That Abortion Is a Matter Just
   Between a Woman and Her Doctor, They're Forgetting
   Someone"
Dr. Rainer Jonas   207

"Privacy-Invading Press Doesn't Serve Anyone"
Howard L. Reiter   208

"Et Tu, Pennzoil?"
Michael Kinsley   209

"In Time You'll Be Able to Overlook the Fact That I'm a
   Woman"
Mary Gauerke   210

"PRO/CON: Restrict Smoking in Public Places?"
Joseph Califano and Paul Screvane   211

"Your AIDS Research Dollars at Work. . ."
David Wiley Miller   214

"Raising the Minimum Wage Will Put People Out of
   Work"
Senator Orrin G. Hatch   215

"Come Home for Christmas"
Archbishop Oscar Lipscomb   217

"Cocaine Lies"
Partnership for a Drug-Free America   218

"The Price of Freedom"
Harlon B. Carter   219

"Too Many Sex Experts Teaching the Subject"
S. L. Varnado   221

"Life Without Risk"
Aetna Life and Casualty   223

"Fight Urban Criminals, Not Innocent Victims"
Jesse Hill Ford   224

"Should Priests Marry?"
Martin Ridgeway   225

"English Leather Drives Me Crazy!"
MEM Company   227

"Should Job Be a Personal Relationship—or Strictly Business?"
William F. Dwyer II   228

"Which Would You Rather Put on Your Kids' Cereal?"
Sugar Association   230

"Marijuana and Common Sense"
NORML   231

"Speed Limit 55 (or Whatever)"
David Seavey   234

"Don't Execute Children"
Tanya Coke   235

"Penalizing Bad Taste Risks Rights of All"
USA Today   237

"Before You Do Crack, Do This"
Partnership for a Drug-Free America   239

"Repeal the Son-of-Sam Law"
Arthur Eisenburg   240

"Phone-in Poll: Should Every American Be Tested for AIDS?" (Includes Pro and Con essays by Rep. William Dannemeyer and Rep. Dan Burton)
Leonard Katz   242

"It's a Dream Come True!!"
Psychic Solution   244

"Another Bureaucracy"
Alexander B. Trowbridge   245

"NFL Owners Have Rights, Too"
Bob Roesler   247

"Application to Be President of the United States, 1989–1993"
Bob Englehart   249

"Man and Nature—A Preservation"
R. Johnson   250

"A Smoke-Free Society"
Rep. Thomas A. Luken   251

PART THREE   Eight Rules for Good Writing   253

Rule 1: Find a Subject You Can Work With   255

EXERCISES   256

Rule 2: Get Your Facts   257

VISIT THE LIBRARY   257
USE YOUR TELEPHONE   259
WRITE FOR FACTS YOU NEED   260
EXERCISES   260
ALTERNATE EXERCISES   261

Rule 3: Limit Your Topic to Manageable Size   263

EXERCISES   264

Rule 4: Organize Your Material   265

THE INTRODUCTION   265
THE BODY   266
THE CONCLUSION   267
EXERCISE   268

Rule 5: Make Your Writing Interesting   269

TRUISMS   269
CLICHÉS   269
GENERALIZED LANGUAGE   270
INFLATED LANGUAGE   271
EXERCISES   272

Rule 6: Make Your Writing Emphatic   274

AVOID WORDINESS   274
WRITE IN THE ACTIVE VOICE   275
EXPRESS YOUR MAIN IDEA IN THE SUBJECT-VERB OF YOUR
   SENTENCE   275
DO NOT WASTE THE ENDS OF YOUR SENTENCES   276
KEEP YOUR SENTENCES RELATIVELY SHORT   276
EXERCISES   277

Rule 7: Avoid Language That Draws Attention to Itself   278

SEXIST LANGUAGE   278
REPETITION   279
DANGLING AND MISPLACED MODIFIERS   279
ELABORATE FIGURES OF SPEECH   279
FAULTY PARALLELISM   280
AWKWARD CONSTRUCTIONS   280
ABRUPT CHANGES IN TONE   281
EXERCISES   281

Rule 8: Avoid Mechanical Errors 283

PUNCTUATION 283
USE COMMAS TO MAKE YOUR SENTENCES EASIER TO READ 283
USE A SEMICOLON TO SHOW THAT TWO INDEPENDENT
CLAUSES ARE CLOSELY RELATED 284
USE A COLON TO INTRODUCE A UNIT 284
USE AN EXCLAMATION MARK TO SHOW EMPHASIS 285
USE A QUESTION MARK AFTER A DIRECT QUESTION 285
USE HYPHENS TO FORM COMPOUND ADJECTIVES AND TO
DIVIDE WORDS AT THE END OF A LINE 286
USE PARENTHESES TO TUCK IN EXTRA MATERIAL 286
USE A DASH WHERE YOU NEED IT 287
APOSTROPHES, QUOTATION MARKS, ITALICS, AND CAPITAL
LETTERS 287
USE APOSTROPHES TO SHOW POSSESSION, TO INDICATE AN
OMISSION, AND TO FORM UNUSUAL PLURALS 287
USE QUOTATION MARKS TO ENCLOSE THE EXACT WORDS
OF A SOURCE, TITLES OF SHORT WORKS, A WORD USED
AS A WORD, AND (SOMETIMES) WORDS USED IN AN ODD
OR IRONIC SENSE 289
USE ITALICS FOR TITLES OF LONGER WORKS, FOR FOREIGN
WORDS, AND (IF YOU HAVE TO) FOR EMPHASIS 290
USE CAPITAL LETTERS WITH THE NAMES OF SPECIFIC
PERSONS, PLACES, AND THINGS 291
ABBREVIATIONS 294
NUMBERS 295
SPELLING 296
EXERCISES 298

Final Reminders 300

CREDIT YOUR SOURCES 300
USE YOUR SPEAKING VOICE 300
GET HELP FROM FRIENDS 301
MAKE IT NEAT 301
REMEMBER YOUR AUDIENCE 302
REMEMBER YOUR PURPOSE 303
BE SMART 304

APPENDIXES 307

EXERCISES FOR REVIEW 309
SUBJECTS FOR ARGUMENTATIVE ESSAYS 315
GOOD WORDS, BAD WORDS, AND PERSUASIVE WORDS 323
WRITING A BUSINESS LETTER 327
MAKING A SPEECH 333

SUBJECTS TREATED IN THIS BOOK

ABORTION

"Concerning Abortion: An Attempt at a Rational View"   7
"John Saad Is Pro-Life"   57
"Diary of an Unborn Child"   110
"When They Tell You That Abortion Is a Matter Just
   Between a Woman and Her Doctor, They're Forgetting
   Someone"   207

ADVERTISING

"Order Your Mint-Perfect Statue of Liberty 'Double Eagle'
   Commemorative"   18
"When You Live a Cutty Above"   53
"Future Generations Must Be Inheritors. . .Not Just
   Survivors"   76
"Never Met a Scoundrel I Didn't Like"   172
"You Don't Have to Be a Man to Appreciate a Great Beer"   188
"English Leather Drives Me Crazy!"   227

AIDS

"Your AIDS Research Dollars at Work. . ."   214
"Phone-in Poll: Should Every American Be Tested for
   AIDS?"   242

ANIMAL EXPERIMENTS

"Holding Human Health Hostage"   159

ATLANTIS

Weekly World News Headlines   81

BALDNESS

"The Baldness Experiment"   137

THE BIBLE

"The Bible and the Death Penalty"   83
"The Trail of 666"   143

"What Jesus Said About Homosexuality"   198
"Marriage and Catholic Doctrine"   200

BIRTH CONTROL

"PRO/CON: Birth-Control Clinics in Schools?"   50
"If They're Old Enough to Get Pregnant, They're Old
   Enough Not To"   168

CAPITAL PUNISHMENT

"The Bible and the Death Penalty"   83
"Don't Execute Children"   235

CENSORSHIP

"Porn Doesn't Cause Violence, But a Fear of New Ideas
   Does"   181
"Is This That Old-Time Religion?"   187
"Penalizing Bad Taste Risks Rights of All"   237

COLLECTIVE BARGAINING

"Union Solidarity"   171

CONGRESS

"Meet George Crockett, Esquire"   117

CONSPIRACY

"Elvis Is Alive"   33

CRIMINAL LAW

"John Hinckley: Wrong Reasons Won't Yield Right
   Answers"   42
"Heinous Ruling Gets an 'Apology' "   97
Weekly World News Headlines   81
"Well, There They Go! . . .Violating Our Civil Rights
   Again!"   116
"In the U.S., Crime Pays Because Criminals Don't"   141
"Fight Urban Criminals, Not Innocent Victims"   224
"Repeal the Son-of-Sam Law"   240

DRUGS

"Cocaine Doesn't Make You Sexy—It Makes You Dead"   180
"Cocaine Lies"   218
"Marijuana and Common Sense"   231
"Before You Do Crack, Do This"   239

EDUCATION

"Introductory Psychology 101"   95
"The Little Red School House"   185

"Is This That Old-Time Religion?"   187
"Too Many Sex Experts Teaching the Subject"   221

EMPLOYMENT LAW

"Union Solidarity"   171
"Should Job Be a Personal Relationship—or Strictly
  Business?"   228

ESP

"Psychometry"   20
"The Hundredth Monkey Phenomenon"   148
"It's a Dream Come True!!"   244

EVOLUTION

"Evolution as Fact and Theory"   173

FASHION

"Should U.S. Women Go Mini Again?"   190

FINANCE

"It's a Perfectly Safe Investment if Nothing Goes Wrong"   36
"The Federal Deficit"   127

FOREIGN TRADE

"It's Time to Get Out of Bed and Kick Jap Butt!"   101
"Only a Tough Law Can Fix Trade Problems"   205

GAS vs. ELECTRICITY

"An All-Electric Home? I Think I'll Pass!"   184

GOETZ, BERNHARD

"A Recent Graduate of the Bernhard Goetz School of
  Self-Defense"   163
"Fight Urban Criminals, Not Innocent Victims"   224

GOVERNMENT SECRECY

"The Ideal American Citizen?"   ii

GUN CONTROL

"Help Me Fight the National Rifle Association"   13
"God Bless America"   135
"In the U.S., Crime Pays Because Criminals Don't!"   141
"The Price of Freedom"   219

HISPANIC AMERICANS

"Why Spanish Translations?"   166

HOMOSEXUALITY

"AB-1 and Homosexuality"   15
"Left-Handers (Those Sickos) Got No Reason to Live!"   183
"What Jesus Said About Homosexuality"   198

IRAN/CONTRA

"Meet George Crockett, Esquire"   117
"No More Killing, No More Lies"   155
"A Simple Yes or No Will Be Sufficient, Colonel"   202

LIABILITY LAW

"Life Without Risk"   223

MARRIAGE

"Marriage and Catholic Doctrine"   200
"The Episcopal Church Meets the Sexual Revolution"   203
"Should Priests Marry?"   225

MEDIA

Weekly World News Headlines   81
"*Time* Resorts to Hokum"   169
"Privacy-Invading Press Doesn't Serve Anyone"   208
"Application to Be President of the United States,
   1989–1993"   249

MINIMUM WAGE

"Raising the Minimum Wage Will Put People Out of
   Work"   215

NAMES

"Do You Have the Right Name?"   192

NATIONAL DEBT

"The Federal Deficit"   127

NATURAL FOODS

"Which Would You Rather Put on Your Kids' Cereal?"   230

POLITICS

"John Saad Is Pro-Life"   57
"Bill Hays: A Citizen's Approach to County Government"   99
"Application to Be President of the United States,
   1989–1993"   249

PORNOGRAPHY

"Porn Doesn't Cause Violence, But a Fear of New Ideas
Does"   181
"Penalizing Bad Taste Risks Rights of All"   237

PRAYER IN PUBLIC SCHOOLS

"The Little Red School House"   185

RACE

"Meet George Crockett, Esquire"   117
"Varsity Racism?"   156
"South Africa Pullout Is Unprincipled"   199

ROMAN CATHOLICISM

"We Consider Ourselves Practicing Catholics"   147
"What Jesus Said About Homosexuality"   198
"Marriage and Catholic Doctrine"   200
"Come Home for Christmas"   217
"Should Priests Marry?"   225

SEX SCANDALS

"It's Time to Get Out of Bed and Kick Jap Butt!"   101
"Privacy-Invading Press Doesn't Serve Anyone"   208
"Application to Be President of the United States,
1989–1993"   249

SMOKING AND HEALTH

"Smoking Is Very Glamorous"   40
"Proposed Federal Cigarette Ad Ban: The 'Slippery Slope'"   112
"Answers to the Most Asked Questions About Cigarettes"   164
"PRO/CON: Restrict Smoking in Public Places?"   211
"A Smoke-Free Society"   251

SOUTH AFRICA

"South Africa Pullout Is Unprincipled"   199

SPEED LIMIT

"Speed Limit 55 (or Whatever)"   234

SPORTS

"Coaches Are Rare, Deserve Higher Pay"   38
"End the Hypocrisy and Pay the Players"   55
"Varsity Racism?"   156

SUGAR

"Which Would You Rather Put on Your Kids' Cereal?"   230

SURROGATE MOTHERS

"Ban Surrogate Births; Selling Babies Is Wrong"   93

TEXACO VS. PENNZOIL

"Et Tu, Pennzoil?"   209

UFOs

"Government Document Reveals Crash of Three 'Flying
    Saucers'"   78
Weekly World News Headlines   81

U.S.S.R.

"Aid and Comfort to Our Avowed Enemy"   59
"Meet George Crockett, Esquire"   117

VEGETARIANISM

"Man and Nature—A Preservation"   250

VITAMINS

"Vitamin E in the Hands of Creative Physicians"   70
Weekly World News Headlines   81

WELFARE

"For the Birds"   189

WILDERNESS

"Access to Public Lands: A National Necessity"   193

WOMEN'S RIGHTS

"A G.I. Bill for Mothers"   114
"In Time You'll Be Able to Overlook the Fact That I'm a
    Woman"   210

PREFACE

The purpose of this new edition remains the same: to teach students to read argument and to provide materials around which they can write their own argumentative essays. The selections cover a range of provocative issues. Some are notably persuasive, some are not. Most of today's hot topics are represented.

This book is larger than the previous edition. I have kept 15 selections from the fifth edition and added 79 new ones. All are intended to create excitement and controversy in the classroom.

The "Argument for Analysis" section has 56 short (or relatively short) works: essays, advertisements, letters, photographs, cartoons, editorials, and so on. Students can be asked to write on any of these, giving either an analysis of the argument or a response to it. Teachers could conceivably assign a different title to each member of their class.

These short selections should produce a good result. I am not anxious that my students know all the facts about some area of controversy (abortion or secular humanism or nuclear power). I will be happy if they can read an argument and say, "That's an unrepresentative sample," or "Where did those statistics come from?," or "Post Hoc rides again!" With the short arguments, students have more of these fallacies to look at.

Many of my examples come from Alabama periodicals or deal with Southern issues. The issues that are important here are important everywhere. Comparable examples certainly can be found in other newspapers in other cities.

I am indebted to a lot of people. Jim Dorrill, the English Department chair at the University of South Alabama, has been continually supportive. Mary A. Coan, Lynda Thompson, Gene Knepprath, and Charlie Harwell offered materials that found their way into the book. Mike Hanna, Tim Lally, and Irene McDonald were continuing intellectual resources. Rebecca McDonald brightened my days by making regular visits to my office. And Ellen Williams did a perceptive job of typing and editing. I have had the benefit of some first-rate minds—and some beautiful friends.

I also want to thank the following people for reviewing the manuscript: Nancy Barry, University of Iowa; Nancy Joseph, York College of Pennsylvania; Patricia Morgan, Louisiana State University; Christina Murphy, Texas

Christian University; Betty Jo Hicks Peters, Moorhead State University; and Joseph Sanders, Lakeland Community College.

The editor who selects and annotates controversial essays must work to keep his own opinion out of his textbook. I think I am getting good at this. Half the people who claim my book has a bias accuse me of beliefs I consider reprehensible.

Daniel McDonald

PART ONE

FORMS OF
ARGUMENT

Japonica
Glistens like coral in all of the neighbouring gardens,
And today we have naming of parts.
—Henry Reed

LOGIC AND COMPOSITION

"If the world were a perfect place, you wouldn't need a Buick."

Most writing is persuasive writing.

When you write, you want something. You want people to be more informed and to accept your point of view. You want them to do something. You want them to see you in a positive way. Good writing is writing that gets the effect you want.

A study of the techniques of persuasion will make you more concerned about your audience and about forms of writing that have a good or bad effect on them. It will keep you from speculating vaguely on some topic that cannot be proven with evidence. It will help you know when you are making sense.

WIN YOUR AUDIENCE

To make a persuasive case, you have to know your audience. This will help you choose your words and shape your style.

One body of readers—say, a group of fraternity men—may respond to a direct appeal in strong language; another group—say, members of a Methodist congregation—may reject your whole argument if you use a word like "crap." One group will respond to wit, another, to biblical quotations, and still another, to a spread of statistics. Some readers will be offended if you write "Ms.," "ain't," "Negro," "symbiotic," "Dear Sir," or "and/or." Most audiences will be bored if you write vaguely about "Civic Responsibility" or "Tomorrow's Promise," but some audiences and occasions may call for rhetorical generalities. A detailed analysis of a social problem would be out of place at a political rally. The writing that would produce a great letter or advertisement would be unsuccessful in a sociology term paper. You have to know your audience.

A central feature in argument is creating a personal voice to express your views. Too often individuals with an impressive case fail to be persuasive

3

because of a writing style that makes them sound like a computer, a demanding top sergeant, a condescending aristocrat, or a stubborn child.

Most readers respond favorably to a concerned and courteous tone. So let your writing sound like a human voice. When addressing a committee, refer to the members in your presentation. ("I'm sure you ladies and gentlemen recognize how complex this question is.") When writing a business letter, try to use a direct, personal style. ("I'm sorry about your problem, Mr. Baker, and I hope we can do more for you next time.") Routinely, work to avoid a hostile tone. Don't write, "You must do this," when you can say, "We would like to have you do this promptly" or "I need this by Wednesday." Never write, "I will not do this," when you can say, "For these reasons, I cannot do this now." Don't protest, "You're too dumb to understand my argument"; say, "I am sorry I did not make myself understood."

This tone can be difficult to maintain. At times, you will want to rage out with righteous indignation or ego-gratifying scorn. Don't do it. Remember that anger never persuaded anyone. In argument, nice guys finish first.

The point deserves repetition. An Alabama attorney looking back on a lifetime of courtroom experience said, "When I was young, I thought that lawyers won cases. Later I believed that facts won cases. Now I think that clients win cases. When the facts aren't overwhelmingly against him, the jury will find for the person they like best." (The celebrated trials of Jean Harris, Larry Flynt, John DeLorean, and Bernhard Goetz seemed to work on that principle.)

The persuasive force of sweet good-nature can hardly be overstated. Americans twice elected Ronald Reagan as president because, among other reasons, they perceived him to be a nice person. Occasionally, lawyers have to press a personal injury suit against Disneyland or Walt Disney World. The attempts fail because Disney is too fixed in the public mind as sweet, clean, and moral. One frustrated lawyer said, "You might as well try to sue Mother Teresa."

DEFINE THE ISSUE

A study of logic shows the importance of defining your issue. Some topics you may want to discuss are flatly unarguable. They would produce vague speeches and incoherent essays.

Some issues rely more on a definition of terms than on evidence. When two people argue about whether Senator Ted Kennedy is handsome, for example, they are not disagreeing about his hair, teeth, or clothes, but about a definition of *handsomeness.* If they can agree on a definition, they will probably agree about Senator Kennedy as well. Similarly, the question of whether capital punishment is wrong hinges not so much on the character of the act (the pain, the possibility of error, the protection afforded society) as on the definition of *wrongness.*

Aesthetic and moral questions are often unarguable because individuals cannot agree on the terms involved. The meaning of any word is what a body of people say it is. A telephone is called a *telephone* because English speakers regularly use that word to denote it. But in these special areas, people do not agree. What is handsomeness? What is beauty? Theoreticians have sought objective standards, but the quest seems fruitless. Is a Greek temple more beautiful that a Gothic cathedral? Is Bach's music better than Steely Dan's? Who can say? The decision rests on a subjective judgment that does not lend itself to evidence.

When friends tell you they prefer Frank Zappa's music and the taste of L.A. beer, you can't argue with them. It's a good time to change the subject.

Like beauty, the idea of goodness is not easy to define. Seeking an objective basis for calling actions right and wrong, authorities have cited scriptural precedents; they have based systems on the inalienable rights of each human being; they have insisted that nature provides a moral example. But these definitions have not been universally accepted. If two individuals could agree that morality resides, say, in a natural law, they might then *begin* to argue about capital punishment. In general usage, however, moral terms remain so ill-defined that such issues cannot be argued meaningfully at all. (If you have to write on beauty or morality, focus your essay on some concrete example— say, arson or pop art or Vanna White—and work in as many "for example" and "for instance" references as you can.)

Moral and aesthetic questions are further removed from argument because they often produce emotional responses. Two individuals who agree in defining *handsomeness* might, for example, still disagree about Senator Kennedy because one objects to his liberal politics or his personal style. It is, of course, unreasonable to let emotions color such a judgment, but it happens all the time. You might be completely persuaded that capital punishment is cruel and barbaric yet at a given moment argue that hanging is too good for a child murderer or a political terrorist.

Vague definitions make argument impossible in many areas. Saab has been proclaimed "the most *intelligent* car ever built," and Royal Copenhagen "the only *elegant* musk oil cologne." The advertisement insists "Only Tareyton has the *best* filter!" Are these claims true? Until the key words are defined, the statements are no more subject to being proved with evidence than is "Razzle dagons, popple stix." Nonsense is neither true nor false.

Many areas of modern controversy hinge on definitions of terms. Do animals "talk"? Can children "sin"? Is running a "religious" experience? Is prostitution a "victimless" crime? Do computers "think"? It depends on how you define the words.

Only when terms are defined and mutually accepted can you begin gathering evidence to prove something. You can, for example, argue whether O. J. Simpson or Walter Payton was the better football player because their records, the merits of their supporting and opposing teams, and the qualities of a good running back are generally agreed upon. Is it true that smoking causes lung cancer, that Vice President Bush knew about the illegal events of the Iran/contra scandal, that Gordon's is the largest-selling gin in the world? The questions can at least be argued.

MAKE YOUR CASE

Finally, the study of argument will let you know when you are making sense. It will tell you if your sample is sufficient to support an inductive conclusion, if the expert you want to quote is a reliable authority, if your words express the meanings you want, and if your statistics are relevant.

A survey of logic will make you a more perceptive reader. You will be better able to recognize strengths and weaknesses in particular arguments. It will be harder for people to lie to you.

The essays in this book will show you writing patterns to imitate and avoid. You cannot become a good writer simply by knowing how words are spelled and where commas go. You need a clearly defined subject, a personal voice, and an effective presentation of your information. *What you have to say is of the essence of good writing.* And the study of logic should make what you have to say more persuasive and meaningful.

EXERCISES

Can you argue the truth of these statements?

1. All men are created equal.
2. Mexico City's Copper Dome is higher than the Empire State Building.
3. Nonsmokers make better lovers.
4. It is wrong to say "between you and I."
5. Subaru—"$5,500. And built to stay that way."
6. Time is a trapezoid.
7. Babe Ruth was a better baseball player than Dizzy Dean.
8. "Blessed are the pure in heart, for they shall see God."
9. All prisoners eligible for parole should be tested for the virus that causes AIDS.
10. Patty Hearst was brainwashed.
11. A diamond is forever.
12. No woman is happy with the way she looks.
13. Immorality is corrupting every area of this country. Only a moral renaissance can save America now.
14. One way to relieve the gasoline shortage is to legalize marijuana.
15. Stolichnaya—"The only vodka imported from Russia."
16. L'Oreal—"Why be gray when you can be yourself?"
17. SURGEON GENERAL'S WARNING: Smoking Causes Cancer, Heart Disease, Emphysema, and May Complicate Pregnancy.
18. Vacation in Florida—"The Rules Are Different Here."

CONCERNING ABORTION:
AN ATTEMPT AT A RATIONAL VIEW

CHARLES HARTSHORNE

My onetime colleague T. V. Smith once wrote a book called *Beyond Conscience,* in which he waxed eloquent in showing "the harm that good men do." To live according to one's conscience may be a fine thing, but what if A's conscience leads A to try to compel B and C to live, not according to B's or C's conscience, but according to A's? That is what many opponents of abortion are trying to do. To propose a constitutional amendment to this effect is one of the most outrageous attempts to tyrannize over others that I can recall in my long lifetime as an American citizen. Proponents of the antiabortion amendment make their case, if possible, even worse when they defend themselves with the contention "It isn't my conscience only—it is a commandment of religion." For now one particular form of religion (certainly not the only form) is being used in an attempt to tyrannize over other forms of religious or philosophical belief. The separation of church and state evidently means little to such people.

IN WHAT SENSE "HUMAN"?

Ours is a country that has many diverse religious groups, and many people who cannot find truth in any organized religious body. It is a country that has great difficulty in effectively opposing forms of killing that *everyone* admits to be wrong. Those who would saddle the legal system with matters about which consciences sincerely and strongly differ show a disregard of the country's primary needs. (The same is to be said about crusades to make things difficult for homosexuals.) There can be little freedom if we lose sight of the vital distinction between moral questions and legal ones. The law compels and coerces, with the implicit threat of violence; morals seek to persuade. It is a poor society that forgets this difference.

What is the *moral* question regarding abortion? We are told that the fetus is alive and that therefore killing it is wrong. Since mosquitoes, bacteria, apes and whales are also alive, the argument is less than clear. Even plants are alive. I am not impressed by the rebuttal "But plants, mosquitoes, bacteria and whales are not human, and the fetus is." For the issue now becomes, *in what sense* is the fetus human? No one denies that its origin is human, as is its *possible* destiny. But the same is true of every unfertilized egg in the body of a nun. Is it wrong that some such eggs are not made or allowed to become human individuals?

Granted that a fetus is human in origin and possible destiny, in what further sense is it human? The entire problem lies here. If there are pro-life activists who have thrown much light on this question, I do not know their names.

One theologian who writes on the subject—Paul Ramsey—thinks that a human egg cell becomes a human individual with a moral claim to survive if it has been fertilized. Yet this egg cell has none of the qualities that we have in mind when we proclaim our superior worth to the chimpanzees or dolphins. It cannot speak, reason, or judge between right and wrong. It cannot have personal relations, without which a person is not functionally a person at all, until months—and not, except minimally, until years—have passed. And even then, it will not be a person in the normal sense unless some who are already fully persons have taken pains to help it become a human being in the full value sense, functioning as such. The antiabortionist is commanding some person or persons to undertake this effort. For without it, the fetus will *never* be human in the relevant sense. It will be human only in origin, but otherwise a subhuman animal.

The fertilized egg is an individual egg, but not an individual human being. For such a being is, in its body, a multicellular organism, a *metazoan*—to use the scientific Greek—and the egg is a single cell. The first thing the egg cell does is to begin dividing into many cells. For some weeks the fetus is not a single individual at all, but a colony of cells. During its first weeks there seems to be no ground for regarding the fetus as comparable to an individual animal. Only in possible or probable destiny is it an individual. Otherwise it is an organized society of single-celled individuals.

A possible individual person is one thing; an actual person is another. If this difference is not important, what is? There is in the long run no room in the solar system, or even in the known universe, for all human eggs—even all fertilized eggs, as things now stand—to become human persons. Indeed, it is mathematically demonstrable that the present rate of population growth must be lowered somehow. It is not a moral imperative that all possibilities of human persons become actual persons.

Of course, some may say that the fertilized egg already has a human soul, but on what evidence? The evidence of soul in the relevant sense is the capacity to reason, judge right and wrong, and the like.

GENETIC AND OTHER INFLUENCES

One may also say that since the fertilized egg has a combination of genes (the units of physical inheritance) from both parents, in this sense it is already a human individual. There are two objections, either one in my opinion conclusive but only one of which is taken into account by Ramsey. The one he does mention is that identical twins have the same gene combination. The theologian does not see this as decisive, but I do.

The other objection is that it amounts to a very crude form of materialism to identify individuality with the gene-combination. Genes are the chemical bearers of inherited traits. This chemical basis of inheritance presumably influences everything about the development of the individual—*influences,* but does not fully determine. To say that the entire life of the person is determined by heredity is a theory of unfreedom that my religious conviction can only regard as monstrous. And there are biophysicists and neurophysiologists who agree with me.

From the gene-determined chemistry to a human person is a long,

long step. As soon as the nervous system forming in the embryo begins to function as a whole—and not before—the cell colony begins to turn into a genuinely individual animal. One may reasonably suppose that this change is accompanied by some extremely primitive individual animal feelings. They cannot be recognizably human feelings, much less human thoughts, and cannot compare with the feelings of a porpoise or chimpanzee in level of consciousness. That much seems as certain as anything about the fetus except its origin and possible destiny. The nervous system of a very premature baby has been compared by an expert to that of a pig. And we know, if we know anything about this matter, that it is the nervous system that counts where individuality is concerned.

Identical twins are different individuals, each unique in consciousness. Though having the same genetic makeup, they will have been differently situated in the womb and hence will have received different stimuli. For that reason, if for no other, they will have developed differently, especially in their brains and nervous systems.

But there are additional reasons for the difference in development. One is the role of chance, which takes many forms. We are passing through a great cultural change in which the idea, long dominant in science, that chance is "only a word for our ignorance of causes" is being replaced by the view that the real laws of nature are probabilistic and allow for aspects of genuine chance.

Another reason is that it is reasonable to admit a reverse influence of the developing life of feelings in the fetus on the nervous system, as well as of the system upon the feelings. And since I, along with some famous philosophers and scientists, believe in freedom (not solely of mature human beings but—in some slight degree—of all individuals in nature, down to the atoms and farther), I hold that even in the fetus the incipient individual is unconsciously making what on higher levels we call "decisions." These decisions influence the developing nervous system. Thus to a certain extent we *make our own bodies* by our feelings and thoughts. An English poet with Platonic ideas expressed this concept as follows:

> *The body from the soul its form doth take,*
> *For soul is form and doth the body make.*

The word soul is, for me, incidental. The point is that feelings, thoughts, experiences react on the body and partly mold its development.

THE RIGHTS OF PERSONS

Paul Ramsey argues (as does William Buckley in a letter to me) that if a fetus is not fully human, then neither is an infant. Of course an infant is not fully human. No one thinks it can, while an infant, be taught to speak, reason, or judge right and wrong. But it is much closer to that stage than is a three-month fetus. It is beginning to have primitive social relations not open to a fetus; and since there is no sharp line anywhere between an infant and a child able to speak a few words, or between the latter and a child able to speak very many words, we have to regard the infant as significantly different from a three-month or four-month fetus. Nevertheless, I have little sympathy with the idea that infanticide is just another form of murder. Persons who are already functionally persons in the full sense have more important rights even than infants. Infanticide can be wrong without being fully comparable to the killing of persons in the full sense.

Does this distinction apply to the killing of a hopelessly senile person (or one in a permanent coma)? For me it does. I hope that no one will think that if, God forbid, I ever reach that stage, it must be for my sake that I should be treated with the respect due to normal human beings. Rather, it is for the sake of others that such respect may be imperative. Symbolically, one who has been a person may have to be treated as a person. There are difficulties and hazards in not so treating such individuals.

Religious people (I would so describe myself) may argue that once a fetus starts to develop, it is for God, not human beings, to decide whether the fetus survives and how long it lives. This argument assumes, against all evidence, that human life-spans are independent of human decisions. Our medical hygiene has radically altered the original "balance of nature." Hence the population explosion. Our technology makes pregnancy more and more a matter of human decision; more and more our choices are influencing the weal and woe of the animals on this earth. It is an awesome responsibility, but one that we cannot avoid. And, after all, the Book of Genesis essentially predicted our dominion over terrestrial life. In addition, no one is proposing to make abortion compulsory for those morally opposed to it. I add that everyone who smokes is taking a hand in deciding how long he or she will live. Also everyone who, by failing to exercise reasonably, allows his or her heart to lose its vigor. Our destinies are not simply "acts of God."

I may be told that if I value my life I must be glad that I was not aborted in the fetus stage. Yes, I am glad, but this expression does not constitute a claim to having already had a "right," against which no other right could prevail, to the life I have enjoyed. I feel no indignation or horror at contemplating the idea that the world might have had to do without me. The world could have managed, and as for what I would have missed, there would have been no such "I" to miss it.

POTENTIAL, NOT ACTUAL

With almost everything they say, the fanatics against abortion show that they will not, or cannot, face the known facts of this matter. The inability of a fetus to say "I" is not merely a lack of skill; there is nothing there to which the pronoun could properly refer. A fetus is not a person but a *potential* person. The "life" to which "pro-life" refers is nonpersonal, by any criterion that makes sense to some of us. It is subpersonal animal life only. The mother, however, *is* a person.

I resent strongly the way many males tend to dictate to females their behavior, even though many females encourage them in this. Of course, the male parent of a fetus also has certain rights, but it remains true that the female parent is the one most directly and vitally concerned.

I shall not forget talking about this whole matter to a wonderful woman, the widow of a philosopher known for his idealism. She was doing social work with young women and had come to the conclusion that abortion is, in some cases, the lesser evil. She told me that her late husband had said, when she broached the subject to him, "But you can't do that." "My darling," she replied, "we *are* doing it." I see no reason to rate the consciences of the pro-lifers higher than this woman's conscience. She knew what the problem was for certain mothers. In a society that flaunts sex (its pleasures more than its serious hazards, problems and spiritual values) in all the media, makes it difficult for the young to avoid unwanted pregnancy, and does little to help them with the most difficult of all problems of self-discipline, we tell young persons that they are murderers if they resort to abortion. And so we should not be surprised that Margaret Mead, that clearsighted observer of our society (and of other societies), should say, "Abortion is a nasty thing, but our society deserves it." Alas, it is too true.

I share something of the disgust of hard-core opponents of abortion that contraceptives, combined with the availability of abortion, may deprive sexual intercourse of spiritual meaning. For me the sacramental view of marriage has always had appeal, and my life has been lived accordingly. Abortion is indeed a nasty thing, but unfortunately there are in our society many even nastier things, like the fact that some children are growing up unwanted. This for my conscience is a great deal nastier, and truly horrible. An overcrowded world is also nasty, and could in a few decades become truly catastrophic.

The argument against abortion (used, I am sorry to say, by Pearl Buck) that the fetus may be a potential genius has to be balanced against the much more probable chance of its being a mediocrity, or a destructive enemy of society. Every egg cell is a possible genius and also a possible monster in human form. Where do we stop in calculating such possibilities?

If some who object to abortion work to diminish the number of unwanted, inappropriate pregnancies, or to make bearing a child for adoption by persons able to be its loving foster parents more attractive than it now is, and do this with a minimum of coercion, all honor to them. In view of the population problem, the first of these remedies should have high priority.

Above all, the coercive power of our legal system, already stretched thin, must be used with caution and chiefly against evils about which there is something like universal consensus. That persons have rights is a universal belief in our society, but that a fetus is already an actual person—about that there is and there can be no consensus. Coercion in such matters is tyranny. Alas for our dangerously fragmented and alienated society if we persist in such tyranny.

DISCUSSION QUESTIONS

1. Why did the author call his essay "an attempt" at a rational view of abortion?
2. Define the words *soul, person, human,* and *moral.*
3. The author refers to persons opposing abortions as "proponents of the

antiabortion amendment," "antiabortionists," "activists," "hard-core opponents of abortion," "the fanatics against abortion," and advocates of "the most outrageous attempt to tyrannize over others." How else might these people be described?

4. The author describes himself as "an American citizen" and as one of the "religious people." How else might he be described?

5. "I may be told that if I value my life I must be glad that I was not aborted in the fetus stage. Yes, I am glad, but this expression does not constitute a claim to have already had a 'right,' against which no other right could prevail, to the life I have enjoyed. I feel no indignation or horror at contemplating the idea that the world might have had to do without me. The world could have managed, and as for what I would have missed, there would have been no such 'I' to miss it." In this kind of passage, an author is telling about both an issue and himself. What does this section tell you about him?

6. The author talks about preserving the lives of unfertilized human eggs, fertilized eggs, fetuses, babies, adults who fail to exercise, adults who smoke, and hopelessly senile people. How parallel are these examples? What is the author's point in mentioning such instances?

7. He also refers to the lives of plants, bacteria, mosquitoes, whales, dolphins, apes, and chimpanzees. Do these help his case? Do any of the examples complicate his case?

8. The author refers to fertilized eggs, a colony of cells, possible persons, and potential persons. How would a pro-life advocate describe such entities?

9. If the entire abortion issue were described as "semantic," would it be less crucial and dramatic? Is it essentially semantic?

—Mrs. James S. Brady—

"Help me fight the National Rifle Association."

"Six years ago, John Hinckley pulled a $29 revolver from his pocket and opened fire on a Washington street. He shot the President. He also shot my husband.

I'm not asking for your sympathy. I'm asking for your help.

I've learned from my own experience that, alone, there's only so much you can do to stop handgun violence. But that together, we can confront the mightiest gun lobby–the N.R.A.– and win.

I've only to look at my husband Jim to remember that awful day... the unending TV coverage of the handgun firing over and over... the nightmare panic and fear.

It's an absolute miracle nobody was killed. After all, twenty thousand Americans are killed by handguns every year. Thousands more–men, women, even children–are maimed for life.

Like me, I know you support *stronger* handgun control laws. So does the vast majority of Americans. But the National Rifle Association can spend so much in elections that Congress is afraid to pass an effective national handgun law.

It's time to change that. Before it's too late for another family like mine... a family like yours.

I joined Handgun Control, Inc. because they're willing to take on the N.R.A. Right now we're campaigning for a national waiting period and background check on handgun purchases.

If such simple, basic measures had been on the books six years ago, John Hinckley would never have walked out of that Texas pawnshop with the handgun which came within an inch of killing Ronald Reagan. He lied on his purchase application. Given time, the police could have caught the lie and put him in jail.

Of course, John Hinckley's not the only one. Police report that thousands of known criminals buy handguns right over the counter in this country. We have to stop them.

So, please, pick up a pen. Fill out the coupon. Add a check for as much as you can afford, and mail it to me today.

It's time we kept handguns out of the wrong hands. It's time to break the National Rifle Association's grip on Congress and start making our cities and neighborhoods safe again.

Thank you and God bless you."

"Together we can win."

Dear Sarah,

It's time to break the N.R.A.'s grip on Congress once and for all. Here's my contribution to Handgun Control, Inc., the million-strong nonprofit citizens' group you help direct:

☐ $15 ☐ $25 ☐ $35 ☐ $50 ☐ $100 or $_____.
☐ Tell me more about how I can help.

NAME

ADDRESS

CITY   STATE   ZIP   *

HANDGUN CONTROL

1400 K Street, N.W., Washington, D.C. 20005, (202) 898-0792

Courtesy of Handgun Control, Inc.

DISCUSSION QUESTIONS

1. What does this ad tell you about Mrs. Brady? What qualities make her particularly appealing as an antigun spokesperson?

2. Her husband had part of his brain shot away in the Hinckley attack and is living on in a diminished state. What does the author tell you about this? Why is she so restrained?

3. Identify the passages where she specifies that the gun situation is *your* problem. Why does she emphasize this?

4. What is the effect of the "Dear Sarah" that introduces the coupon at the bottom?

5. What is the effect of the many short sentences? the frequent paragraph breaks? the talkiness of the language? Is this good writing?

AB-1
AND HOMOSEXUALITY

THADDEUS E. SHOEMAKER

AB-1,* which has now succumbed to Governor George Deukmejian's veto, is not only endemic of the sorry and lowly state of California politics, but glaringly reveals the pervasive pathos of public and social values possessed by a majority of elected politicos. The homosexual "bill of rights," as it is called by its devotees, demonstrates how gutless our politicians are and how easily they are bought.

But this criticism is too mild. Permit me to present a characterization of politicians by William E. Simon in his article in the *Wall Street Journal* (Feb. 2, 1984). Quoting a recent editorial in which the writer characterized most of our representatives as " '. . . craven, abject, lily-livered body of lap dogs, these lickspittle, these toadies, these footmen . . . It is time for (Californians) to crucify these no count posturing, bloodsucking, thimble witted, hypocritical Kallikaks.' "

How do your politicians respond? They tell us that it took great courage to support AB-1 and stand up for what is "right." In both declarations they lie, not only to us, but to themselves as well. The result is public bewilderment, social disintegration, and personal disillusionment. Meanwhile our elected officials continue the gratification of their insatiable greed at the expense of the public weal and, as with sexual deviancy, greed knows no limits. Popular esteem for our lawmakers has never been very high, but the legislature in the role of "pimp" must be regarded, even by the most cynical, as an all-time low. Traditionally in America the contest for votes has been also a contest of ideas. But what we see in AB-1 is political favors from unrestricted libidos running amuck.

What is AB-1 all about? It is not about social abuses suffered by homosexuals; the alleged abuses, purportedly the "raison d'etre" of the bill, have not been demonstrated by the evidence. Besides, the claimed discriminations, if they were to exist, are already illegal and the courts are competent to deal with them. Beyond this, collective bargaining agreements in private and public employment protect against discriminatory activity on the part of management.

No, the charge of gross abuse is a mere facade to hide the true purpose of AB-1, which is to establish, insofar as politically possible, legally protected, mainly in the work-place, special status for those who by preference and choice desire to live openly as homosexuals. Homosexuals seek society's forced acquiescence through legal sanction.

*AB-1 was a bill passed by both houses of the California legislature in 1984 and vetoed by the governor. It would have made it illegal for an employer to discriminate on the basis of sexual orientation.

SOURCE: Reprinted from *Sacramento State Forum*, September 1984. Reprinted with permission of author.

AB-1 is wrong, just as wrong, as its proponents are wrong-headed. It is wrong because it is unreasonable, improper, and unnecessary, and not simply because homosexuality is offensive to the majority, or that it violates the codes of the sacred texts of the Judeo-Christian tradition. Certainly it is true, whatever may be one's personal standards of morality and immorality, that a majority of Americans (and Californians) are influenced by that great and powerful tradition. For those who love and admire that tradition, homosexuality and its companion evils will always be immoral. I will leave to others more qualified than I to defend that tradition. But my judgment is that no liberal interpretations, no textual analyses, however erudite, can obviate the fact that homosexuality is universally abhorred, explicitly prohibited, and condemned by Judeo-Christian ethics.

Let us look at several assumptions upon which AB-1 is purported to be founded. Homosexuals claim they are a persecuted minority analogous to other minorities, whose past discriminations, based on gender, ethnicity, and national origin, have already been given legal status. Therefore, like these minorities, the homosexuals are deserving of minority status and must be recognized as suffering from the invidious discrimination upon which suspect-classifications are legally based. The law's establishment of suspect-classifications is founded in the Civil Rights Act of 1964, which states that if any individual falls within the general minority categories of gender, ethnicity, and national origin, and that person brings forth a charge of discrimination against an employer, or the employer's agent, "it is to be presumed that such charge on its face is invidious" and thereby prohibited by the Act, with the burden of proof of non-discrimination resting upon the employer. The intent of AB-1 is to make homosexuality a suspect-classification as defined by national and California law.

That homosexuals be given such legal minority status is both unreasonable and improper. First, the Civil Rights Act recognizes that the categories upon which suspect-classifications are based are physical features of a unique and special nature beyond the power of the individual to change or control. Racial minorities and women are incapable of changing their ethnicity or gender. But what is the condition of the homosexual? The evidence is overwhelming—except for the practicing homosexuals and their apologists who refuse to accept the facts—that sexual appetite, pleasure, and passion are a matter of preference and choice, and not a product of biological determination.

No matter how absurd it may sound, some homosexuals would have us believe that their sexuality is but an analogue to eating and drinking. Such distortion of logic is for the purpose of deception. Consider the facts: one may choose to never engage in any sexual activity and still be a healthy, happy and productive person. Mother Teresa is a saintly example of this. Sexual gratification is not absolutely essential to life. Eating and drinking are. In stating this I do not mean to imply that environmental factors such as disease and accident do not play a role in the development of sexual tendencies, and these tendencies do indeed influence personal preference and choice. Still, our sexual gratification remains a matter of determining for self if, and how, it will be achieved. The most compelling evidence, both contemporary as well as historical, instructs that biological factors determining human sexuality are limited to gender identification and a natural propensity toward bisexuality, but in no way does the evidence show that there is in us a "biological master," over which we have no control, "enslaving" some of us to heterosexuality and others to homosexuality. Biologically, our nature makes us male and female, but nature no more makes us homosexuals than it makes us murderers.

Limitations of space compel me to restrict this essay to one final claim by the supporters of AB-1. The author of AB-1 claims that the homosexuals need this bill so that they can be guaranteed jobs. Why is the homosexual worthy of such a guarantee? There is no right to work, no guarantee for a job, anywhere in America—except for our politicians, of course. Why are not the energies expended on AB-1 used instead to guarantee a job for those most deserving of all, the poor? It is not homosexuals that are in great need; it is the poverty-burdened heterosexuals that cry out for relief. Why is this so? Because they are politically powerless. Not so with the homosexuals. They are powerful and they have money to feed the politicians' greed. For this reason and this reason alone, there will be relief for the powerful, while the deserving poor continue to go hungry. A guaranteed job for all Californians would make AB-1 unnecessary.

DISCUSSION QUESTIONS

1. The author quotes "a characterization of politicians" written by William E. Simon. What does this say about politicians as a group? What does it say about Mr. Simon? About the author of this essay?
2. The author claims that when California legislators supported AB-1, the result was "bewilderment, social disintegration, and personal disillusionment." What does this mean? To whom is the author referring?
3. Does the author believe the legislators were voting their honest convictions? Why, in his view, did they vote for AB-1?
4. The author says that AB-1 would give "special status to those who by preference and choice desire to live openly as homosexuals." On what basis does he object to such open living?
5. "The evidence is overwhelming . . . that sexual appetite, pleasure, and passion are matters of preference and choice, and not a product of biological determination." What evidence supports this claim?
6. The author says, "It is not homosexuals that are in great need; it is the poverty-burdened heterosexuals that cry out for relief." Is this necessarily an argument against AB-1?

Help "Save the Lady"
By Ordering Your Mint-Perfect

STATUE OF LIBERTY
"DOUBLE EAGLE" COMMEMORATIVE

Celebrating the 100th Anniversary of the Statue of Liberty

The authentic Statue of Liberty "Double Eagle"

You may now acquire direct from the National Historic Mint a first-edition Statue of Liberty Commemorative—the authentic "Double Eagle" Series "L"—honoring the 100th anniversary of one of America's most historic national treasures.

Layered in .999 pure silver

Each specimen is mint-perfect, layered in pure .999 silver and will be accompanied by a Certificate of Authenticity to that effect from the National Historic Mint.

**Limited Series
Rare Mint Quality**

Rarer than any silver dollar ever minted, the Statue of Liberty Commemorative is *uncirculated* and embodies the American Numismatic Association's standard of *perfect mint state* quality. Not more than 1,000,000 will be minted in the "L" Series. Thereafter, the dies will be destroyed, thus assuring permanent rarity.

A Unique Historic Event

This Statue of Liberty issue was commissioned and struck by the National Historic Mint as a unique commemorative medallion and has never been intended, designated or circulated as currency. We therefore recommend storage in its protective sleeve to protect against mishandling.

**Price honored
only until March 9**

We cannot guarantee to honor requests at the original issue price after Mar. 9. Should you wish to sell or redeem your Statue of Liberty Commemorative anytime within the next fifty (50) years, we will give you the full cash price you paid.

Lower Serial Numbers

Many collectors desire a low Certificate of Authenticity serial number.

Layered in mint-pure .999 Silver

▲ Enlarged to show detail

NOTE: Double-eagles on back of coin commemorate bicentennial (200 years) of the eagle as America's national symbol.

Help "Save the Lady"

All funds to restore "The Lady" are required to come from private citizens. Therefore with each Commemorative you order, a donation of one dollar will be made to the Statue of Liberty/Ellis Island Foundation; and a Freedom Certificate, suitable for framing, will be issued and sent to you "In Grateful Acknowledgement of your participation and support in the Preservation of one of America's National Historic treasures."

"The National Historic Mint is a private corporation not affiliated as an agent or otherwise with the U.S. Government or the Statue of Liberty/Ellis Island Foundation.

Therefore please order your Commemorative promptly. There is a limit of two (2) commemoratives per address at this price, but requests which are mailed early enough (before February 28) are permitted to order up to 5.

Since this offering is limited, please respond *promptly*—use the toll-free number below to avoid disappointment. Or mail (promptly) to address below.

Send $15 for each Commemorative together with your name and address. Add only $3 shipping and handling no matter how many you order. (New York residents add sales tax.) Allow up to 6-8 weeks for shipment. Mail to: **National Historic Mint, Save The Lady, Dept. 588-93, Box 1235, Westbury, New York 11595.
(E26970)**

☎ **PHONE TOLL FREE
1-800-453-1983** and ask for **Dept. 588-93.** (Call 24 hrs-a-day, 7 days a week plus Sunday.) Please have your VISA or Master Card ready.

© 1985 National Historic Mint Ltd

Courtesy of The National Historic Mint.

DISCUSSION QUESTIONS

1. What is the main effect that the author sought by using words like "Double Eagle," "Commemorative," "Series L," "uncirculated," and "perfect mint state quality"?
2. What is ironic about using this language?
3. How big is the coin being offered? What is it made of?
4. What does "Layered in mint pure .999 Silver" mean? Why is it recommended that the coin be kept in its protective sleeve?
5. "Not more than 1,000,000 will be minted in the 'L' Series." Can you guess how many coins will, in fact, be minted?
6. Why does the author offer a full refund "anytime within the next fifty (50) years"? Is this a safe offer?
7. Why did the people who produced the coin choose to call their company "The National Historic Mint"? Why didn't they call it "Platt's Commemorative Tokens"?
8. Considering the ad as a whole (the language and the layout), is this an effective piece of argument?

PSYCHOMETRY

DAVID ST. CLAIR

That fancy ten-dollar word means holding something in your hand and getting the vibrations from it—no more than that.

After a while, all objects take on the personality of their owner, and just as fingerprints cling to a drinking glass, your psychic print remains on things you wear and touch. Don't ask me why, because I don't know. This phenomenon, like so many others in this field, has yet to be investigated scientifically.

Quite often a good medium will be able to give you a reading just by holding an object belonging to you. Again, like the radio set, she tunes out the world around her—especially her own thoughts—and tunes in to what the object is transmitting. Then she reports what is coming through to her. If she is right, you should tell her so and she'll know she has tuned in to your particular vibrations. Then the reading will continue with ease and (one hopes) with accuracy.

In Los Angeles there is one well-known medium, the Baroness Lotta von Strahl, who has helped the Los Angeles police solve innumerable cases by the exclusive use of psychometry.

One of her most famous cases was that of the Manson killings. The day after they found the bodies of Sharon Tate and her friends in all that blood and gore, the police came (secretly, of course!) knocking at Lotta's door. They had objects that belonged to the victims and also a knife or two that they were sure must have been dropped by the killers. What could she see?

Lotta took the objects and began to have horrible pains. She felt the stabbings in her back and stomach and, a few times, was tempted to ask the police to go away and not force her to go through this torment. But she kept on. She said that she picked up the name "Mason" or "Maxon," and that the man was small, with piercing dark eyes. She also said that the killers were not just men but that there were women with them, and young girls at that. She was puzzled when she kept getting "the same last name. You know," she told the officers, "it's almost as if they were all members of the same *family.*" Then she saw something that puzzled her. It was an old town in the days of the Wild West but "nobody lives there. It's strange, but the doors are open and the houses have no substance."

Of course, when Charles Manson was finally caught, he did have several girls with him who formed his "family." They had been living at a ranch that served as a location for shooting Western films. What Lotta had seen was the empty false fronts of the movie set.

Another case involved a violent murder at a Mexican-American wedding. The groom had been stabbed and the bride was wounded. The police had arrested several suspects, but none of them admitted committing the crime. The police gave Lotta the dead man's shirt, all torn

SOURCE: Reprinted by permission of author. From *David St. Clair's Lessons in Instant ESP.* New York: New American Library (Signet Books), 1978.

and brown with dried blood, and she picked up something about a man with a birthmark on his upper-right shoulder. The police had photographs of the corpse. No, he didn't have such a mark. "Then," said the medium, "the murderer has such a mark. If you find the man with this birthmark, he will confess."

The police called in all the suspects and asked them to remove their shirts. One had a birthmark just where Lotta had said it would be. He denied killing the bridegroom, but when the police told him about Lotta and what she had seen, he began to scream about witchcraft, broke down, and confessed.

Psychometry is easy, especially if you practice and if you—what's the magic word?—*listen.*

Here it is terribly important to *listen* to the information you get from the object. Don't hesitate to say something because *you* don't feel it applies. *You must stay out of it.* It is vitally important for your success that you keep *yourself* out of it as much as possible. Once again, you are only the radio receiving the message—and radios don't think or decide what they will broadcast.

The first time I ever tried psychometry, I was interviewing two wonderful mediums in San Jose, California: Marcia Warzek and Norma Dart, for my book *The Psychic World of California.* Both women had been doing psychometry for a large audience that afternoon, going from row to row and telling people things about themselves no stranger could possibly have known. The audience was amazed and, I'll confess, I was impressed. Later that evening I said to Norma, "That must be very difficult to do, isn't it?"

"Not at all," she said, and promptly took off her bracelet and handed it to me. "Just relax, close your eyes, and tell me the first thing that comes to your mind. Don't force it and don't try to analyze it. Just let the images come and I'll tell you if you're right or not."

I took that bracelet (a little self-consciously, for after all, they were the psychics, not I!) and as I held it, I started to smile.

"What's so funny?" Norma asked.

"I've got a dumb picture here," I said with some embarrassment. "It couldn't possibly mean anything, because it doesn't have anything to do with you."

"Well, what is it? You let me decide if it's for me or not."

"I see a large sailing ship," I said, "with its sails unfurled, and it's going across choppy water." I opened my eyes and handed her the bracelet. "See? That meant nothing at all."

"Oh no?" Norma got up and went out of the room. In a few minutes she was back with a book in her hand. "When my husband died recently, I decided to take all his books and incorporate them into my own library. I wanted to have the same bookplate in them that I had in my own books. I've been combing San Jose for the past month trying to find that bookplate. Look!" She opened her book and pointed to the bookplate. It was a picture of a ship, its sails unfurled, going against a rough sea.

After that, I did psychometry for my family and acquaintances, even saved a friend of mine a few dollars on the purchase of an antique Chinese vase. She was anxious to have it, but the dealer wanted $500 for it. She took me with her to help her make up her mind. I know quite a bit about American and English antiques but nothing about Oriental art. Yet as I picked up the vase I decided to do some psychometry on it. The first words I got were "not old."

"Should I buy it?" she asked me, with the dealer standing right there.

"No," I said with great authority. "It's not old. It's a fake."

The dealer looked thunderstruck. "What do you know about the Ming period?" he asked haughtily.

"A great deal," I lied, "and this vase is not more than thirty years old and not worth more than fifty dollars."

He was sure I was from the police and began to apologize for having tried to sell us something that wasn't genuine. We walked out in righteous indignation and had a good laugh about it in a nearby bar. My friend bought the drinks with some of the $500 I had saved her.

One of the first times I ever did psychometry in public was in Dallas, Texas. I was lecturing on various aspects of psychic phenomena and when I mentioned that it was possible to get information from inanimate objects, a lady in the front row got up and handed me a very expensive diamond wristwatch. "Let's see what you can get from that," she said.

I held the watch and looked at the lady. She was superbly dressed in the very latest fashion—Gucci shoes, diamond necklace, Louis Vuitton handbag, the works. There I stood before over four hundred people and what did I get? A tumbledown shack, an old Ford up on cinder blocks, and two or three small children running around with bare feet, dirty clothes, and ratted hair.

"Well?" she said.

I gulped, trying to get out of this public fiasco and wondering if Texans still used guns to run charlatans out of town. I decided to play it honest. "What I get can't have anything to do with you. There is a shack, an old Ford, and some dirty half-naked children playing around it."

"Oh yes," she beamed. "That does mean something to me. That was the way we lived until Daddy struck oil!"

I repeat: Keep *yourself* out of the reading!

The longer an object has been worn, the stronger the vibrations will be. When giving a reading, ask for something the person has carried with him for a while. A key ring bought just a few days ago won't tell you anything, but a pair of glasses worn for five years will be an encyclopedia of information.

Also make sure that the object has had only one owner. If someone gives you a ring that has also been worn by her mother or her sister, you may well get conflicting vibrations. Often I've been telling someone things and she'll say, "No, that doesn't mean a thing," and *then* she'll tell me that she bought that object in a secondhand store or antique shop. I have no way, then, of knowing *who* the vibrations belong to.

When you are giving a reading, insist that the person be entirely honest with you. If you say that he drives a green car, and he drives a brown car, tell him to say so. Many people will want to please you, and they will stretch the truth (or just plain lie) to "help" you along. They are only confusing things because until you start getting the truthful "Yes, that makes sense" answers, you have no idea whether you have tuned in to that person or not. Insist that people be honest with you; it'll help you give them a better reading.

Every now and then, you'll find yourself telling someone things, they'll go along and admit that you are absolutely right, and then you'll hit one item and they'll balk: "No. That isn't me. I don't know what you're talking about." If the image in question fades away and doesn't repeat itself in the reading, then most likely you were wrong. But if it *keeps* returning or won't go away, and the person keeps denying it, it is almost 100 percent certain that this person doesn't know or doesn't remember what he or she is talking about.

I've had people tell me, as much as a month later, that I had been correct and they just hadn't realized it then. I remember with one woman I kept getting the name Sarah. No, she didn't know any Sarah. The name came back and wouldn't go away. "I have the impression that this Sarah is in spirit and is guiding you, protecting you," I said. No, she had never had a Sarah in her life. I must be wrong.

Then, about three months later, I got a letter from the woman. She had gone back to visit her aged mother and had told her of the reading. When she mentioned the name Sarah, her mother almost fainted. The first child the mother had ever had was named Sarah, but she was born with a severe deformity and only lived a few days. The mother had never told any of the children that came after Sarah that they had had a sister who died.

The information may be given to you in many different ways. You may get names, dates, places, and so on—by "get" I mean you'll *hear* them inside your head or else you'll *see* them written out in your mind's eye.

You may get colors, or heat or cold. You may get symbols. You may see an eagle, for example, and know this person doesn't keep eagles as pets or shoot eagles on her days off, so the big bird must be symbolic of something. Don't try to interpret the eagle symbol *unless* the interpretation is given to you immediately after the image. If all you get is the bird, then give her the bird and let her interpret it to her own satisfaction.

One last thing that is *very important. Never* give someone a reading who doesn't want it! It will only end in disaster, with you looking like the main candidate for the Nobel Prize for Jerks. If someone says that he doesn't want to have anything psychometrized then *don't* insist. You will get no cooperation from this negative soul but be blocked at every level by his negativity. Don't say I didn't warn you!

Any further questions, dear students? Good. Let's get to *work*. Find yourself someone (the less well you know them, the better) who has an object and wants a reading. Have that person take off the object and hold it in her hands. Tell her to close her eyes and imagine currents of electricity running down both her arms into her palms. Have her recharge the object to put even more of herself into it. Then, when you feel ready to begin, ask her to hand it to you.

Say whatever comes into your head. You may start to get words or names even before the object touches your own hands. Fine—say what you get. Keep asking for confirmation of your facts. Make the person say yes or no or maybe, but get her confirmation in some way or else you won't know if you're on the right track.

If you don't get anything at all, ask for another object and hold *both* those objects together. You can pass the objects from one hand to another if you choose, press them against your forehead, do anything with them (within reason!) to make you closer and more in touch with their vibrations.

If you still don't get anything, pass the objects back. Either ask for another item to hold or forget the whole thing with that particular person. And remember, just because you bomb out with one person doesn't mean you'll do it with another. Maybe you just couldn't find that first person's wavelength.

Keep at it until you get it right . . . and you will.

Okay, you may say, this is all very nice but what *good* is it? Why bother to learn this spooky stuff with the long name?

Good question! I've already cited two of the reasons: to help track down a murderer and to decide if something, like the fake antique vase, is really worth the price.

But there are other reasons. You are about to sign a contract, say. You hold it for a few minutes and "something" just doesn't feel right to you. You ask to take it home and study it overnight. Then, in the calmness of your own study, you read the small print at the bottom! No way do you agree with those terms!

You get a letter from a friend. He is saying one thing but by holding his letter and "listening," you get what he was *thinking* as he was writing—and that was something completely different. I'm not suggesting that you'll get his exact words, but you'll get his mood and his emotions, and you'll be able to judge for yourself whether or not to take his letter at face value.

On being introduced to someone, you reach out and take his hand. Blaaahhh! comes back the response in quick psychometric fashion. Uh-huh, you say to yourself, I'd better *watch* this fellow.

I've had students who were collectors of various and sundry things use their psychometry to cut through all the muddle at flea markets and head straight for the items they would be interested in. It saves a lot of time and shoe leather.

I myself like to collect occult and psychic books, especially those written before 1940. I've gotten so that I can go directly to such books in the most jumbled shop and my hand will reach for the interesting ones first. Furthermore, if the book has been signed by the author, I *know* the signature is in there before I open the cover.

There are many ways psychometry can be used in your daily life. After all, that's why you are taking this course, correct?

DISCUSSION QUESTIONS

1. What biographical facts does this essay tell you about David St. Clair? Does he seem to be someone you'd like to know? Do you feel you can trust him?
2. What does the writing style tell you about the author? Does he use many big words, many long sentences? Does he seem concerned about communicating with *you?*

3. If you wanted to verify the story of Baroness Lotta von Strahl's helping the police solve the two crimes, how could you do it?
4. What keeps you from being too impressed by the fact the Baroness guessed the name "Maxon" and knew of Charles Manson's eyes and his family? When are you learning about these facts?
5. What advantages does a psychic have because of these features of psychometry?
    a. The subject hands the psychic an object.
    b. The subject comments about right and wrong facts as the reading progresses.
    c. Some images can be interpreted either literally or symbolically.
    d. Some subjects try to help the psychic by lying or by exaggerating things about themselves.
    e. One should never do a reading for a "negative" person.
6. If you tried a psychometry exercise and a psychic saw a ship on a choppy sea and the name "Sarah," could you find a way to tie these into your life story?
7. If you tried to do a reading on some other member of your class, what advantages (besides psychic power) would you have to help you make correct statements?

INDUCTION

Induction is the process of drawing a general conclusion from incomplete evidence. Most of the things you know, you know by induction.

You believe, for example, that polar bears are white. But because you haven't seen all polar bears, your judgment is based on limited evidence. The two or three polar bears you have seen were white. Those shown in *National Geographic* and in Disney movies were white. Everyone you know agrees they are white. From this information, you reasonably decide that all polar bears are white.

This process is induction. You consider evidence you have seen or heard to draw a conclusion about things you haven't seen or heard. The intellectual movement from limited facts—called a *sample*—to a general conviction is called an *inductive leap.*

Most conclusions regarding past, present, and future events are based on this kind of leap. You believe, for example, that Balboa discovered the Pacific Ocean, that taking Tylenol eases a headache, and that the Democrats will win the next presidential election. Because you can never secure all the evidence relating to these questions, you reasonably make judgments from the evidence you have.

It is equally reasonable, when you hear induced conclusions, to inquire about the number and kinds of facts that went into making them. For a claim to be credible, its sample must be (1) known, (2) sufficient, and (3) representative. If you are told simply that the FBI is directed by Jewish conspirators, you can withhold belief on the ground that the sample is not known. No evidence is given to support the accusation. If you hear a famous athlete's low IQ cited to demonstrate that athletes (or members of the athlete's race or nationality) are generally ignorant, you can respond that the sample is not sufficient. One example proves nothing about a large group. And if you hear the cruelties of the Spanish Inquisition used as evidence of the repressive views of Catholics in general, you can insist that the sample is not representative. Spanish practice in the fifteenth century is hardly typical of worldwide Catholicism today.

You should recognize such unsupported claims when you see them. Try to keep them out of your own writing.

IS THE SAMPLE KNOWN?

You frequently hear statements that lack evidence. An advertisement announces that "Ban is preferred by seven out of ten American women." A tabloid headline reads "Seven Out of Ten Husbands Are Cheating." A rumor whispers that green M&Ms are aphrodisiacs, that McDonald's hamburgers contain worms, and that Procter & Gamble is involved in Satan worship. Such claims can be dismissed if no evidence is ever offered to support them.

A variation popular with sensational writers is to make an extravagant claim and then point to conclusive evidence—which happens to be unavailable. They argue that superbeings from outer space built Stonehenge and that President Warren G. Harding was murdered by his wife; then they regret that evidence is lost in the past. They talk confidently about Bigfoot, Atlantis, and the Loch Ness monster—and then lament that proof remains out of reach. (Tabloids regularly report arthritis cures, sacred statues that talk, and other wonders occurring "behind the Iron Curtain.") Popular writers insist that UFOs are extraterrestrial spaceships and that a massive conspiracy led to the attempted assassinations of President Reagan and Pope John Paul II—then they protest that government officials and law enforcement agencies are withholding crucial evidence.

When you become familiar with a few of these stories, you begin to see a pattern. The tabloids and the talk shows tell you about the audio tapes giving intimate conversations between President Kennedy and Marilyn Monroe. They mention a dog who can read and an 87-year-old woman who is pregnant. Where are these amazing wonders? You know where they are. They're elsewhere, in some distant place. You can't get there from here.

The Reagan administration has produced a new kind of "lost" evidence. It claims that most Latin American leaders favor U.S. policies in Central America. Then, when leader after leader denies this, the administration says, "Yes, that's what they say in public. In private, they say the opposite."

All these are inductions with an absent sample.

IS THE SAMPLE SUFFICIENT?

Induction with an insufficient sample is common. You regularly hear charges like these:

> Most labor leaders are crooks. Look at Tony Boyle, Frank Brewster, Jimmy Hoffa, and Roy Williams.

> Running is dangerous. You saw what happened to Jim Fixx.

> Don't talk to me about Puerto Ricans. I lived next to a Puerto Rican family for two years.

Clearly, the indicated samples—*four* labor leaders, *one* runner, and *one* family—are inadequate evidence on which to base any broad conclusion.

Insufficient samples lead to stereotyping. They underlie the simplistic descriptions you hear about blacks, Jews, college professors, Republicans, southern Baptists, feminists, Swedish stewardesses, athletes, cab drivers, and so forth.

Persuaders commonly try to enhance the effect on an insufficient sample by insisting their examples are "typical" or "average." In argument, the words typical and average deserve immediate suspicion.

IS THE SAMPLE REPRESENTATIVE?

A sample is said to be unrepresentative when it is not typical of the whole class of things being studied. It is easy to see that you cannot gauge your town's attitude toward a proposed liquor tax by polling only the citizens at a corner tavern or only members of a local fundamentalist church.

Nevertheless, conclusions based on an unrepresentative sample can sound quite persuasive on first hearing; for example, "Women are better drivers than men; they have fewer accidents." Here the sample is large enough—a substantial body of accident statistics—but it is not broad enough to be meaningful. The conclusion concerns *all drivers,* but the sample group includes only *drivers who have had accidents.* To be representative (that is, typical of the whole area under discussion), the sample must include all four groups involved:

1. Men
2. Women
3. Drivers who had accidents
4. Drivers who had no accidents

With this broad sample you can see that there are fewer women in automobile accidents because there are fewer women driving. The isolated accident statistics are meaningless if they are not compared to those for all drivers.

Similarly, if you hear that 80 percent of all San Quentin convicts came from homes that served liquor, you can draw no significant conclusion. The implied judgments describe *everyone,* but the sample includes only *convicts;* there are no general statistics with which to make comparison. Perhaps 80 percent of *all* homes serve liquor. Then, of course, the narrower statistics become meaningless.

Photographic evidence is usually induction with an unrepresentative sample. A candidate's campaign photographs show him and his loving wife walking on the beach with their wonderful children. They show him late at night reading important books and thinking deeply about the problems of the day. The pictures you see are chosen from dozens taken by professional photographers and media people who arranged settings, chose clothes, and told the candidate how to stand and what to do. When you see such photos, ask yourself, "What would this candidate look like if I saw him right now?"

Any induced conclusion is open to question, then, if its sample is too small or unduly weighted in some way. The Nielsen and AGB rating services claim to know the audience size for American television programs. But because the information comes from 2000 people meters (one for every 56,000 homes), the sufficiency of the sample has been questioned. *The Hite Report* on female sexuality was based on responses to questionnaires mailed to chapters of the National Organization for Women, abortion-rights groups, and university women's centers; on information from women who saw notices in newspapers, the *Village Voice, Mademoiselle, Bride's,* and *Ms.* magazines, and who wrote in for the questionnaires; and on responses from female readers of *Oui* magazine, which ran the questionnaire in its entirety. Clearly, the sample is not representative of all American women.

Any poll with a selective sample—that is, where some individuals choose to respond to it and others do not—is unrepresentative. Those who choose to respond cannot represent those who do not.

POLLING

People can misuse a poll to make it support a favored opinion. They can announce the results of surveys that were never taken. (Politicians have for years made good use of "private polls" to enhance the prestige of a lagging candidate.) They can phrase a poll question to draw the response they seek (Evangelist Jerry Falwell asked, "Do you approve of the present laws legalizing Abortion-on-Demand that resulted in the murder of more than one million babies last year? Yes ____. No ____."), or they can inflate others' polls. A memorable example occurred in 1972 when Washington television station WTTG asked viewers to write in their opinion of President Richard Nixon's decision to mine North Vietnamese harbors. The final poll result showed 5157 supporting the president and a much smaller number opposing him. Later investigation showed that some 4000 of the votes favorable to Nixon came directly from the Committee for the Reelection of the President.

What is an adequate sample on which to base a reliable judgment? There is no easy answer. It varies with both the character of the question and the degree of probability you want.

You should remember, however, that a small sample—if generally representative—can sustain a broad conclusion. George Gallup assesses the opinions of the American public by polling 1500 individuals. But because his sample is chosen so that every adult American has an equal chance of being interviewed, the Gallup poll, like similar polls, is a reliable source of information. The mathematical probability is that, 95 times out of 100, a selection of 1500 anonymous people will give results no more than 3 percentage points off the figures that would be obtained by interviewing the whole population.

In the past 23 national elections, the Gallup predictions were an average of 2.3 percentage points off the exact results.

In the 1980 presidential election, however, both the Gallup and the Harris polls were 4 percentage points off the final total. Apparently many voters made up their minds at the last minute, after these polls had been completed. Both Carter's and Reagan's personal pollsters, who surveyed opinion right up to election eve, predicted the final results exactly.

In 1984, all the polls were impressively accurate. The ABC–*Washington Post* survey said President Reagan would get 57 percent of the vote. The CBS News–*New York Times* poll gave him 58 percent. And the *USA Today* poll (of 2219 registered voters) said the president would win 60 percent of the total vote. He won 59 percent.

OCCAM'S RAZOR

Even in everyday experience, you commonly use very limited information to draw a tentative conclusion. This is not unreasonable. If you see that a friend is not wearing her engagement ring and is behaving despondently, you may speculate that she has broken her engagement. The evidence is not sufficient for you to offer condolences, but it will keep you from making jokes about marriage.

If you hear from a friend that a new restaurant is disappointing, you will probably choose not to eat there—at least until you hear a contrary report. Your conclusion is based on a tiny sample, but it is all the sample you have. As your sample grows, so will your degree of conviction.

With induction, you should remember *Occam's razor,* the maxim that when a body of evidence exists, the simplest conclusion that expresses all of it is probably the best. A perfect illustration occurred in 1967 when New Orleans District Attorney James Garrison sought to prove that Clay Shaw, a local businessman, was involved in the assassination of President Kennedy. He submitted that Shaw's address book carried the entry "Lee Odom, P.O. Box 19106, Dallas, Texas," and that the number "PO 19106," when properly decoded, became "WH 15601," the unlisted phone number of Jack Ruby, slayer of Kennedy's assassin Lee Harvey Oswald. (The process involved "unscrambling" the numerals and—since P and O equal 7 and 6 on a telephone dial—subtracting 1300.) Thus Garrison used the entry in Shaw's address book as inductive evidence leading to a sensational conclusion. But Occam's razor suggests a simpler explanation, one that proved to be true: Shaw was acquainted with a businessman named Lee Odom, whose Dallas address was P.O. Box 19106.

You should remember Occam's razor when you read the many books and articles that "reexamine" famous crimes. Routinely, they conclude that people like Lee Harvey Oswald, Alger Hiss, Lizzie Borden, Bruno Hauptmann, Carl Coppolino, James Earl Ray, Sam Sheppard, the Rosenbergs, Alice Crimmins, Jeffrey MacDonald, and Sacco and Vanzetti were really innocent. The true criminal was either a shadowy figure whom nobody saw or members of some complex and incredible conspiracy. Occam's razor submits that the person with the motive and the opportunity and the gun is probably guilty. It submits that the 16-year-old Greek girl who had the illegitimate baby probably was not captured and impregnated by space aliens.

As you read, carefully examine the facts underlying conclusions. Are they given? Are they sufficient and representative? As you write, support your generalizations as much as you can.

EXERCISES

How reliable are these inductive arguments?

1. In a study of a possible relationship between pornography and antisocial behavior, questionnaires were sent to 7500 psychiatrists and psychoanalysts, whose listings in the directory of the American Psychological Association indicated clinical experience. Over 3400 of these professionals responded. The result: 7.4 percent of the psychiatrists and psychologists had cases in which they were convinced that pornography was a causal factor in antisocial behavior; an additional 9.4 percent were suspicious of such a connection; 3.2 percent did not commit themselves; and 80 percent said they had no cases in which a causal connection was suspected.

2. Do you prefer your hamburger flame-broiled or fried?

3. In an article warning of the dangers of cholesterol, *Time* showed the clogged arteries in the heart of an 85-year-old woman.

4. Listerine Antiseptic advertisement: "Proven most effective against colds."

5. How can you argue that large families frustrate the individual child? Benjamin Franklin was the eighth child of his parents. There were six in the Washington family, and Abraham Lincoln had seven brothers and sisters. The Jeffersons numbered ten; the Madisons, twelve; the Longfellows, eight; and the Beethovens, twelve.

6. Do you prefer a hamburger that is grilled on a hot stainless steel grill or one cooked by passing the raw meat through an open gas flame?

7. *Psychology Today* asked its readers to answer questions about paranormal activity. The responses showed that 85 percent of the women and 78 percent of the men believe ESP exists. Wow!

8. I don't care what you say about stereotypes. Most of the blonds I know are dumb.

9. Cola drinkers were asked to compare glasses of Coke and Pepsi for taste. The Coke was in a glass marked Q, and the Pepsi in a glass marked M. A majority of those tested said they preferred the taste of Pepsi.

10. Certainly it's obvious from the newspaper reports that rich and famous people have a higher proportion of divorces than the general public.

11. A study of 3400 New York citizens who had had a recent heart attack showed that 70 percent of them were 10 to 50 pounds overweight. Clearly, obesity is the cause of heart disease.

12. Arguing that eighteenth-century English poetry was essentially prosaic, Matthew Arnold offered a passage from "Pope's verse, take it almost where you will":

    To Hounslow Heath I point and Banstead Down:
    Thence comes your mutton and these chicks my own.

13. Don't tell me that homosexuals aren't sick. I'm a psychiatrist with a large number of homosexual patients, and all are deeply disturbed. Every one of them.

14. "Soviet archeologists have uncovered pieces of an advanced computer system buried in the desert more than 25,000 years ago—and scientists now believe the machinery was abandoned during an ancient mission by space aliens."—*National Enquirer*

15. Since 1979, the Soviet Union has been converting Nicaragua into a forward base of operations on the North American continent. The Sandinista government, as part of its role in the international "anti-imperialist" struggle, has turned Nicaragua over to the Soviet empire.

ESSAY ASSIGNMENTS

Write an essay either affirming or opposing one of these statements. The arguments you encounter in your background reading will probably be inductive, and so will your essay.

1. Prisoners should be brainwashed.
2. ESP has been proved to exist.
3. Absurd drama is a waste of time.
4. Rock music is a national danger.
5. Jogging is a perfect exercise.
6. Homosexuals should not be allowed to teach in elementary school.
7. The drinking age should be raised to 24.
8. X is worth saving. (Fill in the X.)

ELVIS
IS ALIVE!

PATRICK COTTER

Startling new evidence suggests that Elvis Presley's long-time manager, Col. Tom Parker, arranged for The King to fake his own death so he could lead a normal life, reveals a top author.

Since Elvis vanished from the scene ten years ago there has been widespread speculation that he was alive. Now Gail Brewer-Giorgio, author of an amazingly prophetic novel, *Orion,* makes a series of stunning new revelations, indicating that the superstar's alleged death is an elaborate hoax.

In the book, published in 1979, the wily manager of an immensely popular rock n' roll superstar fakes his client's death to allow him to escape the prison of superstardom.

EVIDENCE

Now Brewer-Giorgio, of Marietta, Georgia, discloses that she is in possession of disturbing new evidence indicating that the novel was closer to fact than fiction.

But the veteran writer fears that releasing her most conclusive proof, a tape recording Elvis made four years after his "death," will ruin The King's new life as an ordinary man.

"I am in a terrible position," she told the *Examiner.* "It's the most incredible tape you'll ever hear. The whole thing has got to be handled delicately.

"Elvis feels that he made a mistake by hoaxing his own death. He said he has been recognized, but he knows no one will believe anyone who says they saw him."

The circumstances surrounding the publication of *Orion* lead Brewer-Giorgio to believe that Col. Tom Parker masterminded both Elvis' masquerade and the mysterious disappearance of her book from shelves all across the country.

At first the book, for which she was given a $60,000 advance, was well-received and well-promoted. But suddenly it simply vanished from the shelves of bookstores. Now *Orion* "is nowhere to be found," she says.

"It's fiction that was stopped because it got too close to the truth," adds Brewer-Giorgio. "It's very, very strange."

Shortly after she finished writing the book in 1978, a songwriter friend showed it to Mae Boren Axton, who wrote Elvis' first million seller hit, "Heartbreak Hotel," introduced The King to Col. Parker, and became Elvis' "second mother."

SOURCE: Reprinted by permission from the *National Examiner,* August 11, 1987.

ASTONISHED

Axton repeatedly told Brewer-Giorgio how astonished she was at how well the author had captured the soul of Elvis in the book—and marveled at her knowledge of events and traits that were known only to insiders.

By an eerie coincidence, Axton had been Brewer-Giorgio's eighth-grade English teacher.

Later, after the book was copyrighted but before it was published, TV reporter Geraldo Rivera did a story: "The Cover-Up On The Death Of Elvis Presley."

A short while after that, Brewer-Giorgio received a copy of the medical examiner's report on Elvis, a document that Rivera was unable to obtain for his show.

"The contents are astounding and, if correct, give evidence that Elvis indeed was not the subject of that particular report," says Brewer-Giorgio.

Axton suggested that Brewer-Giorgio allow one of the top literary agencies in the country to handle the sale of *Orion*. The president of the agency's office in Nashville, Tennessee, at the time, Bob Neal, was Elvis' first manager. Neal has since died.

Although Brewer-Giorgio was bowled over by the agency's eagerness to handle the book, she balked at their insistence on an exclusive three-year contract and gave *Orion* to another agent.

But shortly after being published, she says the book "mysteriously disappeared." The publisher said it simply wasn't selling well, said Brewer-Giorgio, but assured her she could keep the money they had given her.

"'And please,' they urged," she adds, "'do nothing or say nothing about Elvis Presley.' But I knew the book was doing fine. In fact I still get calls about it."

Brewer-Giorgio asked a friend in the publishing business to investigate.

LAWSUIT

"The friend heard it was the Colonel that had gone to the head of the publishing house, threatening a lawsuit," adds the author. "But why? What had I unwittingly touched on? What had I uncovered?"

Brewer-Giorgio took no action at the time because she was trying to recover her reprint rights to her own book. Then, suddenly, they were given back, "out of the blue."

Shortly after that, she was given the tape by two strangers who insisted they remain anonymous.

"They know everything," she says. "I insisted on witnesses during their visit. I was presented with a tape and told I may do with it what I wish."

Brewer-Giorgio is now agonizing over whether to have the tape scientifically analyzed and compared to a known recording of The King's voice to determine if it is truly Elvis speaking.

The voice mentions the attempted assassination of President Reagan in 1981, proving the tape could not have been prepared beforehand.

"Elvis tells in his own words how he managed to fake his own death, how it seemed right at the time, and how he misses the music now.

"There are times when he says he would like to come back, but that he would be foolish to enter a life he tried so hard to escape."

DISCUSSION QUESTIONS

1. Seven different strands of evidence support the thesis that Elvis is alive. How persuasive is each?
   a. The novel *Orion* tells of a superstar who fakes his death. It also contains much insider information about Elvis Presley.
   b. Gail Brewer-Giorgio (author of *Orion*) has a tape on which Elvis discusses events—like the shooting of President Reagan—that happened years after his death.
   c. On the tape, Elvis says that, in the years since his death, various people have recognized him. (Other Elvis legends claim that a Tennessee farmer saw him strolling on a hillside and an Alabama truck driver gave hitchhiking Elvis a lift.)
   d. *Orion* suddenly disappeared from bookstore shelves. Someone said that Colonel Tom Parker had threatened the publishers with a lawsuit.
   e. After the book disappeared, the publishers let the author keep her advance money. But they warned, "Do nothing or say nothing about Elvis Presley."
   f. Television reporter Geraldo Rivera did a story called "The Cover-Up on the Death of Elvis Presley."
   g. The medical examiner's report on Elvis's death is suspect.
2. Do the seven arguments taken together have a greater effect than the arguments taken one at a time?
3. Consider the language of the essay. Is this readable prose?

Courtesy of the American Bankers Association.

DISCUSSION QUESTIONS

1. Is it fair to say that the main feature of this argument is the photograph? What does the photo suggest about brokers and investors?
2. Is there any evidence that this picture is typical of brokers and investors? Discuss the stereotyping involved.
3. What is suggested in the contrast between "the professionals at your bank" and "people pushing investments"?
4. The ad warns of "risks" and offers "security with no ifs." What is an inevitable characteristic of the investment with no risks? Why might one prefer an investment with risks?

COACHES ARE RARE, DESERVE HIGHER PAY

CHARLES GILMAN

TO THE EDITOR:

Some people have questioned whether it is right that coaches are paid more than twice what professors receive, but I would like to present some reasons why the present situation is best.

1. Every university has many more professors than coaches. Since coaches are rarer, they are more valued, just as gold is worth more than silver.

2. Most liberal arts graduates go into ordinary jobs with average salaries, while the best college athletes may earn millions as pros. The coaches train these valuable graduates, so they deserve the relatively small share of the loot they receive.

3. Coaches are constantly criticized by the newspapers and television commentators when they have bad luck, while professors are scarcely ever mentioned by the media. The coaches deserve extra money to make them feel better after all the public abuse they have to take.

4. Coaching is dangerous. A coach who is unlucky and loses may be fired. It doesn't matter how many unqualified students pass through a professor's hands, she or he usually continues to climb the career ladder. The coach needs the big bucks to counteract the risk.

5. Coaches have to work in wet, cold stadiums or smelly gyms, not nice air-conditioned classrooms. Part of their pay is hardship allowance for this unpleasantness.

6. Professors are always questioning things, and this may cause the students to doubt the wisdom they have learned from their parents. Coaches are known for being loyal to the school that pays them, and this loyalty provides a good example of patriotism.

7. Professors make people feel uncomfortable by using big words and talking about things nobody else can understand. Ordinary people like to see somebody like themselves do well. The high pay of coaches is a valuable warning against the undemocratic idea that some people know more than others.

Trying to change things by making the pay scales for coaches and professors more equal would send out the wrong message. It would be a step backwards to the middle ages when people were less enlightened than they are now and thought the main purpose of a university was to teach students how to use their minds.

America has the best college athletic programs of any country in the world. Even if we are surpassed in learning and science by other nations

SOURCE: Reprinted from the Nashville *Tennessean*, December 13, 1986. Reprinted by permission of the author.

it won't matter, because our high-paid coaches will be producing better TV entertainment than all the professors put together.

If you add all these reasons up, it is clear that coaches deserve even more, and professors even less than they now get.

DISCUSSION QUESTIONS

1. Clearly, the seven reasons justifying coaches' high salaries are not equally persuasive. Which are the most convincing arguments?
2. Which arguments are weak to the point of being ridiculous? Analyze these one at a time.
3. Considering these weak arguments, what do you think is the real purpose of this essay?
4. Comment on the dangers of using irony in argument.
5. Can you make a substantial argument on this subject? What are the real reasons that coaches get paid more than professors?

SMOKING IS VERY GLAMOROUS

AMERICAN CANCER SOCIETY

Courtesy of the American Cancer Society.

DISCUSSION QUESTIONS

1. The author uses irony. What is really meant by the claim that "Smoking is very glamorous"?
2. If the author is making a statement about how smokers look, what is his evidence?
3. Where do you think the Cancer Society people and their photographer found this woman? Give reasons for your answer.
4. Put in terms of inductive argument, is his sample known, sufficient, and representative?
5. What does this argument tell you about photographic evidence in general?

JOHN HINCKLEY: WRONG REASONS
WON'T YIELD RIGHT ANSWERS

ROBERT GILLMORE

Should John Hinckley go free for a day? I don't know, I'm not his psychiatrist.

What I do know is that nearly every argument offered up to Wednesday for keeping Hinckley at St. Elizabeth's is wrong.

- Wrong reason No. 1 (and, incidentally, the worst): Assorted public officials—none of them health professionals—think he's still dangerous.

"He shot four individuals," says a Secret Service spokesman, "and to us he's still a threat."

Law-enforcement officers think a lot of people are "threats" and, if they could, they would lock them up, too.

It would certainly take away a lot of the uncertainty, wouldn't it?

Unfortunately, it would also take away personal liberty, which free governments like ours are founded to protect.

- Wrong reason No. 2, often expressed as: "The sonofabitch shot the president, goddammit. He should *pay* for it. He shouldn't be able to just walk away."

But Hinckley *should* be able to "walk away." Because the court found he was temporarily insane, he was found innocent. Like any other acquitted defendant, he owes us absolutely nothing.

The whole point of the insanity defense, after all, is to recognize that the insane are literally not responsible and, therefore, cannot in fairness be held responsible for their actions.

- Wrong reason No. 3: "He faked it."
- Wrong reason No. 4: "He wasn't *that* crazy."

Both reasons say, in effect: The court that found Hinckley insane was bamboozled. But second-guessing trial-court fact-finding leads only to bigger mistake-making—which is why not even appellate courts which have the entire trial transcript before them indulge in it.

And if appellate courts won't do it, what does that say about lay persons guided only by rumor, occasional media accounts, and no rules of evidence?

- Wrong reason No. 5: "He's still dangerous."

Unfortunately, that reason is based on even bigger second-guessing than overruling a trial court. Candid psychiatrists will tell you they can't predict behavior—particularly the behavior of ex-mental patients—with certainty. But who can?

SOURCE: Reprinted by permission from *USA Today,* April 16, 1987.

And if you think your predictions are better than those of highly trained professionals who have observed and examined Hinckley at length, you give new meaning to the word "hubris."

DISCUSSION QUESTIONS

1. How far do you have to read in the essay to know the author is an effective writer?
2. The issue that provoked this article is mentioned in the opening paragraph: Should John Hinckley be permitted to leave the hospital to spend one day eating a holiday meal with his parents? Does the essay as a whole go beyond this?
3. This is a special kind of induction. Instead of offering reasons to support a conclusion, the author rejects reasons that support a conclusion he rejects. Is this an effective kind of argument?
4. How might this kind of argument be used to produce a specious result?
5. You must know people who want Hinckley to remain locked up. Does this essay answer their argument? (Could an argument like this respond to someone who wants a particular criminal executed?)

DEDUCTION

"You have an M.B.A. from Harvard. Of course I believe you."
—Wendy Wasserstein, Isn't It Romantic?

Deduction is the opposite of induction. Where induction moves from specific facts to a general conclusion, deduction moves from a general truth to a specific application. Because there are many kinds of deduction—some quite complicated—this discussion aims to be little more than a useful oversimplification.

The vehicle of deduction is the syllogism. This is an argument that takes two existing truths and puts them together to create a new truth. Here is the classic example:

> MAJOR PREMISE: All men are mortal.
> MINOR PREMISE: Socrates is a man.
> CONCLUSION: Socrates is mortal.

In everyday affairs, you encounter many examples of deductive thinking. The syllogism is often abbreviated, however, with one of the parts implied rather than stated.

> You haven't registered, so you can't vote. (IMPLICIT MAJOR PREMISE: Anyone who does not register cannot vote.)

> No man lives forever. Even old Dan Thompson will die someday. (IMPLICIT MINOR PREMISE: Dan Thompson is a man.)

> Anyone can make a mistake. After all, Roger is only human. (IMPLICIT CONCLUSION: Roger can make a mistake.)

Many informal arguments can easily be resolved into syllogistic form. You do this so that you can judge their reliability more systematically.

A deductive argument is considered reliable if it fulfills three conditions: (1) the premise must be true, (2) the terms must be unambiguous, and (3) the syllogistic form must be valid. These requirements will be considered each in its turn.

44

ARE THE PREMISES TRUE?

First, the premises must be true. Because the major premise of a syllogism is usually derived by induction (that is, it is a general statement drawn from specific facts), you can judge its reliability by asking whether the facts that produced it are known to be sufficient and representative. Here is a vulnerable example:

> Gentlemen prefer blondes.
> George Bush is a gentleman.
> George Bush prefers blondes.

This syllogism reaches an unreliable conclusion because the major premise is unproven. The generalization about blondes exists only as a cliché (and as a title by Anita Loos); it was not induced from any known sample. You have heard the common argument for lowering the drinking age:

> Anyone old enough to fight is old enough to drink.
> Eighteen-year-olds are old enough to fight.
> They should be old enough to drink.

This syllogism will be persuasive to anyone who accepts the major premise, but many people find the premise unacceptable.

Political partisans regularly use dubious major premises (a war hero would make a good president, a woman would make a poor one, etc.) to produce the conclusions they want.

IS THE LANGUAGE UNAMBIGUOUS?

The terms of deductive argument must be clear and consistent. If definitions change within a syllogism, arguments can be amusingly fallacious:

> All cats chase mice.
> My wife is a cat.
> Therefore . . .

> All men are created equal.
> Women are not men.
> Therefore . . .

But sometimes such an argument can be misleading. The advertisement "See *Witness,* the Academy Award Winner" was based on this syllogism:

> The Academy Award–winning movie is worth seeing.
> *Witness* is this year's Academy Award–winning movie.
> *Witness* is worth seeing.

Here the phrase "Academy Award–winning movie" is ambiguous. In the major premise, it refers to the movie voted Best Picture of the year; in the minor premise, to a movie winning one of the dozens of minor awards given annually. *Witness* won an award for its screenplay.

Ambiguous examples are not always frivolous. Consider these syllogisms:

Killing an innocent human being is murder.
Abortion kills an innocent human being.
Abortion is murder.

A private club should have the legal right to accept or exclude anyone it wants.
The Junior Chamber of Commerce is a private club.
The JCs should have the legal right to accept or exclude anyone they want (i.e., they shouldn't have to admit women).

These syllogisms went all the way to the U.S. Supreme Court, where the terms "human being" and "private club" were analyzed very carefully.

A current advertisement is based on this syllogism:

You should be anxious to buy a genuine diamond ring for only $5.
We are offering a genuine diamond ring for $5.
You should be anxious to buy this ring.

The advertisers offer a ring containing a 0.25-carat diamond chip. This is not a diamond in the sense you usually think of one.

IS THE SYLLOGISM VALID?

A reliable syllogism must have a valid form. This requirement introduces a complex area of discussion, because there are many types of syllogisms, each with its own test of validity. Commonly, "valid form" means that the general subject or condition of the major premise must appear in the minor premise as well. It is easy to see that this argument is false:

All murderers have ears.
All Methodists have ears.
All murderers are Methodists.

What makes the argument unreliable syllogistically is the fact that the term "murderers" does not recur in the minor premise. A major premise about "all murderers" can only lead to a conclusion about murderers. Similarly, the premises "If Taylor loses his job, his wife will leave him" and "Taylor does not lose his job" produce no necessary conclusion. The condition "lose his job" does not occur in the minor premise.

When an invalid syllogism appears as argument, it usually maintains that things with one quality in common share a kind of identity. Such argument takes extreme forms:

The father of Miss Smith's baby has blood type O.
Mike Hanna has blood type O.
Therefore . . .

The American Communist Party opposes resumption of the draft.
Phil Feldman opposes resumption of the draft.
Therefore . . .

Because the crucial term does not appear in both premises of these syllogisms, their conclusions are no more valid than the claim that all murderers are Methodists.

These three tests, then, permit you to judge the reliability of a deductive argument.

Some deductive arguments involve several syllogisms. Consider the following example.

> A change in a person's handwriting shows a change in his or her emotional state.
> There has been a change in Nancy Reagan's handwriting.
> There has been a change in Nancy Reagan's emotional state.

> If Nancy Reagan's emotional state has changed, it must be because of a disturbing current event.
> Nancy Reagan's emotional state has changed.
> Nancy Reagan's emotional state has changed because of a disturbing current event.

> Nancy Reagan's emotional state has changed because of a disturbing current event.
> The Iran/contra scandal is a disturbing current event.
> Nancy Reagan's emotional state has changed because of the Iran/contra scandal.

This is the kind of thinking that produced the *National Enquirer* article "Handwriting Shows Nancy Reagan Is Devastated by Iran Scam." Notice that every premise—major and minor—is questionable.

INDUCTION OR DEDUCTION?

Because most syllogisms begin with an induced major premise, certain arguments can be analyzed as either induction or deduction. Consider this example: "John Floyd doesn't drink; he'll make some girl a fine husband." You can read this as a syllogism and attack the implicit major premise "Anyone who doesn't drink will make a fine husband." Or you can treat it as induction and argue that the sample (the fact that John Floyd doesn't drink) is insufficient to sustain a conclusion about his prospects as a husband. With such arguments, it is best not to quibble over terms; either approach is satisfactory.

When you evaluate a syllogism, don't judge it as true or false, but as reliable or unreliable. An unreliable conclusion may nevertheless be true. From the doubtful major premise ("Anyone who does not drink . . .") you cannot reasonably deduce that John Floyd will make a fine husband. But he might, in fact, make a very fine husband. In rejecting the syllogism as unreliable, you simply say that the claim is not proved by this argument.

You can recognize the distinction between truth and a reasonable conclusion by recalling a passage from Eugene Ionesco's *Rhinoceros.* In the play, the logician argues, "All cats die. Socrates is dead. Therefore Socrates is a cat." And his student responds, "That's true. I've got a cat named Socrates."

Recognizing the syllogistic form of an argument will help you to analyze its reliability. It will also help you to structure an argumentative essay. Commonly, in deductive writing the first paragraph offers the major premise, and the last paragraph, the conclusion. The body of the theme tries to demonstrate the minor premise. (This is, for example, the structure of the Declaration of Independence.)

EXERCISES

How reliable are these deductive arguments?

1. Of course Sylvia is a poor driver. She's a woman, isn't she?
2. A medical procedure that preserves life and health should be legal. Abortion preserves life and health that would be endangered in a clandestine operation. Abortion should be legal.
3. Professor Costello's new book on marriage should be pretty informed. After all, he's been married four times.
4. Both Catholics and Protestants are Christians. No one can be both Catholic and Protestant. Therefore, no one can be a Christian.
5. We should not pass laws that can never be enforced. Laws prohibiting smoking in public places can never be enforced. Laws prohibiting smoking in public places should not be passed.
6. The Easter Island statues could not have been carved, moved, and erected by mere humans. The work must have been done by superhuman agents.
7. The Easter Island statues were carved, moved, and erected by superhuman agents. Space travelers who could visit the earth must be superhuman agents. So the Easter Island statues must be the work of space travelers.
8. Genuinely oppressed people (like blacks) have lower academic scores and shorter life spans. Women do not have these. Women are not oppressed.
9. The Book of Revelation says that the Antichrist of the last days will be identified by the number 666. Count the letters in the name R-o-n-a-l-d W-i-l-s-o-n R-e-a-g-a-n. What do you get?
10. I know I'm not supposed to lust after my neighbor's wife. But Mary

Davis lives way over in Biloxi, and she and Billy Miller aren't married.

11. My condition is beyond the help of medical science. Fortunately, Mr. Harris is a quack.

12. The Roman Catholic Church should follow the example of Jesus. Jesus chose only men to preach his gospel. The Church should never permit women to be priests.

13. "Any public school curriculum on sex education should meet a four-point test: It should be true, healthy, legal, and constitutional. The only classroom teaching that satisfies all four is to teach children sexual abstinence until marriage."—Phyllis Schlafly

14. "If you don't like fast driving, why don't you go to Russia?"—Charles Bowden

15. "The EPA is equally confident that conclusions from animal studies . . . can be readily transferred to humans. It believes that swamping animals with nearly toxic doses of a chemical provides a clear measure of whether the substance will cause cancer [in humans] at very low doses."—Vincent Carroll, syndicated columnist

---

ESSAY ASSIGNMENTS

Write an essay either affirming or opposing one of these statements. The argument you encounter in your background reading will probably be deductive, and so will your essay.

1. There's nothing wrong with buying a term paper.
2. Evolution is a foolish theory.
3. Cable TV should not be permitted to show uncut, R-rated movies.
4. Teachers have no right to strike.
5. America needs stronger libel laws.
6. There should be no required courses in college.
7. The miracles of Jesus prove he was God.
8. X is a disease; it should not be punished but cured. (Fill in the X.)

PRO/CON:
BIRTH-CONTROL CLINICS IN SCHOOLS?

LAURIE ZABIN AND BISHOP LEO MAHER

PRO

Interview with Prof. Laurie Zabin, Johns Hopkins School of Public Health

Q Professor Zabin, why do you favor the establishment of health clinics in or near the schools?

Family planning is one of the best ways of reducing pregnancy, and we know that a vast proportion of adolescent conceptions, in particular, are unintentional. There's no doubt that the provision of clinical services can help cut down unintentional pregnancies among teenagers.

Q But why must the health clinics be in high schools?

It's a principle of public health that one places clinics where the patients are or as near to them as possible. They should either be in schools or accessible to them, preferably with some staff in school to encourage initial contact. Adolescents often seek health care only during a crisis. So there's a real need for early diagnosis, including regular health care, identifying drug and alcohol use, smoking and reproductive problems.

Q Don't these clinics encourage sex among adolescents?

There's absolutely no evidence of that. In fact, the first rigorous evaluation of a clinic—a study we just published on a program in two schools in Baltimore—shows that the 28-month program postponed first intercourse by seven months. Seven months can be a critical time period for an adolescent.

Q Don't clinics supplant the rights of parents and the church to counsel youths about sex and contraception?

No, not in any way. The clinics don't relieve parents or other institutions of their responsibilities; in the Baltimore clinics, counselors actually helped children to open up and talk with their parents. Certainly parents and teachers should be involved in developing a school's total program.

Q Should parental consent be required for contraceptives?

No. In some states, confidentiality is a matter of law. But I would go further and say that parents should want their children to receive confidential treatment. A parent already in communication with her child has nothing to fear. The parent that is not should welcome the clinic because it could open up that communication. In any case, the parents are better off than if the clinic wasn't there.

Q While the clinics don't perform abortions, aren't clinic counselors going to encourage kids to get abortions?

Abortion is completely legal, and it's absolutely necessary that clinic counselors tell young people about all available options. I don't think more clinics will lead to more abortions; abortions in the Baltimore schools dropped soon after the opening of the clinics. If you give teens the opportunity to avoid getting pregnant, you'll bring down the abortion rate. Anyone seriously interested in doing that ought to be in the vanguard of this movement.

CON

Interview with the Most Rev. Leo Maher, Roman Catholic Bishop of San Diego

Q Bishop Maher, why do you oppose school-based health clinics that give contraception and abortion counseling?

My main objection is moral. By providing contraception and abortion counseling, such clinics tacitly encourage children to act promiscuously, as various surveys show. Sexual activity outside marriage is immoral, and school-based clinics promote it.

The clinics, moreover, are antieducation, antifamily values and antireligion. The presence of the clinic undermines the rights of parents and weakens self-discipline among teenagers. The message sent to schoolchildren is that it's all right to be self-indulgent.

Q Yet some clinics have reduced the pregnancy rate in high schools. Isn't this a point in their favor?

Any decrease in births that results from the presence of the clinics occurs only because they encourage abortions. You can't use evil means to bring about good. You cannot do away with the fifth commandment—thou shalt not kill—by making it easy for teenagers to have sex, even if the pregnancy rate does come down. If teenagers drive recklessly, do you encourage them to avoid the police by teaching them to drive even more recklessly? Obviously not. What's more, the facts mostly don't substantiate that the clinics lower the pregnancy rate.

Q Several million girls who are sexually active don't receive family-planning services. What should be done to protect these adolescents?

The schools have an obligation to teach; they should promote virtue, more self-control and abstinence among our young people. Instead, the moral development of teenagers is left to the entertainment industry or peer-pressure groups.

Q Children receive instruction at school on various problems outside the family circle, such as drugs, sex, child abuse and first aid. Why draw the line at school clinics providing counseling about sex?

Because a child's parents are his primary teachers. Schoolteachers are there to assist them, not to take over that duty. Sex education in our schools is done with the consent of and under the supervision of parents.

Q Would you support school-based clinics if the students had to get parental consent to use them?

No. The schools can use any *educational* method they want to reduce pregnancies, abortion and venereal disease. The clinics, however, are a *health* program, and there are plenty of other places where youths can get counseling about sex.

All the clinics are trying to do is supply children with contraceptives. They're promoting a breakdown of morals.

DISCUSSION QUESTIONS

1. Professor Zabin's argument is based on this syllogism:
     A system is needed to reduce teenage pregnancy, abortion, and disease.
     Health clinics in the schools constitute such a system.
     Health clinics in the schools are needed.
   How would Bishop Maher challenge this syllogism?
2. Bishop Maher offers this syllogism:
     A system is needed to reduce teenage pregnancy, abortion, and disease.
     A course of education favoring virtue, self-control, and abstinence constitutes such a system.
     A course favoring virtue, self-control, and abstinence is needed.
   How would Professor Zabin attack this syllogism?
3. What evidence does each offer to support his/her premises?
4. Is Professor Zabin counseling immoral behavior? Is Bishop Maher counseling immoral behavior? What is meant by "moral"?
5. Is it fair to say that one author is more concerned with moral behavior and the other more concerned with solving social problems?
6. Does Bishop Maher offer any evidence to support his claim that school clinics reduce pregnancies simply by counseling abortion? Is there any evidence that Professor Zabin is right on this matter?

Courtesy of the Buckingham Wile Company.

DISCUSSION QUESTIONS

1. The ad begins with the line "When You Live a Cutty Above," and it ends with the implicit recommendation that you buy Cutty Sark whiskey. Can you reconstruct that into a syllogism?
2. How reliable is that syllogism?
3. What does "a Cutty Above" mean? Explain why you think what you do about it.
4. Discuss the range of good qualities that are expressed in the picture.
5. Is there any reason to associate Cutty Sark whiskey with living "a Cutty Above"?

END THE HYPOCRISY
AND PAY THE PLAYERS

JEFF RIGGENBACH

You'd have to be suffering from terminal naivete to believe that big-time college sports can be "cleaned up"—at SMU or anywhere else.

And you'd have to be a confirmed elitist to want them cleaned up—if cleaning them up means making sure no college athletes are paid for their valuable services.

And make no mistake about it, their services *are* valuable. Successful football and basketball teams earn profits for the schools they represent. More important, they attract gifts from alumni better than anything else that's ever been tried. Success in sports is not infrequently the difference between a wealthy school and one that's just scraping by.

It's the athletes who make all that wealth possible. That's why they're in demand. But the kind of athletic skill that makes up a championship team in big-time football or basketball is scarce. And when any good or service is both scarce and in demand, people will try to outbid each other in order to get it.

This is called the law of supply and demand. And like the law of gravity, the law of supply and demand is a law that can't be repealed or evaded.

If you try to repeal it by outlawing the sale of certain goods or services, it will simply go underground, onto the black market. This is why our vice laws have never stopped gambling, prostitution, or the drug trade. And this is why we will never be able to stop colleges from offering young athletes payments or other incentives in return for their services on the playing field. No matter what we do, it will go on happening, on the sly or in disguise, but it will go on nevertheless.

And why shouldn't it? Other people who have valuable services to offer are allowed to be paid for their work. Journalism students, business students, and music students are free to earn money from journalism, from business, and from music while they go to school; why should student athletes be punished when they try to do the same thing? Who exactly is damaged when a college pays an athlete for his performance?

The inventors of the myth that there is something sacred about "amateurism" were a bunch of unabashed elitists wealthy enough to be able to fritter away their time playing games without getting paid for it. They didn't want to have to dirty their hands associating with lower-class types who could afford to play only if they did get paid. Such elitists might see themselves as losing something if the idea of amateurism in sports were consigned to the scrap heap where it belongs, but it is difficult to see how anyone else would lose.

DISCUSSION QUESTIONS

1. The author presents a syllogism:
    A worker who gives valuable service to a school should be paid for
       it.
    A football player (like other athletes) gives valuable service to his
       school.
    He should be paid for it.
   How might a person who differed with the author attack this
   syllogism?
2. Here is a countersyllogism:
    Student athletes should not be paid when they volunteer to
       participate in extracurricular activities.
    A football player is a student athlete who volunteers for an
       extracurricular activity.
    He should not be paid.
   How might one attack this syllogism?
3. The author uses analogies. He says the law of supply and demand is
   like the law of gravity. He says an athlete should be like a business
   major who can profit from his or her work. How reasonable are these
   analogies?
4. Consider another analogy: If football players are simply paid
   performers who make a profit for the university, why shouldn't the
   school buy a stable of racehorses and let them carry the school
   colors?
5. Who are the "elitists" the author complains of? Are they the people
   in the previous argument who "live a Cutty above"?

JOHN SAAD IS PRO-LIFE

HE IS THE KIND OF MAN
WE NEED IN MONTGOMERY

JOHN SAAD
SENATE DISTRICT 34

Advertisement from the *Catholic Week*.

DISCUSSION QUESTIONS

1. Here the syllogism is obvious:
   We need a man who is pro-life in the state senate in Montgomery.
   John Saad is pro-life.
   We need John Saad in Montgomery.
   Is this a reasonable argument?
2. Are the premises true?
3. Are the terms unambiguous?
4. What does the picture prove?
5. Would this ad be equally persuasive in a different periodical?

AID AND COMFORT
TO OUR AVOWED ENEMY

C. B. WILLIAMS

This is a sequel to my recent "Kangaroo Court" letter:

The incessant inquisitors in Washington, who are doing their utmost to destroy President Reagan, are seriously breaking the law; not only just a law, but the Constitution of the United States.

Article 3, Section 3, paragraph 1, reads: "Treason against the United States shall consist only in levying war against them, or in adhering to their enemies, giving aid and comfort." Can any sensible patriotic American doubt that those senators and congressmen now holding a moot court in Washington are adhering to and giving aid and more comfort to Russia, our dangerous enemy?

A more patriotic and freedom-preserving president than President Reagan never occupied the White House, and those devious, communist-courting congressmen and senators who would destroy him should be indicted before the federal grand jury for treason; for giving aid and comfort to our avowed enemy, who are biding their time until President Reagan is out of office, so they can resume their march for world conquest.

Those individuals who would destroy President Reagan's Strategic Defense Initiative are communist-courters too, giving aid and comfort to the communists by saying it won't work. If it won't work, why are the Russians so all-fired against it? They know it will work, and will interfere with their future plans to subjugate other nations.

Let the so-called Boland Amendment sink into a hot place called Hell if it is going to be the means of destroying the freedom of our nation.

Every one of those taking a part in the moot court, including the inquisitive, high-faluting legal advisers, should be warned they are defying the Constitution of the United States by giving aid and comfort to a known enemy, and if they don't cease and desist immediately, the American people should take the necessary action to see that they do comply or receive the impending consequences.

DISCUSSION QUESTIONS

1. This argument concerns the congressional committee investigating Colonel Oliver North and the diversion of funds from arms sales to Iran to the contras in Nicaragua, an act that specifically violated the Boland Amendment. The author presents two syllogisms. This is the first:

    Anyone who gives aid and comfort to America's avowed enemy is guilty of treason.

SOURCE: Reprinted from the *Mobile Register,* July 3, 1987. Reprinted by permission of the author.

The congressmen who oppose President Reagan's efforts are giving aid and comfort to the Russians.

The congressmen are guilty of treason.

Is this a reasonable argument? Is the syllogism vulnerable?

2. This is the second syllogism:

We should not obey a law that will destroy the freedom of our nation.

The Boland Amendment is such a law.

We should not obey it.

Where might one attack this syllogism?

3. What evidence does the author give to support any of his claims?

4. Do the snarl words used here ("inquisition," "devious, communist-courting congressmen," etc.) help the argument?

ARGUMENT
BY AUTHORITY

*"Thanks to the Buddha, I won
$10,000.00."*
—L. W., Fla.

Much of what you believe—or are asked to believe—must be accepted simply on the word of an expert. Your doctor says you have glaucoma. Your mechanic says the car needs a valve job. Your newspaper reviews *Police Academy* and calls it awful. Scientific authorities say the universe is expanding. In such instances, you are asked to accept a view on the basis of someone's authority.

It is reasonable to credit such testimony if it fulfills two conditions: (1) The speaker must be a genuine expert on the subject at hand, and (2) there must be no reasonable probability of bias. When Zsa Zsa Gabor, for example, turns from her acting career to praise the effects of acupuncture, you can justly question her expertise in the area. When Pete Rose appears on television praising the excellence of Tegrin shampoo, you know he is being paid for the advertisement and suspect a degree of bias.

Remember, however, that these unreliable arguments are not necessarily false. Zsa Zsa Gabor may be expressing an important truth about acupuncture, and Pete Rose may be giving his honest opinion of Tegrin shampoo. Nevertheless, it would be unreasonable to accept an argument—or to build a persuasive essay—solely on the authority of such speakers. You should relate their views to other evidence and to the word of other authorities.

EXPERT TESTIMONY

Many arguments raise the question of genuine expertness. Authorities may be unnamed. (Advertisements for health products often print testimony from "Brazilian researchers" or "five New York doctors.") They may be unfamiliar. (*"Promise of Saccharine* is a provocative book—readable and profoundly informed."—Colonel Winston X. Montgomery III.) They may be known largely by their degrees. (A Kansas medico, in recommending goat gland surgery to restore vitality, signed himself "John R. Brinkley, M.D., C.M., Dr.P.H., Sc.D. . . .") And they may appear with strange credentials. (A self-help book by Scott Reed describes him as "one of the nation's leading mind-power experts.") Persuaders always magnify the reputations of authorities who agree with them. A temperance circular quoting William Gladstone's condemnation of alcohol calls him "the greatest prime minister in English history."

Sometimes speakers of unquestioned authority express themselves in areas outside their competence. Actor Tony Randall praises Easy-Off Oven Pads. Actress Brooke Shields warns of the medical effects of cigarette smoking. Rural evangelists pinpoint weaknesses in evolutionary theory. And a U.S. Senate subcommittee (by a 3–1 vote) declares that human life begins at conception. Such people must be judged on the quality of their evidence, not on their word as experts.

Religious Authority

Equally questionable as authorities are "God" and "everyone." Because the claim is not subject to verification with hard evidence, one can champion almost any opinion by saying it conforms to divine will. A correspondent to the *Mobile Press* in 1975 assured readers that West Coast earthquakes were God's punishment for California's sinful life-style. Another correspondent declared it would violate "Christ's plan for the world" if the United States gave up its holdings in Panama. And during the 1984 election, the Moral Majority (and pro-life organizations) made clear that Ronald Reagan was God's choice for president of the United States.

Christian writers routinely quote passages from the Bible to declare the will of God and thus open up a rich area of argument. As mentioned earlier, religious questions often do not lend themselves to meaningful discussion because people cannot agree on necessary definitions. Clearly, an argument involving biblical authority can be persuasive only when addressed to someone who already accepts the truth of scripture and who interprets it in the same way as the speaker. There are large differences between those who claim the Bible *is* the word of God, those who say it *contains* the word of God, those who enjoy it as an anthology of great literature, and those who reject it altogether.

Even when participants in a discussion agree on preliminary matters, problems remain. Because the biblical texts were written by many authors over the course of 1300 years and include a wide variety of opinions, literary styles, and translations, people can find a passage or two to support any argument they choose to make. (Bishop James Pike illustrated this by asking ironically, "How many persons have been reborn from meditating on the last line of Psalm 137: 'Blessed shall he be that taketh and dasheth the little ones against the stones'?") Consequently, when facing a scriptural argument, you should take time to trace the references. You will often find that authors quote passages out of context (they might be championing the superficial counsel of Job's friends) and quote passages inaccurately from memory. They may cite lines scarcely related to the issue at hand. ("Only God can save America now. See Chronicles 7:14.")

An interesting modern claim says, "Of course, God favors capital punishment; otherwise he would never have used it as a means to save the world." The problem with this argument is that it also puts God on the side of betrayal of friends, unjust trials, torture, and other atrocities.

Mass Authority

The authority of "everyone" is claimed in statements beginning, "They say," "Everyone knows," or "All fair-minded people agree."

Such arguments can be convincing in instances where "they" (some notable majority) have demonstrably committed themselves on a matter they are competent to judge. Arguments announcing "More women choose Simplicity than any other pattern" and "Budweiser—Largest Selling Beer in the World" are genuinely impressive because, in these areas, the opinion of a mass audience is superior to that of any particular expert. (What renowned epicure is qualified to assure you that Old Style Lager is America's best-tasting beer?)

It is important to remember that America's democratic procedures and its jury system both rely on the expertness of "everyone."

Mass authority, however, can be distorted in a number of ways. It can be claimed arbitrarily. ("Everyone knows that Jimmy Carter stole the 1976 election.") It can be coupled with ambiguous language. ("More men get more pleasure out of Roi-Tan than any other cigar at its price.") And it can be invoked in areas that call for technical information. (A Gallup poll reported that 41 percent of Americans believe that cigarette smoking is a cause of birth defects.) In such instances, "everyone" is a dubious authority. When you're having severe chest pains, it is no time to take a poll.

Still, mass opinion is worth listening to, especially when it becomes more or less unanimous. Remember the famous counsel, "If you can keep your head when all about you are losing theirs, probably you haven't grasped the situation."

Divided Authority

The word of a genuine expert will not, of course, settle every argument. Alexander Pope put the question best:

Who shall decide when Doctors disagree.
And soundest Casuists doubt, like you and me?

The plain fact is that many issues are complex, and experts hold opposing views. Legal authorities disagree over whether certain means of gathering evidence violate constitutional safeguards. (Was John DeLorean entrapped?) Eminent psychiatrists appear in court arguing the mental competence of particular defendants. (Was John Hinckley insane?) Medical experts do not agree whether a month-old fetus is human. (Is abortion murder?)

Which authorities should you believe? In such cases, it is probably best to side with the majority of experts. However, when you hear a genuinely important authority voicing a minority view (for example, Rachel Carson on insecticides, or Linus Pauling on vitamin C), you would do well to withhold judgment altogether and await further pronouncements.

Critical Authority

You should recognize that some authorities have more established reputations than others. For example, many publications contain reviews of books, plays, and movies, but the reviews of the major New York newspapers, the television networks, and nationally circulated periodicals (*Time, Newsweek, Harper's,* the *Christian Science Monitor,* etc.) are generally thought more critically reliable.

If a book, movie, or play wins praise from critics writing in these publications, the reviews may be quoted in newspaper ads and on book jackets. If an advertisement quotes reviews from other sources, it strongly suggests that the work was not praised by the major critics and may not be very good.

Of course, you can enjoy any book, play, or movie whatever the critics' judgment of it, but you should recognize the varying standards of critical authorities. You should be warned, for example, when you see the cover of the paperback edition of Nancy Freeman's *Joshua Son of None* boasting rave reviews from the *El Paso Times,* the *San Gabriel Valley Tribune,* the *Macon Georgian,* and the *Oceanside Blade-Tribune.*

You should recognize these distinctions when writing a critical essay. If the book or movie you're championing is praised by the major critics, quote the reviews. If it found favor only with lesser authorities, you should probably not mention the reviews at all.

BIASED TESTIMONY

Even when speakers are admitted experts in the field under discussion, an argument should be examined for the possibility of bias. An argument has a probable bias if the authority profits from expressing it or if it reflects the predictable loyalty or routine antagonism of a group. To dismiss the testimony of biased individuals is not to call them liars or even to say that they are wrong; it means a condition exists that makes it unreasonable to accept a conclusion *solely* on their authority.

You don't ask a barber whether you need a haircut.

Rewarded Opinions

Experts profit from making an argument when it brings them money or prestige. The financial incentive is easy to recognize when Reggie Jackson recommends Panasonic TV sets (and Spalding running shoes and Pentax cameras), when Uri Geller proclaims his psychic powers on lecture tours, and when owners of outdoor movies protest the unnaturalness of daylight saving time.

Today many people earn a living by convincing you of preposterous "facts." Tabloid advertisers boast incredible products that will let you grow new hair, develop a larger bust, win at the racetrack, lose 16 pounds in a week, and win true love by wearing Madame Zarina's talisman. Papers like the *Star* and the *National Enquirer* routinely carry stories of reincarnated housewives, arthritis cures, and space creatures that appeared in Canada. Recent best-selling books reveal that Errol Flynn was a Nazi spy, that Marilyn Monroe was murdered, that the Mafia killed President Kennedy, and that the Lindbergh baby is still alive. Such stories are fun to read, and there may be splinters of truth in some of them. But you can give no special belief to the authors of such tales. They are making money peddling their extravagant claims.

The effect of prestige is clear when individuals discuss their incomes, their reading habits, and their sex lives. In these areas, egos are threatened—and people lie.

The impact of money and prestige on an expert is sometimes difficult to establish. For example, few scientific authorities have affirmed the existence of Atlantis or of UFOs, but the few who have won a level of recognition—along with television appearances, speaking engagements, and book contracts—that they could never have won voicing more orthodox opinions. (You won't get on a talk show saying that fluoride prevents cavities.) The experts may be expressing their honest judgments, but you should remember all that acclaim when evaluating their testimony.

The 1987 revelations concerning TV evangelist Jim Bakker and church secretary Jessica Hahn illustrated problems relating to argument by authority. Both told of a sexual episode, though each remembered it differently. We know, however, that Bakker was trying to save his reputation as a religious leader. And we know Hahn changed her story twice when offered large amounts of money. In such a case you have to rely on outside evidence. You can't be comfortable believing either authority.

Similarly, when you read current articles about AIDS, you should recall that a lot of people stand to profit by exaggerating the health danger. There are researchers who want a grant to build a new laboratory, evangelists who need to proclaim God's vengeance, reporters who are looking for a sensational headline, and politicians who want to appear in the news. When you see the dire warnings, ask yourself who is telling the story.

In the mid-1980s, headlines warned that AIDS was spreading into the heterosexual community. Cases appeared among people who insisted they had no involvement with homosexuals or drugs. Medical experts later discovered that many of these people were lying to protect their reputations.

Predictable Judgments

An argument by authority is presumed to be biased if it is totally predictable—that is, when it reflects a traditional loyalty or antagonism. When you want to learn about the new Ford Escorts, you can't rely on the word of your Chevy dealer. You can't learn the truth about a woman's character by asking her ex-husband.

A definitive example of a predictable and biased judgment occurred in 1977 when the University of Alabama's football team was ranked second in the final Associated Press and United Press International polls. Thereupon the Alabama state legislature issued its own poll, and the Crimson Tide moved up to No. 1. Equally predictable are pamphlets on smoking and health distributed by the Tobacco Institute, articles on gun control and crime appearing in the *American Rifleman,* and the publicized study of pain relievers produced by the makers of Bayer aspirin.

In 1986, when Attorney General Edwin Meese appointed a commission to investigate the effects of pornography on the social order, he remembered that a 1970 commission appointed by President Nixon had found that pornography did not cause dangerous behavior. So Meese selected a commission that would bring in a different ruling. Most of the members he chose were well known as militant opponents of pornography. And they brought in a report recommending a repressive agenda for controlling sexual images and texts. There may be merit in these recommendations, but they came from a notably biased source.

This presumption of bias appears most notably in political argument. When any Democrat is nominated for president, the candidate and the party's platform will be praised in liberal periodicals (*Washington Post, St. Louis Post Dispatch, Commonweal, The Progressive,* etc.) and condemned in conservative publications (*Chicago Tribune, U.S. News & World Report, Los Angeles Times, National Review,* etc.). When any president finishes a State of the Union message, opposition speakers will call his program inadequate, wrongheaded, and potentially dangerous. You must judge these claims on specific evidence; such predictable views carry little authority.

DISTORTING QUOTATIONS

Besides a doubtful expert and a biased opinion, other misleading features attend argument by authority. Statements are sometimes abridged. (The advertisement for Kyle Onstott's *Mandingo* quotes a review from the *Dallas News:* ". . . like no other book ever written about the South. . . .") Claims may be irrelevant to the issue at hand. (The paperback edition of *Nightmare in Pink* prints Richard Condon's opinion that "John D. MacDonald is the great American story-teller.") Quotations can appear without a source. (See *Hand in Hand*—"The Most Widely Praised Picture of Them All!") And undated quotations can be impressive. (In the last presidential campaigns, opponents printed statements Ronald Reagan had made years before when he was a Democrat.)

Exact quotations can be presented in a distorting context. Under the heading "How L.B.J. Would Remake America," *Common Sense* printed a sentence from President Johnson's State of the Union message: "We are going to try to take all the money that we think is unnecessarily being spent and take it from the 'haves' and give it to the 'have nots' that need it so much." As the context of the speech made clear, the president did not advocate taking from the rich to give to the poor; he proposed taking money from the more heavily funded federal programs and putting it into those with smaller appropriations.

For decades, conservative speakers have quoted Nikita Khrushchev's line "We will bury you," interpreting it as a Soviet threat to destroy the United States. The sentence is lifted totally out of context. Actually, Khrushchev was saying that the communist economic system would outproduce the capitalist system, and thus survive it.

In the same way, temperance advocates like to strengthen their argument by quoting lines from Chaucer ("Character and shame depart when wine comes in") and Shakespeare ("O thou invisible spirit of wine, if thou has no name to be known by, let us call thee devil!"). The lines, of course, are not direct expressions of these authors; they come from literary characters who are speaking in a dramatic context.

The hallmark of distorted quotations is the *Congressional Record,* which purports to be a record of what went on during House and Senate sessions. The periodical does record what the legislators said. But it also deletes what they said and reports what they wished they had said. It is a magnificently self-serving document and should be immediately questioned when quoted as an argumentative source.

Audiotaped and Videotaped Evidence

With the advent of tape and video recorders, a person can produce new kinds of distorted testimony. In the 1972 senatorial campaign in Alabama, opponents broadcast Senator John Sparkman's voice saying, "Will the cause of desegregation be served? If so, the busing is all right." The two sentences were spliced together from separate parts of a taped interview. President Nixon recorded his phone calls and office conversations and produced the tapes that eventually implicated him in the Watergate scandal. Noting that the president made totally contradictory statements on the tapes, Congressman Tip O'Neill speculated about Nixon's intention:

> Now that tells you what he was going to do with those tapes. He was going to take them with him when he left and spend years editing them, and then he could string together a record of his own which would show he was the greatest man ever to live. He'd be able to prove it with the tapes. You never would have known about any of the other tapes. That would have been thrown away. They would have only given you all these tapes with him making a hero of himself.

In the Abscam trials in the early 1980s, the FBI convicted government officials with the help of videotapes that showed them taking money and making incriminating promises to an agent posing as an Arab sheikh seeking favors. Here it is important to remember that the FBI agents had complete control of the situation. They could introduce topics, guide the conversation, stop it when convenient, tape some episodes, not tape others, and then choose which tapes they wanted to show in court. The Abscam defendants may not have been faultless, but it is hard to imagine St. Francis of Assisi surviving such a test.

In 1984, a California jury saw films showing John DeLorean with quantities of illegal cocaine. They also saw a number of FBI agents who were taking part in the elaborate charade. They ruled that DeLorean was a victim of entrapment.

In 1986, advocates produced a radio ad about cigarette companies and broadcast New York City Mayor Ed Koch's voice repeating, "They are selling death." In fact, Koch had said this not about tobacco but about New York City bathhouses, which he thought were spreading AIDS.

You must take great care in analyzing audio and video evidence. There is a lot to consider besides the words and pictures you see.

Lies

Expert testimony can lend itself to bald misstatement of fact on the part of authorities or of those who quote them. A national columnist accused author Quentin Reynolds of being a Communist and a war profiteer. A U.S. senator called newsman Drew Pearson a child molester. Many have circulated the story that three Pennsylvania students on LSD became blind from staring at the sun for several hours and that a Michigan schoolteacher took off all her clothes to demonstrate female anatomy to her coed sex education class. All these sensational claims were untrue.

Fictional quotations appear as evidence. For many years the statement "We shall force the United States to spend itself to destruction" has been attributed to V. I. Lenin and used to ground conservative political argument. Lenin never said that or anything like it. More recently, liberal sources circulated a paragraph protesting the communist threat and concluding, "We need law and order"; they ascribed this to Adolf Hitler. The quotation is pure fiction. Several years ago a tabloid headlined the news that marijuana may cure cancer. The story quoted Dr. James H. Kostinger, director of research for the Pittsburgh Academy of Forensic Medicine, who had been conducting studies in this area for four years. Investigation later revealed that the academy did not exist and that no medical school in Pittsburgh had ever heard of Dr. Kostinger.

Although expert testimony can be misused by dishonest writers and speakers, it remains a forceful element of legitimate argument. When genuine authorities agree with you, quote them in your writing. Your case will be more persuasive.

EXERCISES

How reliable are these arguments from authority?

1. "Cast thy bread upon the waters: For thou shalt find it after many days."—Ecclesiastes

2. Baron Philippe de Rothschild's Mouton-Cadet—"Enjoyed more by discerning people than any other bordeaux wine in the world."
3. "The most disadvantageous peace is better than the most just war."—Erasmus
4. *Shakespeare of London* by Marchette Chute: "The best biography of Shakespeare"—Bernadine Kielty, *Book-of-the-Month Club News*
5. "72% of men have had sex by age 19."—Tom Biacree, *How Do You Rate?*
6. The Mont Blanc Diplomat—"Many pen experts here and abroad consider the Diplomat to be the finest pen ever designed. It's Europe's most prized pen, unmatched in writing ease."
7. "Causes of Cancer Remain Unknown"—headline in the *Tobacco Observer*
8. "Adolf Hitler Is Alive!!!"—headline in the *National Examiner*
9. "More people will read this issue of *Parade* than there are Communists in the Soviet Union."
10. *Hitler's Daughter* by Gary Goss: "A brilliant academic satire"—Dennis Renault, *Sacramento Bee;* "A hilarious time"—Harry Cargas, *Buffalo Press;* "Raunchy and unfair"—Otto Tumiel, *Reading Intelligencer.*
11. Pond's Cold Cream—"They say you can tell by a girl's complexion when she's in love."
12. "A bad peace is even worse than war."—Tacitus
13. "I might possibly be the Lindbergh child."—Harold Olson
14. Tareyton—"America's best-selling charcoal-filter cigarette."
15. "If I have a sore throat, or a rasp, or something that feels like laryngitis, I will visualize the color blue. Certain colors represent specific areas of the body, and blue is the color for the throat."—Shirley MacLaine
16. "In field test after field test, women agree Musk by English Leather outscores the competition every time."
17. Psychic Sven Petersen, who foresaw the 1986 Delta Airlines disaster in Dallas, predicts that Puerto Rico will become the nation's fifty-first state and will elect Vanna White its first governor. (*Examiner,* August 25, 1987)

ESSAY ASSIGNMENTS

Write an essay either affirming or opposing one of these statements. The arguments you encounter in your background reading will include expert testimony, and so should your essay.

1. Marijuana should be legalized.
2. Vitamin C pills are necessary for good health.
3. Speaking in tongues is a genuine spiritual gift.
4. Flying saucers are here.
5. Fluoridation of drinking water is dangerous.
6. A faith healer can help you.
7. Solar power is the answer.
8. To remain healthy, one should avoid X. (Fill in the X.)

VITAMIN E IN THE
HANDS OF CREATIVE PHYSICIANS

RUTH ADAMS AND FRANK MURRAY

Of all the substances in the medical researcher's pharmacopoeia, perhaps the most maligned, neglected and ignored is vitamin E. In spite of this apparent ostracism in the United States, however, some of the world's leading medical authorities are using alpha tocopherol—more commonly known as vitamin E—to successfully treat and cure a host of mankind's most notorious scourges.

For those medical researchers who are at work trying to treat and prevent heart attacks—our No. 1 killer—and to help many more thousands who are dying of related circulatory disorders, vitamin E is playing a major role. And for many athletes, vitamin E (in the form of wheat germ oil, specially formulated oils for stamina and endurance, vitamin E capsules and perles, etc.) has long been as indispensable as calisthenics.

"There are over 570,000 deaths from heart attacks each year," says a publication of the American Heart Association, "many thousands of them among people in the prime of life—and growing indications that heart disease may be a disease of prosperity."

In scientific minds, vitamin E may be related to fertility and reproduction, said an article in *Medical World News* for April 18, 1969. But a famous ball player, Bobby Bolin of the San Francisco Giants, credits the vitamin with keeping his pitching arm in condition. He developed a sore shoulder in 1966, resulting in a poor pitching season for two years. He began to take vitamin E. The article said that he expected to be a "regular starter" at the beginning of the 1969 season, and that vitamin E was responsible for the good news.

It isn't surprising that many athletes have discovered the benefits of taking vitamin E regularly. The vitamin is in short supply in most of our diets. Vitamin E is an essential part of the whole circulatory mechanism of the body, since it affects our use of oxygen. When you have plenty of vitamin E on hand, your cells can get along on less oxygen. This is surely an advantage for an athlete, who expends large quantities of oxygen. And, according to recent research at the Battelle Memorial Institute, which we will discuss in greater detail in a later section of this book, vitamin E, along with vitamin A, is important to anyone who lives in the midst of constant air pollution.

From *The Summary*, a scientific journal published by the Shute Institute in Canada, a publication we will frequently refer to, we learn additional facts about vitamin E. Dr. Evan Shute, who heads the clinic, and Dr. Wilfrid E. Shute, his brother, have pioneered in work with vitamin E for more than 20 years. *The Summary* condenses and abstracts for doctors and medical researchers some of the material on relevant subjects that has appeared in medical journals throughout the world.

SOURCE: *Vitamin E, Wonder Worker of the 70's.* New York: Larchmont Books, 1972.

For instance, a Hungarian doctor reports on the encouraging effects of vitamin E in children born with certain defects. Of all vitamin deficiencies, she believes that vitamin E is the most important in preventing such occurrences. She has given the vitamin with good results in quite large doses to children who would otherwise be almost incapacitated. Mothers, too.

She tells the story of a woman who had three deficient children, two of them with Down's Syndrome or mongolism. When she was pregnant for the fourth time, the physician sent her away for a rest—"tired, aging, torpid" as she was, with "a diet rich in proteins, liver, vegetables and fruit with large doses of vitamins, especially vitamin E, and thyroid hormone." She returned in six weeks to give birth to a perfectly healthy baby!

As for another insidious disorder—chronic phlebitis—Dr. Evan Shute says that most doctors have no idea of how common this condition is. It should be looked for in everyone, he says, certainly every adult woman. After describing the symptoms—a warm swollen foot and an ache in the leg or foot which is relieved by raising the feet higher than the head—he tells his physician readers, "Look for chronic phlebitis and you will be astounded how common it is. Treat it with vitamin E and you will be deluged with grateful patients who never found help before."

Describing a symposium on the subject of vitamins E, A and K, Dr. Shute tells us that speakers presented evidence that vitamin E is valuable in doses of 400 milligrams daily for treating claudication—a circulatory condition of the feet and legs—and that a similar dosage helps one kind of ulcer.

High dosage of vitamin E improves survival time of persons with hardening of the arteries and should always be given to such patients, according to Dr. Shute. He adds that there are some 21 articles in medical literature, aside from the many he himself has written, showing that vitamin E dilates blood vessels and develops collateral vessels—thus permitting more blood to go through, even though the vessel is narrowed by deposits on its walls.

An article that appeared in *Postgraduate Medicine* in 1968 by Dr. Alton Ochsner, a world-famous lung surgeon, states that he has used vitamin E on every surgical patient over the past 15 years and none has developed damaging or fatal blood clots.

Dr. Shute goes on to say that, at the Shute Clinic, all surgery patients are routinely given vitamin E both as a preventive and as a curative measure.

He quotes an article in *Annals of Internal Medicine,* saying that thrombosis or clot formation "has become the prime health hazard of the adult population of the Western world." Dr. Shute adds these comments: "Here is a real tragedy. Twenty years after we introduced a simple and safe clotting agent, alpha tocopherol, to the medical world, everything else is tried, including dangerous drugs and the anti-coagulants, and with all these the results are extremely unsatisfactory. When will the medical profession use vitamin E as it should be used for this condition?"

He quotes a statement from the *Journal of the American Medical Association* showing that the average teenage girl or housewife gets only about half the amount of iron she should have from her diet in the United States.

Then Dr. Shute says, "Another nutritional defect in the best fed people on earth! In one issue the *JAMA* shows the average American is often deficient in iron and vitamin A. Now what about vitamin E?" He, of course, has pointed out many times that this vitamin is almost bound to be lacking in the average diet. As we mention elsewhere, up to 90% of the vitamin E content of various grains is lost during the flaking, shredding, puffing processes that are used to make breakfast cereals.

Dr. Shute then quotes a newsletter on the U.S. Department of Agriculture survey revealing that only half of all American diets could be called "good." He comments thusly, "One continually reads claptrap by nutritionists contending that the wealthiest country in the world feeds everybody well. This obviously isn't true. It is no wonder that deficiency of vitamin E is so common when even the diet recommended by the National Research Council of the U.S.A. contains something like 6 milligrams of vitamin E per day before it is cooked!"

In another issue of *The Summary*, we learn how two Brazilian researchers are working on heart studies done on rats that were made deficient in vitamin E. Of 26 rats, only six normal ones were found. All the rest showed some heart damage when they were tested with electrocardiograms and other devices.

Two German researchers report on the action of an emulsified vitamin E solution on the heart tissues of guinea pigs. They found that the vitamin protects the heart from damage by medication, and helps to prevent heart insufficiency. Dr. Shute adds that this paper indicates that vitamin E should be investigated further in hospital clinics.

Animals deficient in vitamin E produced young with gross and microscopic defects of the skeleton, muscles and nervous system. They had harelips, abdominal hernias, badly curved backs and many more defects. This was reported in *The Journal of Animal Science,* Volume 22, page 848, 1963.

Two American obstetricians report in the *American Journal of Obstetrics and Gynecology* that they know of no way to prevent serious damage and death for many premature infants. Dr. Shute comments, "These authors apparently have not seen our reports on the use of vitamin E in the prevention of prematurity." He goes on to say, "No comparable results have been reported."

A report in the journal, *Fertility and Sterility,* indicates that in six percent of patients studied, the cause of abortion and miscarriage lay in the father's deficient sperm, not in any deficit of the mother. The authors studied carefully the medical histories of many couples who had been married several times. Dr. Shute comments, "We have long advocated alpha tocopherol for poor sperm samples, especially in habitual abortion couples."

A Romanian farm journal reports that extremely large amounts of vitamin E, plus vitamin A, were given to 77 sterile cows. Within one to one-and-a-half months, their sexual cycles were restored and 70 percent of them conceived.

A German veterinarian reports in a 1960 issue of *Tierarztliche Umschau* that he uses vitamin E for treating animals with heart conditions. A one-year-old poodle with heart trouble regained complete health after 14 days on vitamin E. A three-year-old thoroughbred horse with acute heart failure was treated with vitamin E for two weeks, after which time its electrocardiogram showed only trivial changes even after exercise. The vet uses, he says, large doses of the vitamin.

And an Argentinian physician reports in *Semana Med.* that vitamin C is helpful in administering vitamin E. It works with the vitamin to retain it in body tissues. Dr. A. Del Guidice uses the two vitamins together in cases of cataracts, strabismus and myopias. He also noted that patients with convulsive diseases are much helped by vitamin E—massive doses of it—so that their doses of tranquilizers and sedatives can be lessened.

A letter from Dr. Del Guidice to Dr. Shute tells of his success in treating mongolism in children with vitamin E. For good results, he says, it must be given in large doses from the age of one month on. He continues his treatment for years sometimes, and claims that spectacular results can be achieved in this tragic disease.

Two Japanese scientists report in the *Journal of Vitaminology* that hair grew back faster on the shaven backs of rabbits when they applied vitamin E locally for 10 to 13 weeks.

And again from Argentina comes word of vitamin E given to 20 mentally defective children in large doses. In 75 percent, the intelligence quota was raised from 12 to 25 points, "with improved conduct and scholarly ability. Less attention fatigue was noted in 80 percent, and 90 percent had improved memory." A short experience with neurotic adults showed that vitamin E brought a definite reduction in phobias, tics, obsessions and other neurotic symptoms.

In one issue of *The Summary*, Dr. Shute prints a letter of his to the editor of the *British Medical Journal* (July 1966) urging this distinguished man to consider vitamin E as a treatment for pulmonary embolism. He says, "I have used nothing else for years and no longer even think of embolism (that is, blood clots) in my patients, even in those with records of previous phlebitis. Dosage is 800 International Units a day." He adds a PS to readers of *The Summary:* "The Editor could not find space for this letter unfortunately."

A *British Medical Journal* editorial comments on our present methods of treatment for blood clots in leg veins. Raising the foot off the bed, bandaging the legs and getting the patient on his feet doesn't seem to be very helpful, says the editor. Using anticoagulants seems to help some, but we should speedily develop some new methods of treatment. Dr. Shute comments that one would think that vitamin E has a clear field, since nothing else is very effective. It is easy to use, he goes on, safe and effective.

Each issue of *The Summary* contains many articles that have appeared in world medical literature on vitamin E and related subjects. In other countries, vitamin E is treated quite seriously in medical research, is routinely used in hospitals and clinics. In our country, such use is rare.

These are just a few of the case histories that Dr. Shute reports, at his own expense, in *The Summary*. The book is not available for nonmedical people, since it is written in highly technical terms. However, we suggest that you recommend these publications to your doctor, if you or someone you know is suffering from a disorder that might be treated successfully with vitamin E. The address is: Dr. Evan Shute, Shute Foundation for Medical Research, London, Ontario, Canada.

DISCUSSION QUESTIONS

1. The case for vitamin E is supported by reference to a range of authorities:
    a. a publication of the American Heart Association
    b. an article in *Medical World News*
    c. Bobby Bolin of the San Francisco Giants
    d. many athletes
    e. recent research at the Battelle Memorial Institute
    f. *The Summary*
    g. The Shute Institute in Canada
    h. Dr. Evan Shute
    i. Dr. Wilfred E. Shute
    j. a Hungarian doctor
    k. speakers at a symposium on the subject of vitamin E
    l. 21 articles in medical literature
    m. an article in *Postgraduate Medicine*
    n. Dr. Alton Ochsner
    o. an article in *Annals of Internal Medicine*
    p. a statement in the *Journal of the American Medical Association*
    q. a U.S. Department of Agriculture survey
    r. the National Research Council of the United States
    s. two Brazilian researchers
    t. two German researchers
    u. the *Journal of Animal Science*
    v. two American obstetricians
    w. the *American Journal of Obstetrics and Gynecology*
    x. a Romanian farm journal
    y. a German veterinarian
    z. *Tierarztliche Umschau*
    aa. an Argentinian physician
    bb. *Semana Med.*
    cc. Dr. A. Del Guidice
    dd. two Japanese scientists
    ee. the *Journal of Vitaminology*
    ff. an editorial in the *British Medical Journal*
    Evaluate the relative authority of these.
2. A number of consecutive paragraphs give quotations from respected medical journals along with Dr. Shute's commentary. Do these usually say the same thing?
3. The authors begin by noting that vitamin E has been "maligned, neglected and ignored" by American doctors. How can this occur if the vitamin has been so successful in tests and studies?

4. Studies do show that animals and humans deficient in vitamin E improved significantly when given the vitamin. Does this prove that vitamin E should be added to most people's diet?
5. Who publishes *The Summary?*
6. How successful was Bobby Bolin as a pitcher in 1969?
7. Make a list of the maladies that vitamin E is said to cure. Do these wide-ranging claims for the vitamin make the case for it more persuasive?

Snow leopards in the Himalayas. Tigers in the wilds of India. Mountain gorillas and lions in Africa. Jaguars in the swamps of Brazil.

George Schaller, pictured here with a snow leopard, has spent years in remote and rugged places studying the natural history of rare animals—and fighting for their survival.

He sees these animals as symbols of the habitats in which they live. Preserve their habitats and thousands of other plants and animals will be assured of a home.

As director of Wildlife Conservation International, a division of the New York Zoological Society, Schaller and the staff have helped establish more than 50 reserves around the world.

One of the 1000 remaining giant pandas.

He points out that the destruction of environments is now so drastic that, in the decades ahead, the nature of life on earth will be irrevocably changed.

For Schaller, saving fragments of nature is an urgent task.

Recently he faced one of his greatest challenges. With Chinese scientists, he collaborated in a project to save the 1000 giant pandas still alive in the wild. Currently he is working on the Tibetan plateau to help preserve the wildlife of those remote uplands.

"Future generations must be inheritors... not just survivors."
George Schaller

China: Site of panda rescue mission.

Since his work takes him to some of the most forbidding places on earth, choosing the right equipment is crucial. Not surprisingly, Schaller wears a Rolex.

"My watch must be absolutely reliable, as animal observations are recorded under the most demanding conditions. My Rolex has never let me down."

Inhospitable conditions seem to pose no problem for George Schaller. Or his Rolex.

ROLEX

The Rolex Explorer II Oyster Perpetual Chronometer in stainless steel.
Write for brochure. Rolex Watch U.S.A., Inc., Dept. 106, Rolex Building, 665 Fifth Avenue, New York, New York 10022-5383.
© 1985 Rolex Watch U.S.A., Inc.

Explorer II, Oyster Perpetual are trademarks

Courtesy of Rolex Watch U.S.A., Inc.

DISCUSSION QUESTIONS

1. Is this a simple argument by authority? Are you being encouraged to buy a Rolex watch simply because George Schaller uses and recommends one?
2. Does Schaller have a particular need for a Rolex watch?
3. What kind of animal observations require absolute timing precision? What are the "demanding conditions" Schaller works under?
4. Why the pictures of the panda and the snow leopard?
5. What values are the advertisers affirming? How do these relate to the Rolex watch?
6. Why is Schaller recommending Rolex watches?

GOVERNMENT DOCUMENT REVEALS
CRASH OF THREE "FLYING SAUCERS"

JANE HULSE

Government officials may put down UFOs as science-fiction bunk, but a UFO researcher says they can't deny the contents of a top-secret memo sent to then-FBI Director J. Edgar Hoover in 1950.

The memo relates how the Air Force recovered three "so-called flying saucers" that crashed in New Mexico. Aboard each of the three crafts were "three bodies of human shape but only 3 feet tall," the memo states.

The memo is one of hundreds of secret government documents proving the existence of UFOs, according to Robert Hastings, an independent UFO researcher from Albuquerque. Hastings, 35, was in town to speak on the Arapahoe Community College campus Monday night, one stop on his national lecture circuit.

The documents, declassified under the Freedom of Information Act beginning in 1975, indicate a massive coverup by military and intelligence officials, Hastings says.

"The public has a right to know the facts," he said in an interview. He said the government is being "shortsighted to keep the public so totally in the dark regarding seemingly vital information that affects not only Americans, but the entire human race."

The 1950 memo is "frustratingly vague," Hastings said, but it's the most tantalizing key to the UFO mystery.

The memo describes the flying saucers as "circular in shape with raised centers, approximately 50 feet in diameter." The small bodies were dressed in "metallic cloth of a very fine texture." Each was "bandaged in a manner similar to the blackout suits used by speed flyers and test pilots."

The memo doesn't say where in New Mexico the crash occurred. But the crash is blamed on the government's "very high-powered radar setup in that area" that could have interfered with the "controlling mechanism of the saucers."

The brief memo doesn't reveal what happened to the bodies or the flying saucers. Hastings, working with former National Security Agency employee W. Todd Zechel, is striving to end the mystery through investigation and by pressing for release of more secret documents.

The government documents released to Hastings refer to UFOs repeatedly nosing around nuclear weapons laboratories and ICBM sites. Others note attempted aerial interceptions of UFOs by military jet aircraft.

"Whoever is flying these things is highly interested in our nuclear weapons," Hastings said. UFO sightings increased after World War II, a fact Hastings links to the "birth of the nuclear age."

SOURCE: Reprinted by permission of Scripps Howard News Service. Reprinted from the *Mobile Register*, October 23, 1985.

Hastings speculates that the UFOs and their passengers may be "sending a signal to the government that they have the capacity to interfere with a nuclear launch."

Hastings says that military and intelligence officials are covering up the facts about UFOs because of the "potential for panic."

He says the public can handle the information and "it's just a matter of time before it all comes out anyway."

In 1977, *U.S. News & World Report* speculated that before the end of the year then-President Carter was "expected to make what are described as 'unsettling disclosures' about UFOs" based on CIA data.

That didn't happen, and now the public isn't any closer to knowing the truth about UFOs. The Reagan administration has "stonewalled" the issue, Hastings said, and made release of classified documents more difficult.

Hastings's interest in UFOs began as a "pure fluke" in 1967 when he was visiting an air traffic control tower on Malmstrom Air Force Base, near Great Falls, Mont.

"Five UFOs were tracked on military radar," he said. "For a half-hour period they hovered over nearby ICBM silos, violating sensitive air space. Then they flew off at an estimated speed of 5,000 mph, far beyond the capability of any conventional aircraft."

Then 17 years old, Hastings was "scurried out of the room."

Hastings, a photographer and filmmaker, spends about four months a year on the lecture circuit to finance his UFO research. Aside from released government documents, he says his information comes from interviews with retired military personnel.

He shied away from speculation, preferring to talk instead about facts contained in government documents. But he did issue one assurance.

"They are benevolent," he said of the extraterrestrials. "There is nothing to indicate hostility. At some point they will make themselves known."

DISCUSSION QUESTIONS

1. The author refers to a number of authorities that seem to support Hastings's belief in UFOs.
   a. a memo to J. Edgar Hoover, director of the FBI
   b. "hundreds of secret government documents"
   c. W. Todd Zechel, National Security Agency employee
   d. "more secret documents"
   e. *U.S. News & World Report*
   f. President Jimmy Carter
   g. people at the Malmstrom Air Force Base who tracked five UFOs in 1967
   h. retired military personnel who were interviewed
   How persuasive is each of these?
2. Consider everything the essay tells you about Robert Hastings. Is he a genuine expert in the areas under discussion? Is there any reason to suspect bias?

3. How can the Reagan administration and the military and intelligence communities continue to stonewall when Hastings has solid documentary evidence to refute them?

4. What do you know of the 1967 sighting at Malmstrom Air Force Base?

5. How persuasive is Hastings's speculation about the UFOs, their passengers, and their purpose?

It cures everything — and you can get it at your drug store

WONDER PILL MAKES YOU YOUNG AGAIN

WEEKLY WORLD 55¢

NEWS

OUTRAGEOUS!
Wimpy judge lets crazed axe killer go to college!

December 22, 1987   30587   VOL. 9, Issue 11

Thousand-page report reveals answers to world's greatest riddles

Mysteries of Bigfoot, The Devil's Triangle, Atlantis and UFOs
—ALL SOLVED!

Voices of the dead taped in cemetery

★ ★ ★

Miracle pickup truck can heal the sick

★ ★ ★

Firecracker scares new bride to death!

Gossips ruined me!

Town shuns teen and her family after vicious AIDS rumor

Coma man wakes up speaking ancient language, docs say

Courtesy of Weekly World News, Inc.

DISCUSSION QUESTIONS

1. Of the eight stories headlined, which ones do you think are more likely to be true? Which are least likely to be true? Give your reasons.
2. Though all the stories involve argument by authority, one also involves statistical proof. Which one is that? What kind of statistical evidence would lead you to believe the headlined claim?
3. For the other seven stories, specify the authorities who might be involved. Is there any reason for you to doubt their claims?
4. Are the authorities experts in the area under discussion? Is there any reason to suspect bias?
5. How reliable an authority is the *Weekly World News?*

THE BIBLE AND
THE DEATH PENALTY

JOHN LOFTON

The most conspicuous death penalty, the greatest act of capital punishment in all of history, was God's decree that His only begotten son, Jesus Christ, must die on the cross for the sin, the evil committed by others.

Thus, the one thing the death penalty for murder can *never* be is "anti-God." Yet, this is one of the reasons why the lame duck governor of New Mexico, Toney Anaya, a Catholic, says he has commuted the death sentences of five convicted murderers in his state.

In an interview on ABC's "Nightline," Mr. Anaya, defending his view that capital punishment is "anti-God," noted that "the leaders of every major organized religion" are opposed to the death penalty.

But this begs the most important question: What does God say about the death penalty? And the answer to this question is that God has commanded it for certain specified crimes, including murder.

Citing, among other passages in the Bible, Genesis 9:5 and 6, in which God commands an accounting from man for the life of his fellow man—that "whoever sheds the blood of man, by man shall his blood be shed"—Walter C. Kaiser, Jr., in his *Toward Old Testament Ethics* (Academie Books, 1983), observes:

"So sacred was life, that all violent forms of snatching it away caused guilt to fall upon the land—whether in a manslaughter case or that of premeditated murder—and must lead to yielding up another life."

In the case of premeditated murder, there would be no atonement, that is 'substitute' or 'ransom,' for the life of the murderer (Numbers 35:31). Genesis 9:6 would explain why this is so. This one capital offense required the death penalty, but was unlike the other crimes that also had capital punishment which allowed substitution.

"It was because humans are made in the image of God that capital punishment for first-degree murder became a perpetual obligation. To kill a person was tantamount to killing God in effigy. *That murderer's life was owed to God; not to society, not to the grieving loved ones, and not even as a preventative measure for more crimes of a similar nature.*" (Emphasis mine.)

The New Testament makes no essential change regarding this particular matter. Except where specifically dispensed with, the Old Testament law, God's law, still stands.

And the sole purpose of the civil government is justice, to wield the sword, to administer God's law, to be, in the words of Martin Luther, "God's hangman." As St. Paul defines the role of the civil magistrate in Romans 13:4 (the New King James Version of the Scripture):

"For he is God's minister to you for good. But if you do evil, be afraid; for he does not bear the sword in vain; for he is God's minister, an avenger to execute wrath on him who practices evil."

OK, but how about Mr. Anaya's particular religious faith? Does capital punishment violate Catholic teaching? Not at all.

SOURCE: Reprinted by permission from *Liberty Report*, February 1987.

In the *Pocket Catholic Dictionary* (Image Books, 1985), John A. Hardon, S.J., citing passages from the Old and New Testaments, says: "It is certain from Scripture that civil authorities may lawfully put malefactors to death . . . in receiving its authority from God through the natural law; the state also receives from him the right to use the necessary means for attaining its ends. If even with capital punishment crime abounds, no lesser penalty will suffice."

But the problem with modern man—modern rulers and modern institutions—is that they could not care less what God has commanded. They are playing God, not seeking to obey God. And this is a grievous sin.

When, earlier this year, I wrote to another Catholic governor, Mario Cuomo of New York, and asked why he is opposed to capital punishment, my letter was answered by his director of criminal justice, Lawrence Kurlander.

Mr. Kurlander said Mr. Cuomo was against the death penalty because:

1. It can never restore the loss of a loved one or compensate for the suffering such a loss causes.

2. Our judicial system is capable of error.

3. Capital punishment does not prevent or discourage murder any more effectively than life imprisonment.

4. It is not possible to enforce the death penalty without very protracted litigation and lengthy appellate delays.

And Gov. Anaya of New Mexico has this same mindset. In his "Nightline" interview, Mr. Anaya, when asked if he really had the right to overrule the will of his state legislature, five juries, and public opinion, denied that he did what he did! He says he didn't do this.

He says the governor's role is the "ultimate link" in the criminal justice system. And Mr. Anaya, who says he is a man who is "true to myself," says he shouldn't be criticized for using "my power."

Now notice, please, what's missing in the views of Mr. Cuomo and Mr. Anaya. Neither Mr. Anaya nor Mr. Cuomo's director of criminal justice have anything to say about the true definer and creator of all real justice, God Almighty Himself.

But governors aren't ultimate over anything, even when they play God. Only God is sovereign, and over *all* areas of thought and life.

No, the question isn't whether Mr. Anaya or Mr. Cuomo are being true to themselves. Such self-worship is idolatry. The question is whether these heads of state civil governments are true to *God's Word.*

But in the area of capital punishment, neither of these men has been—which is why, in God's sight, they are just as lawless as the criminals whom they judge.

DISCUSSION QUESTIONS

1.   In arguing that God favors capital punishment, the author cites a number of authorities:

Genesis

Walter C. Kaiser, Jr.

Numbers
The New Testament
Martin Luther
St. Paul (Romans 13)
John A. Hardon, S.J.
Are these equally persuasive as authorities?

2. Does Walter Kaiser necessarily favor the death penalty? Does the quote from St. Paul necessarily urge the death penalty? (You might want to check several translations here.)

3. Authorities mentioned who oppose the death penalty are Governor Anaya, Governor Cuomo, and "the leaders of every major organized religion." How impressive are these experts?

4. How can it be that "leaders of every major organized religion" do not understand God's command and the author does?

5. What happened to the Sermon on the Mount teaching about love, forgiveness, and turning the other cheek? How does the author avoid this?

6. If God permitted Jesus to be betrayed, tortured, and executed, does it necessarily follow that He favors betrayal, torture, and capital punishment?

7. What problems occur when one declares "God says" and then quotes Genesis and Numbers and a metaphorical passage from Paul?

SEMANTIC ARGUMENT

"Buick Electra. The name alone speaks volumes."

Semantic argument tries to make a persuasive point by using impressive language rather than by presenting or arranging evidence. It should convince no one.

Semantic argument always sounds good. Its effectiveness derives from the nature of words. A word can have two levels of meaning: a denotative meaning—that is, some specific thing or condition to which it refers *(mail carrier, swim, beige),* and a connotative meaning—that is, certain emotional responses that it arouses. Connotations can be affirmative *(national leader, negotiation, right of unlimited debate)* or negative *(politician, deal, filibuster).* Semantic argument uses connotative words to characterize an issue or to enhance the tone of a discussion.

SNARL AND PURR WORDS

Connotative words (sometimes called purr words and snarl words) do not prove anything; they simply label a thing as good or bad. American politicians of both parties regularly run for office, for example, on a program favoring *obedience to God, family, and country; adherence to law and order; separation of powers; fiscal responsibility; personal integrity; economic progress without inflation;* and *faith in the American dream.* They oppose *absenteeism, wasteful spending, communism, anarchy, economic floundering,* and *stagnation.* The essence of such an argument is its vagueness—and its usefulness. When asked for an opinion on a controversial issue like busing, for example, a candidate can resort to language:

> I'm glad you asked that question because I share your concern in this matter. My record shows I have always fought for the cause of education and for our children, who are the hope of this great nation. I recognize the profound complexities in this area and the honest differences presently existing between good men. I assure you I will work for a positive, fair, and democratic solution. Trust me.

What is the speaker's view on busing? You can't even guess.

This kind of argument can praise any entity—a party platform, a current novel, a union demand—as *authentic, just, reasonable, natural,* and *realistic* or condemn it as *irresponsible, asinine, phony, dangerous,* and *superficial.* It can praise one citizen as a *Samaritan,* a *patriot,* and an *independent thinker* and reject another as a *do-gooder,* a *reactionary,* and a *pseudointellectual.* (One person's *terrorist* is another person's *freedom fighter.*) Such terms have little specific meaning. A rich collection highlights every election. In Alabama, Fob James, a little-known candidate, won the governorship with a campaign that affirmed "the politics of compassion and a renaissance of common sense." In the 1984 campaign, President Reagan demonstrated his usual eloquence. He assured us that "America's future rests in a thousand dreams inside your hearts."

Semantic language depends on its emotional associations. An automobile is more appealing when named an *Eagle SX/4;* a bill, when called a *right-to-work law;* and a military settlement, when termed *peace with honor.* In successful argument, much depends on finding the right words. It is easy to champion *baseball, hot dogs, apple pie, and Chevrolet,* and it is hard to attack a position bulwarked with powerful language. How can anyone oppose *fair-trade* laws, the *right-to-life* movement, or a *clean air* act?

Currently a favorite advertising word is *nature.* A laxative is called "Nature's Remedy"; a shoe, "The Naturalizer"; and Reingold, "the natural beer." L.A. Beer is particularly celebrated. It boasts that "a special natural brewing process along with the finest natural ingredients and slow, natural aging produce a beer with less alcohol, that tastes as good as a regular beer." Beer hardly seems to qualify as natural, since it takes a chemist to make it. Still, if you look at things in a broad perspective, every process and ingredient can be called natural.

The word *light* is equally popular, and equally chancy. Sometimes it means a product has significantly fewer calories, sometimes it doesn't. The Wesson Oil that's called "light and natural" has the same calories as regular Wesson Oil—it's just paler in color. While most light beers have 50 to 80 fewer calories than regular beer, Michelob Light has shed only 15.

There is a special group of words you should look out for—words like *helps, virtually, up to,* and *relatively.* These modify any claim they appear with. You've seen the promises. Product A *helps* control dandruff, Product B leaves dishes *virtually* spotless, Product C lets you lose *up to* 15 pounds in a week, and Product D is *relatively* inexpensive.

Similar modifiers are currently used to make jewelry sound genuine. You can buy "18K gold flash chains," "a Lady Astor artifact diamond," or a "one carat simile diamond solitaire ring." You can get "gold-washed" jewelry. This has a gold coating less than 7 millionths of an inch thick.

Advertisers have called up an impressive range of associations to offer Blue Cross, Lemon-fresh Joy, Cashmere Bouquet, Old Grand-Dad, and Lincoln Continental Mark VII LSC—plus Obsession, Canadian Mist, 280-ZX, Triumph Spitfire, English Leather, and Brut 33 by Fabergé. Such names often make the difference. Millions of dollars have been earned and lost as Carnation Slender won the market from Metrecal, as DieHard outsold the J. C. Penney battery, and as Taster's Choice defeated Maxim instant coffee. Today the largest-selling perfume in the world is called Charlie.

Names make a difference. A weight-loss book titled *The New Dimensions II Bio-Imagery Programming Figure Enhancement System* has a lot going for it (perhaps too much). Products like Algemarin soap, Mr. Turkey luncheon meats, and Jhirmack shampoo seem to labor under a handicap. But a creative persuader can do wonders. Who can forget the jam advertisement "With a name like Smucker's, it has to be good"?

Names

Even people's names carry associations. In comic fiction, you know immediately that Mary Worth is good and that Snidely Whiplash is bad. Real-life examples demonstrate the American rejection of vague or aristocratic names. For years Hollywood hired performers like Leroy Scherer and Doris von Kappelhoff and made them stars as Rock Hudson and Doris Day. For a long time, Household Finance Corporation presented loan officers to the public as "friendly Bob Adams." Currently, men with mild names like Scott Simpson, Robert Remus, and Jim Harris appear on the professional wrestling circuit as "Nikita Kiloff," "Sergeant Slaughter," and "Kamala, the Ugandan Giant." Sylvester Ritter wrestles as "the Junkyard Dog."

Names are important in politics. John Varick Tunney had always been called Varick until he chose to run for office. After Opinion Research of California polled citizen response to the name Varick, he reverted to his unused first name and became Senator John Tunney. It is noteworthy that the serious candidates for the presidency in 1976 (Senators Udall and Jackson, President Ford, Governors Reagan and Carter) were introduced as Mo, Scoop, Jerry, Ron, and Jimmy. In the 1980 race, the candidates were Jimmy, Ted, Ron, George, Bob, John, and Big John. Only Senator Baker (Howard) had a name that needed work.

In 1984, the candidates were Ron and Walter (called Fritz), though much attention was given to Jesse (a fine biblical name for a minister) and to Gary Hart (formerly Gary Hartpence).

Jesse ran again in 1988, as did a number of candidates with safe names— George, Bob, Al, Jack, Pat, Paul, Joe, Bill, Pete, and Sam. However, the American public also faced more complicated ethnic names like Mario Cuomo and Mike Dukakis. (His close friends call him Michael.)

INDIRECT STATEMENT

Semantic argument can also work indirectly; that is, in a particular context a purr word expressed is also a snarl word implied. To advertise "Oil Heat Is Safe," for example, is to imply that gas and electric heat are dangerous. To describe a movie as "not recommended for immature audiences" is to boast that it is impressively sexual or violent. When Tampax was advertised as a "natural cotton" product, it was reminding readers that it was not one of the sponge tampons that had been associated with toxic shock syndrome and several deaths.

Commercial advertising uses many of these indirect attacks. Diners Club says, "Why go abroad with a credit card you've outgrown?" Playtex asks, "Are you still using the same brand of tampons they invented for your grandmother?" And Scope mouthwash boasts it is "Minty-fresh, not mediciney."

Such argument produces rich paradoxes. The ad for *Valley of the Dolls* reported that "Any similarity between any person, living or dead, and the characters portrayed in this film is purely coincidental and not intended"; this told moviegoers that the film was about real-life Hollywood stars. Another ad declared that the "United States Supreme Court has ruled that *Carnal Knowledge* is NOT OBSCENE," which meant that it was.

When George Wallace ran for governor of Alabama in 1980, his two opponents in the Democratic primary could not tastefully point out that he had recently married a country singer and that he was crippled. So one opponent produced television ads showing his own elegant wife and saying "When you elect a governor, you elect a first lady." The other opponent was less subtle. His TV ads showed him running up the steps of the statehouse.

Sometimes, semantic claims are not meant to be penetrated. This is especially true when impressive language is used to mask a negative admission. For example, when government economists announce that the inflation rate is "slowing down," they wish to communicate optimistic reassurance rather than what the words really say, that prices are still high and still climbing. When manufacturers label a garment "shrink-resistant," they want to suggest that it will not shrink, not what the term literally says, that the garment will resist shrinking, and thus that shrinkage will certainly occur. Advertisers for an inexpensive portable radio wish to imply that it is powerful and can pull in signals from distant stations, but what they say is, "You can take it anywhere."

You have to admire the creative language that public relations experts use to mask problems. When the Reagan administration admitted giving the media false stories about Libyan unrest, it called the stories "disinformation." One corporation specified a large sum of money on its annual balance sheet and declared it a "negative investment increment." You know what that means.

PERSUASIVE STYLE

The attempt to communicate more than is literally said occurs also when persuaders use impressive language to add character to an argument. Couching their views in religious allusions, folksy talk, or esoteric jargon, they argue more with style than with facts. In a letter to the *Saturday Review,* for example, Gelett Burgess maintained that Shakespeare did not write the plays attributed to him. His language was intellectual:

Sir:
My recent communication relative to Oxford-is-Shakespeare elicited responses which evince and hypostatize the bigoted renitency usual in orthodox addicts. For the Stratfordian mythology has engendered a

strange nympholepsy like a fanatical religion which is not amenable to reason or logic and abrogates all scientific method.

As a contrast, consider the tone of this fund-raising letter sent out by Senator Jesse Helms:

Dear Friend:

Will you do me a personal favor and place the enclosed bumper sticker on your car today?

And, will you use the enclosed form to let me know if I can send you a Reagan for President button to wear?

I'll be deeply gratified if I could hear from you immediately. . . .

Won't you please, please dig down deep and give as you have never given before?

Whether Ronald Reagan wins or loses is up to folks like you and me.

The decision rests in our hands.

I pray that you will answer this call for help. God bless you.

The author tries to make his message more persuasive by speaking as a Christian Southern gentleman.

You should, of course, judge an argument solely on the evidence brought forward to support a conclusion, not on the effect of connotative language. Similarly, in writing argument, fight the temptation to overuse snarl and purr words. Avoid pedantic language and high-sounding phrases. Your reader will think, perhaps rightly, that you are compensating for weaknesses in your case.

Connotative language defies meaningful analysis. Is it true that "Education without God produces a nation without freedom," that Nike running shoes are "faster than the fastest feet," that Fleishmann's Gin is "Clean . . . Clean . . . Clean"? Who can say? Until the claims are clarified and documented, such vague language can produce only empty and repetitive argument. Fleishmann advertisements, it should be noted, once offered to explain "What do they mean CLEAN . . . CLEAN . . . CLEAN?" The answer: "They mean the crispest, brightest drinks under the sun are made with clean-tasting Fleishmann's Gin." This is about as meaningful as semantic argument gets.

EXERCISES

How effective are these semantic arguments?

1. I can't decide which brand to smoke. I'm choosing between Barclay, Benson & Hedges, Carlton, Cambridge, Kent, Parliament, Tareyton, and Winston.

2. "At Ford, Quality is Job 1"; "Nobody sweats the details like GM."
3. I oppose the bleeding-heart radicals who are opposing President Reagan's peace efforts in Central America. All he's trying to do is destabilize unfriendly governments and neutralize the terrorists.
4. The human organism is a homeostatic mechanism; that is, all behavior is an attempt to preserve organismic integrity by homeostatic restoration of equilibrium, as that equilibrium is disturbed by biologically significant organizations of energies in the external or internal environments of the organism.
5. Macho cologne—"It's b-a-a-a-d."
6. I can't decide which car to buy. I'm choosing between a Dodge St. Regis, a Honda Accord SE-i, an Olds Cutlass Salon, a Toronado Troféo, a Caprice Silver Classic, a Thunderbird, and a Chevelle Malibu Classic Estate.
7. Every dogma has its day, and the dogma *du jour* is that women are oppressed. This notion seems to elicit favorable noises from the least likely people, including such phony feminists as Pope Paul and Hugh Hefner.
8. When a correspondent wrote to *Personality Parade* asking whether Elvis Presley had learned to act, columnist Walter Scott responded, "Mr. Presley has always been good to his mother."
9. Christian Dior's Eau Sauvage—"Virile. Discreet. Refreshing. Uncompromising. A fragrance of masculine refinement."
10. We guarantee our product will reduce your waist by up to three inches in the first two weeks or double your money back.
11. The abortion issue comes down to this: Should a baby be mutilated for the convenience of its mother?
12. Try Naturade Conditioning Mascara with National Protein. (Contains stearic acid, PUP, butylene glycol, sorbitan sesquioleate, triethanolamine, imidazolidinyl urea, methylparaben, and propylparaben.)
13. Don Siegelman believes we need an attorney general tough enough to fight the drug dealers, drunk drivers, career criminals, and anyone else who would harm our families.
14. Miller beer. Made the American way.
15. As a resident of this city for some time, I have become accustomed to the pathetic whining your paper is prone to whenever city government fails to apishly follow your always myopic and generally self-defeating plans for civic "betterment." Tolerating such infantile and retrograde twaddle was the price, I told myself, of a free and unshackled press.
16. A problematic of canon-formation, in contradistinction to an ideology of tradition, must assimilate the concept of tradition within an objective history, as an effect of monumentalization by which a canon of works confronts an author over against the contemporary social conditions of literary production, as simply given.

ESSAY ASSIGNMENTS

Write an essay either affirming or opposing one of these statements. The material you encounter in your background reading will include a good deal of semantic argument, and so may your essay.

1. Abortion is murder.
2. Feminist organizations want to destroy American family life.
3. Who needs poetry?
4. Capital punishment is necessary.
5. The publishers of *Hustler* and *Penthouse* should be sent to jail.
6. America needs some old-fashioned patriotism.
7. We should make "America the Beautiful" our national anthem.
8. X should be abolished. (Fill in the X.)

BAN SURROGATE BIRTHS; SELLING BABIES IS WRONG

DIANE CULBERTSON

I'm not a Catholic, but I have to hand it to the church this time. At last, a voice with moral authority has spoken up on surrogate motherhood and all the other fertility "cures" promoted by big-bucks runaway technology.

The church dares to speak the unspeakable in this day of gratification at any price: Surrogate motherhood is wrong.

Not that we need a church or anybody else to tell us that surrogate motherhood is wrong and should be outlawed. All we have to do is look into our own hearts and recognize baby selling for what it is.

The celebrated Whitehead-Stern case shows us just how ugly the whole business is. We've seen the tragedy of the "natural" parents in this unnatural situation. Each side has dug up all the dirt it could find to smear the other. However the judge rules, hearts will be broken and lives scarred.

But the real tragedy is that other couples are rushing to enter the same kinds of ill-advised agreements. Is it that this yuppified generation can't deny itself? After three cars in the driveway and a VCR in every room, why not believe that babies, too, are available—if you've got the price? I want one; therefore, I'll get one.

Isn't it ego, a prideful longing for someone "with my own genes" that prompts many of these couples? "We have so much love to give," they claim. But they don't want to love the thousands of kids bumped through the foster-care system. They ignore the thousands more available for adoption but who are not quite "right." They're too old, they have mental or physical problems, they're not white.

The church has the courage to speak out against trafficking in human flesh. It defends the marriage vows: "The fidelity of the spouses in the unity of marriage involves reciprocal respect of their right to become a father and a mother only through each other."

And the rights of children: "Surrogate motherhood offends the dignity and the right of the child to be conceived, carried in the womb, brought into the world, and brought up by his own parents."

Banning surrogate motherhood won't completely stop the practice, no more than outlawing drunk driving and drug use has stopped those activities. But laws would send society's message that paying a rent-a-womb to carry a child is wrong.

Does this mean we should stop all research? Not at all. But let research concentrate on discovering why an estimated one in eight couples is infertile. And let science find ways to help them without dancing on the altar of science run amok. Stop before we get to the point of running "fetus farms" to harvest brains and other organs for transplantation.

And if an infertile couple can't be helped to conceive and carry their own child? Well, sometimes God just says no.

SOURCE: Copyright © 1987, *USA Today*. Reprinted with permission from the March 18, 1987, edition of *USA Today*.

DISCUSSION QUESTIONS

1. The essay is filled with snarl words:
    "big-bucks runaway technology"
    "gratification at any price"
    "baby selling"
    the "yuppified generation [that] can't deny itself"
    "if you've got the price"
    "trafficking in human flesh"
    "a rent-a-womb"
    "the altar of science run amok"
    "fetus farms"
    How might these things be differently expressed?
2. What words might have been used instead of these purr words?
    "moral authority"
    "look into our own hearts"
    "courage"
    "marriage vows"
    "fidelity of the spouses"
    "right of the child"
    "dignity"
    "God"
3. The author uses two analogies. She says that to yuppies a baby is just a luxury item, like "three cars" and "a VCR in every room." She says that surrogate motherhood will be just as hard to outlaw as drunk driving. How reasonable are these analogies?
4. Do you feel the author is giving a rational response to the issue of surrogate motherhood? Why or why not?
5. Is the author saying much more than "You can't do this; it's just wrong"?

If you signed up for...

Introductory Psychology

Psychology 101: (4 units) PSD 328-056-101

A general introduction including topics in cognitive, experimental, personality, developmental, social and clinical psychology. Study of the dynamics and prevention of abnormal behavior including neuroses, psychoses, character disorders, psychosomatic reactions and other abnormal personality patterns. Students participate in six hours of psychological research or conduct literature reviews of the writings of Freud, Jung, and Skinner.

but what you really got was...

Psychology 101: (4 units) PSD 328-056-101

A general introduction to the American Guilt Trip and the glory of the Proletarian Struggle including topics in imperial, material, capital and militar -isms. Study of the dynamics and prevention of abnormal behavior including heterosexuality, religion, conservatism, and patriotism. Students participate in hours of Reagan bashing or conduct literature reviews of the writings of Marx, Lenin, and Caldicott.

Fed up with bias? Then join us! We're YAF.

What is YAF?

YOUNG AMERICANS FOR FREEDOM, the nation's oldest, largest, and most active conservative youth organization was founded on the Sharon, Connecticut estate of William F. Buckley, Jr. by young people concerned about the future of our nation and world—young men and women concerned about the problems we face today as individuals and as a nation.

Young Americans for Freedom
Education. Not Indoctrination.

Young Americans for Freedom P.O. Box 847 Sierra Madre, CA 91024-0847

Courtesy of the Young Americans for Freedom.

DISCUSSION QUESTIONS

1. What is the YAF's specific complaint about university education?
2. Is it complaining that psychology, history, and economics are being taught with a bias? or that they are being taught without a YAF bias?
3. In a psychology class, what would the YAF say about homosexuality? In history, what would it teach about Reagan? In physics, what would it say about Caldicott's fear of nuclear power? In economics, what would it say of Marx?
4. What is ironic about its plea for "Education, Not Indoctrination"?

HEINOUS RULING
GETS AN "APOLOGY"

MIKE ROYKO

Oh, boy, I really did it, and am I embarrassed. I've been criticized by the chief justice of the Nebraska Supreme Court for being inaccurate and loose with the facts when I criticized that court for its decision on a murder case.

He says that it is obvious that I had not even read the court's decision before I ridiculed its decision to reverse the death penalty for a creep who murdered a woman to fulfill a sex fantasy.

And to heighten my embarrassment, Chief Justice Norman Krivosha said all this in a speech to journalism students at the University of Nebraska. My, what must these aspiring journalists now think of me?

So I have no choice but to admit my guilt and apologize to the chief justice for my errors.

He's right. I did not read the court's opinion on the case. I based my column on lengthy news accounts in the Nebraska press.

Based on the news accounts, I thought the decision by the Supreme Court to spare the life of Robert Hunt Jr. was pretty dumb, and I said so.

According to the news accounts, Hunt had randomly picked a young woman's wedding announcement picture out of the newspapers. It inspired a fantasy. He went to her home, entered at gunpoint, she pleaded for her life, he stuffed panties down her throat, strangled her, had a sexual experience, and, believing she was still alive, shoved her under water in a bathtub.

He confessed, was found guilty and sentenced to die. But in a 4–2 decision, the Supreme Court said that he should not be executed because the state law requires that the death penalty can only be imposed when a murder is "especially heinous, atrocious, cruel, or manifested exceptional depravity by ordinary standards of morality and intelligence."

The court decided that while the murder was heinous, it was not "especially heinous," etc.

After the judge's speech, I read the full decision. In fact, I have read the decision twice. And I see why the chief justice was upset by the errors in my column.

For one thing, the chief justice pointed out that I had written that the killer "stalked" his victim, when the killer did no such thing.

The chief justice is right. All the killer did was go to her home and watch it for a while. Walk around it a few times. Look in the windows.

That was after he bought a pellet gun with which to frighten her, the panties to stuff down her throat, the nylon stocking for strangling her, and a porn magazine to inspire him.

So, he didn't stalk her. All he did was watch and wait. Wait and watch. Watch and wait. Then kill.

SOURCE: Reprinted by permission: Tribune Media Services. Reprinted from the *Mobile Press,* September 24, 1985.

The judge also criticized me for saying that the killer raped the woman, when the killer did no such thing.

I admit that I was wrong on that, too.

What the killer did, after he stuffed the panties into her throat and choked her into unconsciousness, was perform a sexual act that I find so revolting I am not going to try to describe it.

The judge also says that I was wrong for saying that the killer shoved the woman in a bathtub and drowned her.

Well, he might be right. But maybe not. The experts aren't sure.

You see, when he finished his sexual activities, the killer noticed that the woman was twitching. And he thought he detected a pulse. So he put her head under water in the tub and went home.

Now, it is possible she was already dead, but her body was still twitching. If so, I'm wrong. He didn't drown her.

So, there are my glaring errors. He didn't stalk her. He just watched and waited. He didn't actually rape her. He used her unconscious body in another sexual way. And maybe he didn't drown her. Maybe all he did was strangle her.

In any case, the murder wasn't "especially heinous, atrocious, cruel, or manifested exceptional depravity by ordinary standards of morality and intelligence." At least, that's what the judge and three of his associates say.

I'm glad the judge straightened me out. And I'm so impressed by his eye for detail—the significant difference between stalking and waiting and watching, and the clear difference between "heinous" and "especially heinous"—that I now wish I lived in Nebraska.

Yes, I'd love to be a resident of Nebraska. Especially when the voters there get a chance to decide, as they soon will, whether Justice Krivosha should remain in his job.

DISCUSSION QUESTIONS

1. How far do you have to read to know that the author is not sincerely making an apology? What clues reveal the fact?
2. In his earlier statement, Royko claimed that Robert Hunt, Jr., stalked, raped, and drowned his victim. Was he right? Why is it hard to say?
3. What distinguishes a "heinous" crime from an "especially heinous" crime? Why is it hard to say?
4. Is there any evidence that Chief Justice Norman Krivosha was correct in ruling the crime was not "especially heinous"?
5. What is the purpose of the last paragraph of the essay?
6. Comment on the advantages and disadvantages of using irony in making an argument.

BILL HAYS.
A CITIZEN'S APPROACH
TO COUNTY GOVERNMENT.

When Bill Hays was called upon to serve in local government, he came to public office not as a politician, but as a private citizen.

Because he entered office mid-term, he inherited numerous county-wide problems. But through hard work and clear vision of a better Mobile, he is steadily putting county government back on the right track.

It's this calm sincerity and dedication that sets Bill Hays apart from the loud rhetoric of some politicians.

His intelligent, non-political approach to solving problems is making our community vital again, not just for a few, but for the good of all.

Bill Hays is working for Mobile, independently, as a responsible citizen. Without fear or favor to any special interest group or individual. His is a responsible voice that leads with courage and integrity.

This election, let's rise above politics.
Vote Bill Hays.

Hays
COUNTY COMMISSION · DISTRICT TWO
A RESPONSIBLE VOICE

Advertisement from the *Mobile Press Register,* September 16, 1984.

DISCUSSION QUESTIONS

1. The main argument here is that Bill Hays is running for office not as a "politician," but as a "citizen." What is the denotative meaning of both words? What is the connotative meaning?
2. The argument boasts that Hays was never elected to the office he now holds; he was "called upon to serve." What does this tell you?
3. What other associations attend the idea of "being called"?
4. Beginning with "hard work" and "clear vision," list the vague political words and phrases. How many of these have any specific definition?
5. Does the candidate give you any idea of what he plans to do if elected?
6. Is this the kind of language a candidate should use?

IT'S TIME TO GET OUT OF BED
AND KICK JAP BUTT!

ED ANGER

All these sex scandals with Gary Hart, Jim Bakker and our Marines in Moscow have got me madder than a bunny in a briar patch.

Let's face it, the time has come for us to get our minds out of the gutter and back on America. It's obvious from all this satin sheet hijinks that Americans have forgotten what's important and what sex is for.

The thing that should be foremost on every American's mind is working harder so we can clobber Japan and take back the title of the world's greatest economic power. Sure the Japs are good. But we whipped those little nippers in World War II and we can whip their butts now if we put our minds to it.

The second thing we've got to do is put sex where it belongs—in marriage. As far as I'm concerned, single people have no right to make love.

And married folks shouldn't be fanning the sheets every time they get a spare moment, either.

Sex is for one thing and one thing only—making babies. And if you're not planning parenthood, then you've got no business monkeying around with your mate.

Let's face it, husbands and wives have got lots more important things to do than mess around with each other. I'm talking about working hard to make their family and home secure and safe. Solid families are the building blocks of a strong America.

I figured all this "love" business that those snivelling hippies started in the '60s was over with when herpes and AIDS started sweeping our nation.

Those dreadful diseases are a message from the good Lord telling Americans to stop messing around and get their minds back on building their nation.

Where would our country be if our pioneers and forefathers had gotten bogged down smooching with every Donna, Jessica or Fawn?

I'll guarantee you that Daniel Boone didn't get famous by sitting around spooning with girls. Nope, he was off killing Injuns and discovering new lands.

Do you know where Gary Hart and Jim Bakker would be if they had followed this advice? They'd be back on the job instead of hiding in disgrace!

DISCUSSION QUESTIONS

1. This essay makes reference to a lot of things and people:
     Gary Hart
     Jim Bakker

SOURCE: Reprinted by permission from *Weekly World News,* June 9, 1987.

the romantic Marines in Moscow
Japanese trade
World War II
Japanese and enemies in the war
the purpose of sex
marriage
building a strong America
hippies in the 1960s
pioneers and forefathers
Donna Rice
Jessica Hahn
Fawn Hall
Daniel Boone

How are these unified? What is the author's major complaint?

2. What do the many references listed in question 1 tell you about Ed Anger?

3. Count the number of snarl words in the essay. What do they tell you about Ed Anger?

4. What is your immediate response to anyone who begins a sentence with "Let's face it"?

5. What evidence is there that Ed Anger is more than an ignorant loudmouth?

6. Whom is the author addressing? Should you take the essay very seriously?

FALLACIES

*"How to Tune Up Your
Marriage—Just Like a Car"*
—Essay by Priscilla Kroger

Certain forms of misleading argument occur so commonly that they have been specifically labeled. Although most could be analyzed as faulty induction, deduction, and so on, they are treated separately here because the terms describing them should be familiar to you. You will meet them often; they are part of the language of argument.

FALSE ANALOGY

To argue by analogy is to compare two things known to be alike in one or more features and to suggest that they will be alike in other features as well. This is reasonable argument if the compared elements are genuinely similar. (Josh Woodward is an outstanding player and coach; he will make a fine manager.) It is fallacious if the features are essentially different. (You have *fruit* for breakfast; why not try *Jell-O* for breakfast?)

You test an analogy by asking whether the comparison statement (if there is one) is true and whether the elements compared in the argument are sufficiently alike. A comparison statement is particularly questionable if it is simply an adage. Reelection campaigns regularly submit, for example, that "you wouldn't change horses in the middle of the stream." But even the smallest consideration will remind you of situations in which you would be eager to change horses. Equally vulnerable are arguments insisting that "you can lead a horse to water but you can't make it drink" (meaning some people are unteachable) and that "where there's smoke, there's fire" (meaning some gossip is true). Hearing these analogies, you might want to point out that with brain probes scientists can make a horse drink itself sick and that where there's smoke, there could be dry ice.

More often, you reject an analogy by showing a fundamental difference between the things compared. A common argument insists, "We have pure food and drug laws. Why can't we have comparable laws to keep moviemakers from giving us filth?" Here you must examine the definitions relating to "pure" and "filth." Food is called "impure" when the person eating it gets physically sick. Because the individual who devours X-rated movies does not get sick, there is no comparable definition of pornographic "filth." Thus the analogy fails. Similarly, facing the argument, "We should no more teach communism in the schools than we should teach safecracking," you can respond that knowing a thing is not practicing it and that, unlike safecracking, being a communist is not a crime.

The poster saying "I Don't Spit in Your Face—Please Don't Blow Smoke in Mine" seems excessive. The two actions are not equally offensive.

Analogies can be dangerous. In recent years, the Ayatollah Khomeini has executed prostitutes, adulterers, and homosexuals. His argument: Iran is like a human body, and these citizens are an infectious gangrene. They must be destroyed to preserve the health of the state.

Some analogies are complex. Here is an instance from an argument that has appeared in many temperance campaigns: "There are 10,000 deaths from alcohol poisoning to 1 from mad-dog bites in this country. In spite of this, we license liquor but shoot the dogs." Because it is desirable to get rid of any dogs or any liquor that proves deadly, this analogy seems reasonable. The argument, however, recommends that *all* liquor be outlawed. This action is reasonable only if you are willing to pursue the comparison and shoot all dogs. Similarly, you should scrutinize popular arguments that compare independent nations with dominoes and federal deficit spending with a family budget.

In argument, analogies can be an effective way to make a point. When conservative critics wanted to remove non-Christian books from public schools by saying they preached "secular humanism," Art Kropp, a director of People for the American Way, spelled out the problem. He said, "Trying to define *secular humanism* is like trying to nail Jell-O to a tree."

In writing persuasive essays, you will find analogies useful for illustrating a point or speculating on an event. But be careful. The comparison may make your subject seem trivial. (Evangelist David Noebel wrote that "Sex education without morals is like breakfast without orange juice.") Or it may add strange dimensions of meaning. (Author Jessamyn West praised the book *Four Cats Make One Pride* by saying, "It is about cats in the same way that *Huckleberry Finn* is about boys and *Madame Bovary* is about women.")

Keep your analogies simple and direct. Elaborate comparisons are rarely effective as argument.

PRESUMED CAUSE-EFFECT

Relating an event to its cause can lead to three different fallacies.

Argument in a Circle

Circular argument occurs when speakers offer a restatement of their assertion as a reason for accepting it. They make a claim, add "because," then repeat the claim in different words. ("Smoking is injurious because it harms the human body"; or "One phone is not enough in the modern home because modern homes have plenty of phones.")

Sometimes the expression is more oblique, with the "because" implied rather than stated. William Jennings Bryan once declared, "There is only one argument that can be made to one who rejects the authority of the Bible, namely, that the Bible is true." It is hardly persuasive to argue that a thing is true because it is true. Repetition is not evidence.

Today, circular argument appears regularly in discussions of pornography. Definitions of obscenity never get beyond the one given by Supreme Court Justice William Brennan in *Roth* v. *United States:* "Obscene material is material which deals with sex in a manner appealing to prurient interest." This says that obscene material is obscene material.

Post Hoc Ergo Propter Hoc

The post hoc fallacy ("After this, therefore because of this") occurs when a person mentions two past events and insists that because one happened first, it necessarily caused the second. On such evidence, one can argue that Martin Luther left the Catholic priesthood in order to get married, that President Herbert Hoover caused the Great Depression, and that young people rioted during the 1960s because they were brought up under the permissive theories of Dr. Benjamin Spock. Such logic can make much of coincidence. *Christian Crusade* compared crime statistics for two six-week periods and headlined "Murder Rate Jumps 93 Percent in Oklahoma Following Death Penalty Ban." The cause-effect relationship was, it said, "self-evident."

Nothing illustrates the weakness of the post hoc fallacy better than Stephen J. Gould's example. He noted solemnly that as Halley's Comet approached the earth, the price of ice cream cones in Boston rose regularly.

Post hoc reasoning is fallacious because it ignores more complex factors that contribute to an event. A Smith-Corona advertisement proclaims that "Students Who Type Usually Receive Better Grades" and suggests that buying a child a typewriter will improve his or her schoolwork. The fallacy here is the implication that simply owning a typewriter makes the difference. Other factors seem more likely to account for the higher grades: Parents who buy their child a typewriter are concerned about the youngster's education, take pains to see that the child studies, and can afford to provide other cultural advantages as well. The typewriter alone gives no one higher grades.

Recognizing the post hoc fallacy will keep you from jumping to unwarranted conclusions. No one can deny, for example, that some people who wear copper bracelets suffer no arthritis pain; that some heroin addicts have significantly fewer accidents than other drivers; that some patients with Parkinson's disease who have been treated with L-dopa experience aphrodisiac effects; and that individuals who witnessed John Kennedy's assassination have died in suggestive ways. Nevertheless, these cases do not justify sensational cause-effect conclusions. A post hoc judgment would ignore the range of other factors involved.

Another example: A 1985 study by Emory University psychologists reported that women who read sexy historical novels have sex 74 percent more often than nonreaders of such novels. Here it is hard to establish what is cause and what is effect.

The post hoc fallacy is particularly notable in literature dealing with curses. Many books describe the sad events that have occurred in the Romanov, Hapsburg, and Kennedy families after they were put under a curse. Stories tell the horrible fate of people who owned the Hope Diamond. Magazine articles appear regularly noting that every person who was involved in breaking open King Tut's tomb is now either dead or sadly crippled. When you read such stories, you should remember Darrell Huff's wonderful line: "Post hoc rides again!"

Non Sequitur

Non sequitur means "it does not follow." This fallacy occurs when a person submits that a given fact has led or must inevitably lead to a particular consequence. One can take a fact ("Gary Hart spent a weekend with Donna Rice") and project a conclusion ("He would make a poor president"). Or one can take an anticipated fact ("If the Equal Rights Amendment becomes law") and spell out the consequences ("American family life is doomed"). The reasonable objection, of course, is that the conclusion does not necessarily follow.

The term *non sequitur* is widely used. It lends itself to describing arguments with multiple causes ("The more you know—the more you do—the more you tax your nerves—the more important it is to relax tired nerves. Try safe, nonhabit-forming Sedquilin") or arguments so extreme that they fall outside the usual categories ("Of course Jehovah's Witnesses are communists; otherwise there wouldn't be so many of them"). But the term is of little value in defining general argument; almost any kind of fallacious reasoning is a non sequitur.

Still it's useful to have the term when you read the Emeraude perfume advertisement: "I love only one man. I wear only one fragrance."

BEGGING THE QUESTION

Individuals beg the question by assuming something it is their responsibility to prove; they build their argument on an undemonstrated claim. Generally it takes the form of a question. ("Have you stopped beating your wife?" or "Is it true blondes have more fun?") It can, however, appear as a declaration. ("Busing is no more the law of the land than any other communist doctrine.")

Another form of begging the question is to make a charge and then insist that someone else disprove it. ("How do you know that flying saucers haven't been visiting the earth for centuries?" or "How was Jeanne Dixon able to predict the assassination of President Kennedy?") In all argument, the burden of proof is on the person making the assertion. Never let yourself be put in a position where you have to disprove a claim that was never proved in the first place. One of the most common instances of this fallacy today is the antiabortionist's question: "How can you approve of slaughtering babies?"

IGNORING THE QUESTION

People can ignore a question in different ways: They can leave the subject to attack their opponent, or they can leave the subject to discuss a different topic.

Ad Hominem Argument

An ad hominem argument attacks the opposing arguer rather than the question at issue. ("Senator Thurmond favors resumption of the draft because he is too old to have to serve," or "District Attorney Phillips wants to become famous prosecuting my client so he can run for governor.") Here, nothing is said of the main issue; the speaker ignores the question by attacking an adversary.

It should be noted, to avoid confusion, that an argument about a particular individual—a candidate, a defendant—is probably not ad hominem argument. In such a case, the person *is* the issue.

The fallacy often takes this form: "Of course you believe that—you're a woman" (or a Jew, Catholic, Southerner, rich business person, etc.). It also can involve snarl words: "You're a bleeding-heart liberal" (or a wild-eyed environmentalist, Bible-thumping fanatic, labor-union radical, simpleminded bastard, etc.).

A good rule: *Never make an ad hominem argument.* Attacking your opponent is almost an admission that your case is weak. If you have a substantial argument and want people to know it, a good policy is to flatter your adversary.

Extension

The fallacy of extension has the same effect as an ad hominem argument. Here advocates "extend" the question until they are arguing a different subject altogether. When a convict's execution is stayed, people ask, "What about the rights of the victim?" When women are admitted to medical schools under a quota system, the cry goes up, "What about the rights of men?" In both cases, the question is reasonable, but it moves the argument to a new topic.

A rich example of extension appears on a bumper sticker: "Register Communists, Not Guns."

Either-Or

The either-or fallacy is a form of extension. Here partisans distort an issue by insisting that only two alternatives exist: their recommendation and something much worse. They will describe a temperance election as a choice between Christianity and debauchery. They will depict abortion as a choice between American family life and murder. Should you question American support of the Nicaraguan contras, they challenge, "Which side are you on, anyway?"

To all such examples of ignoring the question, the reasonable response is "Let's get back to the issue."

FALLACIES IN OTHER FORMS

Most of the fallacies mentioned in this chapter can be analyzed as examples of induction, deduction, semantic argument, and so on. A false analogy, for example, is a deduction with an invalid form; a post hoc error is induction with an insufficient sample; and any bad argument can be called a non sequitur. But special terms do exist for these fallacies, and it may be valuable to have two ways of looking at them.

Unless you are championing a particularly weak cause, keep these fallacies out of your writing.

EXERCISES

Identify the fallacies in these arguments.

1. Okay, if you think psychokinesis isn't possible, explain to me how Uri Geller can bend keys just by looking at them.
2. Of course you oppose no-fault auto insurance. You're a lawyer.
3. A woman for vice president? My God, what if the president died?
4. I know the Bible is true. St. Paul says, "All scripture is given by inspiration of God."
5. I don't like the idea of abortion either, but I think it's better than having some poor woman kill herself trying to raise 11 or 12 children.
6. Sterling—It's Only a Cigarette Like Porsche Is Only a Car.
7. Arguing from the principle that a person is sick "when he fails to function in his appropriate gender identification," Dr. Charles Socarides, a New York psychoanalyst, concludes that homosexuality is a form of mental illness.
8. I oppose public smoking laws. If the government can make smokers stay in restricted places, can't they do the same for other groups: garlic eaters, children, gum chewers, crippled people, whistlers, and so on?
9. If evolution is true, why has it stopped?
10. Arrested for hijacking a commuter flight in 1984, the hijacker explained it was all the fault of the federal government, which had not instituted programs to help him overcome his drug habit.
11. I pay for my college education just the way I pay for my groceries in a supermarket. Why does the administration think it can tell me what courses I have to take?

12. Gay people are essentially criminal. Look at the homosexuality that goes on in prison.
13. America—Love It or Leave It!
14. Jim and Tammy Bakker are suffering right now—just like Job and his wife. And like Job, they will rise to new prosperity and happiness.
15. After receiving the Lourdes medal, this cash-starved woman received a $75,000 miracle.
16. Creationism in the public schools? Pretty soon we'll have to give equal time to the stork theory.
17. "Robert Bork's America is a land in which women would be forced into back alley abortions, blacks would eat at segregated lunch counters, rogue police could break down citizens' doors in midnight raids, school children could not be taught about evolution, writers and artists could be censored at the whim of government."—Senator Edward Kennedy
18. Defending Robert Bork's nomination to the Supreme Court, the *Mobile Register* attacked his major critic: "Senator Kennedy has the morals of an alley cat, the courage of a slug, and a political kinship with Mikhail Gorbachev."
19. How can we sympathize with the striking NFL players? They make an average of $230,000 a year. They show up on the picket lines wearing designer clothes, and driving high-priced sports cars.
20. You have to get excited over something. Why not Kellogg's Corn Flakes?

ESSAY ASSIGNMENTS

Write an essay either affirming or opposing one of these statements. The arguments you encounter in your background reading may well include logical fallacies. Your essay should have none, or at least none you didn't intend.

1. We should never have deserted our allies in Vietnam.
2. A massive conspiracy led to the assassination of President Kennedy.
3. Prostitution should not be considered a crime; there is no victim.
4. Daylight saving time is unnatural.
5. If I had a different name, I'd be more successful.
6. America's space program is a waste of money.
7. King Tut's tomb put a genuine curse on all those who disturbed it.
8. X causes crime. (Fill in the X.)

DIARY OF
AN UNBORN CHILD

October 5
Today my life began. My parents do not know it yet. I am as small as a
seed of an apple, but it is I already. And I am to be a girl. I shall have
blond hair and blue eyes. Just about everything is settled though, even
the fact that I shall love flowers.

October 19
Some say that I am not a real person yet, that only my mother exists. But
I am a real person, just as a small crumb of bread is yet truly bread. My
mother is. And I am.

October 23
My mouth is just beginning to open now. Just think, in a year or so I
shall be laughing and later talking. I know what my first word will be:
MAMA.

October 25
My heart began to beat today all by itself. From now on it shall gently
beat for the rest of my life without ever stopping to rest! And after many
years it will tire. It will stop, and then I shall die.

November 2
I am growing a bit every day. My arms and legs are beginning to take
shape. But I have to wait a long time yet before those little legs will raise
me to my mother's arms, before these little arms will be able to gather
flowers and embrace my father.

November 12
Tiny fingers are beginning to form on my hands. Funny how small they
are! I'll be able to stroke my mother's hair with them.

November 20
It wasn't until today that the doctor told mom that I am living here under
her heart. Oh, how happy she must be! Are you happy, mom?

November 25
My mom and dad are probably thinking about a name for me. But they
don't even know that I am a little girl. I want to be called Kathy. I am
getting so big already.

December 10
My hair is growing. It is smooth and bright and shiny. I wonder what
kind of hair mom has.

December 13
I am just about able to see. It is dark around me. When mom brings me
into the world, it will be full of sunshine and flowers. But what I want
more than anything is to see my mom. How do you look, mom?

SOURCE: Reprinted from the *Mobile Press.*

December 24
I wonder if mom hears the whispering of my heart? Some children come into the world a little sick. But my heart is strong and healthy. It beats so evenly: tup-tup, tup-tup. You'll have a healthy little daughter, mom!

December 28
Today my mother killed me.

DISCUSSION QUESTIONS

1. The argument about abortion hinges on the issue of whether a fetus in its early stages is a human person or a collection of cells. What evidence is offered here that the fetus is a person?
2. Consider all the things this fetus knows. It talks of sunshine, flowers, a mother, a father, a female name, death, the relative health of some fetuses, and the intellectual debate about personhood. What fallacy is illustrated here?
3. "I am a real person, just as a small crumb of bread is yet truly bread." How reasonable is this analogy?
4. Comment on the problems of definition that exist when an entity with no brain or brain cells says, ". . . . it is I already."
5. Who is saying, "Today my mother killed me"?

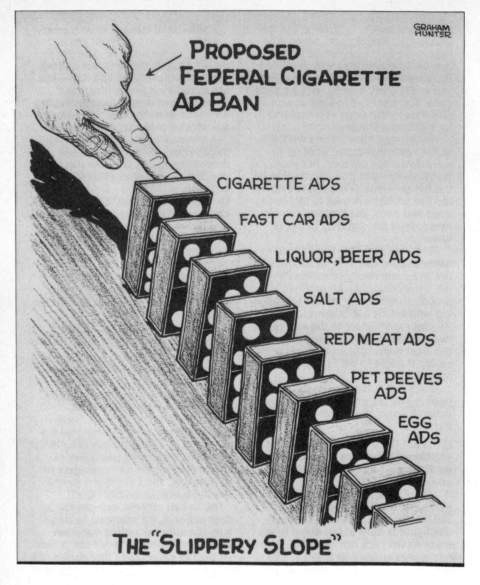

SOURCE: Courtesy of Graham Hunter and the *Tobacco Observer*. From the *Tobacco Observer*, May 1987.

DISCUSSION QUESTIONS

1. This is a kind of argument by analogy. Is it reasonable to say the health concern that would ban cigarette advertising could also ban ads for fast cars, liquor, beer, salt, red meat, and eggs?
2. Are these products roughly equal as threats to American health?
3. The cartoon also says that if cigarette ads are banned now, ads for the other products will be banned before long. Name this fallacy.
4. What is suggested by the image of "the slippery slope"?

A G.I. BILL
FOR MOTHERS

ELLEN GOODMAN

On Monday Helen Feeney took one last shot at Veterans' Preference and missed.

To no one's surprise, the Supreme Court upheld its own June ruling. It is, they said, perfectly legal for the government to give veterans a lifetime edge on the public jobs list. That for the moment is that.

Now, after years of bucking veterans' preference, it may be time for women to adopt it.

Veterans' preference laws were based on the notion that a soldier reentering the job market shouldn't suffer because of the time he spent serving his country. Eventually, many of these programs became a kind of lifetime affirmative action for a generation of soldiers. But the basic concept was and is a worthy one. The government should have a right to help those who helped the rest of us.

Well, there is another group of Americans who have also taken time out of the work force in order to provide what is generally considered a social good. They are also at a disadvantage when they try to get back in. And they are called mothers.

This, according to Barbara Mikulski's favorite fantasy, should—in the best of all possible worlds—qualify them for their own sort of veterans' preference, their own G.I. Bill for Mothers.

"One of the fundamental tenets that underlies my thinking," says the feisty U.S. Representative from Baltimore, "is that what we explicitly state as our values, we implicitly deny in our social programs. If motherhood is an occupation which is critically important to society the way we say it is, then there should be a mother's bill of rights.

"The basics of the G.I. Bill of Rights gave veterans the chance to pursue higher education, to get a mortgage, to get credit for their army years in their pensions, to have the right to return to a job, to have V.A. medical care, and to have a point preference in the job market.

"We gave them that to compensate for the lost time they gave to their country. Now if we transpose that to women, then we ought to provide them with the same sort of rewards for their time out and caring for their children.

"Clearly, not all women need that aid, but many do. We keep inventing new programs to help these women—displaced homemaker programs and all the rest. They're considered gifts when they ought to be a matter of rights," says Mikulski.

Not even this gutsy lady plans to present such a bill. If she did, you would hear a shriek from the Halls of Montezuma to the Shores of Tripoli. "It is not," as she says, "a perfect plan." In fact, it isn't a plan at all, but a point of view.

Still, it isn't a bad place from which to oversee the plight of the woman at home. It has become commonplace lately to cluck about the status of the homemaker. Feminists and antifeminists alike are busily portraying themselves as the Friends of the Homemakers, as if the women were baby seals about to be clubbed to extinction by the opinion makers.

For years people condemned working mothers for neglecting their children and then swung around and condemned full-time mothers for neglecting their minds, their pocketbooks or their futures. We have now settled for the notion that whatever a woman decides is fine, as long as she truly chooses it. We give lip service to choice, as if the choices were free ones instead of tough ones.

The hardest aspect of homemaking isn't the job description, but the insecurity. If one generation looked for security in a marriage certificate, this one looks for it in a résumé.

The homemakers I know who are most at ease are those who know they can reenter when they want to, or when they have to. The young women who have the greatest sense of choice about mothering are those few who have been told the door to the office will still be open. Only they can look at mothering as "time off" or a second career, rather than a permanent job disability.

It is odd that the choice to be comfortably at home, in that most private of relationships, depends on access to the public world. But that is the message from the home front. We have veterans here, too, who need more than thank-yous.

DISCUSSION QUESTIONS

1. The entire argument hinges on an analogy: If veterans deserve a variety of social rewards for taking time out to serve society, so should women who have left or delayed their careers to raise children. Examine the comparison.
2. In what ways are mothers and soldiers alike?
3. In what ways are they different?
4. Does it make any difference (to this argument) if it is shown that all mothers are not equally good mothers?
5. Does the author help her argument by using words like "favorite fantasy," "gutsy," "feisty," "cluck about," and so on?

"WELL, THERE THEY GO! . . . VIOLATING OUR CIVIL RIGHTS AGAIN!"

SOURCE: Courtesy of Bob Gorrell and the *Richmond News Leader.* From the *Mobile Press,* May 1, 1987.

DISCUSSION QUESTIONS

1. What is the main message of this cartoon? Is the cartoonist saying that when there's no death penalty, the criminal has a civil right to rob and kill?
2. What *is* the cartoonist saying?
3. Is there an implication here that law-abiding citizens should have civil rights and criminals shouldn't?
4. What are the problems in a society that offers civil rights to some citizens and not to others?

MEET GEORGE CROCKETT, ESQUIRE

WILLIAM F. BUCKLEY, JR.

Since Congress is in the mood to investigate, one is entitled to ask the ancient question, Quis custodiet ipsos custodes?—a saying loosely translated as, What makes you think you're so hot?

The complaint of the congressional investigating committee, if we can make it out, is that influences on foreign policy have been exercised by two men extrinsic to the system, Lt. Col. Oliver North and Rear Adm. John Poindexter. Who, as the crystallizing cliche goes, elected THEM? They have their response, which is that they were doing the will of the executive, who is charged with making foreign policy, even though the details they engaged in were not known to the president.

Meanwhile, up until quite recently, very little attention has been given to the identity of the new chairman of the House Subcommittee on Western Hemisphere Affairs—which, obviously, is the vehicle through which congressional thought on Central America will be transmitted. That gentleman is Mr. George Crockett, and during the past fortnight, *National Review,* in an article by J. Michael Waller and Joseph Sobran; the *American Spectator,* in an article by David Brock; and the *Conservative Digest,* in an article by John Rees, have given us a little of the background of Mr. Crockett, and it is time to ask Congress: When you are done investigating Col. North and Adm. Poindexter, why not look into your own house?

In 1949, to reach back into the middle age of 74-year-old Crockett, acting at the time as a lawyer defending indicted Communists, Crockett told the jury that "the Communist Party is in truth and in fact the conscience of America." That revelation has been with him for many years, and was in effect reiterated in 1985 when Rep. Crockett (he was elected to Congress in 1980) did not condemn the killing of Maj. Arthur Nicholson Jr. by the Soviets in East Germany. Nor was that out of character. In 1983, when the Soviets shot down the Korean airliner, Crockett was one of two members of the House who abstained on a House resolution condemning the action.

It has been a very long history. During the '40s, Crockett was a law partner of a Communist who had been kicked out of the United Auto Workers by Walter Reuther. In 1946 he was a sponsor of a Communist front, the Civil Rights Congress, and joined the National Lawyers Guild, cited by the Congress of that day as "the foremost legal bulwark of the Communist Party." While defending Communists prosecuted under the Smith Act in 1949, Crockett was sentenced for contempt of court to four months in jail. His patronage extended to Julius and Ethel Rosenberg, for whom he sponsored a money-raising reception. He charged in 1951 that the U.S. government was engaged in "genocide" against American blacks.

SOURCE: Reprinted from the *Mobile Press Register,* July 26, 1987. Reprinted by permission of the author.

In short, there is nothing to distinguish Mr. Crockett from an active Communist save possibly a party card, which as a matter of fact is no longer issued.

Now, how does a gentleman with that record get elected to Congress in the first place? Well, he is a black running from a black constituency in Detroit, and although blacks have never in America responded to enticements by the Communist Party to come aboard, they have not all been discriminating in the men they send to Congress (the other congressman who refused to condemn the Soviet Union for shooting down the Korean airliner was Rep. John Conyers, also from Detroit).

Odd people in odd situations have always been elected to Congress, which, however, leaves unanswered the question: How on earth did he manage to be elected chairman of the subcommittee on Western Hemisphere Affairs? I mean, one might as well, if Mr. Crockett is as consistent in the future as he has been in the past, call in the foreign correspondent of Tass and give him the job.

The job, among other things, of recommending an appropriate policy for the U.S. government in Nicaragua. While Col. North and Adm. Poindexter face prosecution for what they did, the political system we are so anxious to nourish yields us a lifetime fellow traveler as chairman of a crucial committee.

Now the Democratic Party has been reluctant to engage in any disavowal. There was a lot of sullenness but no mutiny when three years ago the Rev. Jesse Jackson consorted with Louis Farrakhan, the strident anti-Semite; and there were even Democrats who frowned, however discreetly, when Jackson went down to Havana and toasted the health not only of Fidel Castro but of Che Guevara. But how can the same Congress that elected Crockett to his present eminence now ask such basic questions as whether he belongs in the Democratic Party?

But such questions are going to be asked. And there are signs that some are beginning to notice the perversion of toleration by the Democrats. To quote Mr. Sobran: "One thing is clear. If George Crockett had shown half as much sympathy for Reaganism as he's shown for Communism, the Democrats would never have given him that chairmanship."

DISCUSSION QUESTIONS

1. What effect do the title and the Latin quote in the first paragraph have on the reader? Did they make you want to pursue the rest of the essay?

2. This article was written at a time when a congressional committee was investigating Colonel North, Admiral Poindexter, and the illegal diversion of Iran arms profits to the contras in Nicaragua. How does the author defend North, Poindexter, and the Reagan administration?

3. "It is time to ask Congress: When you are done investigating Col. North and Adm. Poindexter, why not look into your own house?" What fallacy is illustrated by this sentence?

4. How is Rep. Crockett related to the committee investigating Colonel North and Admiral Poindexter?
5. In preceding years, the House of Representatives had refused Reagan administration requests to send huge sums of money to the Nicaraguan contras. How influential was Rep. Crockett in shaping congressional thought on this matter?
6. The author notes that Crockett has been associated over the years with leftist thought and leftist causes. Has the congressman done anything illegal? Anything immoral? Anything un-American?
7. How persuasive is this kind of "attacking" defense?

STATISTICS

*"There are 54 vampires living in the
United States today."*
—Headline in The Sun

There are a number of ways in which statistics can be used to distort argument. Persuaders can cite impressive averages, irrelevant totals, and homemade figures. They can offer a number in a context that makes it appear larger or smaller, according to their wish.

AVERAGES

A common fallacy involves the use of so-called average figures: average income, average price, average audience size, and so on. It is easy to argue from such statistics because the word *average* can mean three things.

What, for example, is the average if a group of 15 homemakers, responding to a poll question, say they watch television 48, 40, 30, 26, 22, 18, 12, 10, 9, 8, 5, 5, 5, 1, and 0 hours a week? From these numbers one can say that the group watches television an average of 15.933 hours a week, or 10 hours a week, or 5 hours a week. The 15.933 figure is the *mean* (the total number of hours watched divided by the number of viewers); the 10 figure is the *median* (the middle number in the series); and the 5 figure is the *mode* (the number that appears most frequently).

Each kind of average has its value, depending on the type of material being measured. But all three are available to the person who wants to manipulate an argument.

QUESTIONABLE FIGURES

Vague statistics can produce impressive averages. Numbers derived from memory, guesswork, and exaggeration can be averaged with amazing precision. (In the preceding paragraph, the 15.933 average was computed after 15 homemakers made rough guesses of their television viewing time.) Dr. Kinsey interviewed American men and reported that those without a high school education averaged 3.21 sexual experiences a week. The annual FBI report *Crime in the United States,* which compiles material from police departments across the country, showed that Baltimore in one year had suffered a crime increase of 71 percent. But police departments report crimes differently and with different degrees of accuracy. The sensational Baltimore figure derived from more accurate police reporting in the second year rather than from a huge increase in crime.

This kind of computation often derives from a biased source. Recently, divorce lawyer Michael Minton estimated the monetary values of 22 separate jobs and argued that a wife is worth $46,219.16 a year.

Similarly, amazing claims can be drawn from a small or partial sample. Some years ago a survey reported that 33.3 percent of all coeds at Johns Hopkins University had married faculty members. Johns Hopkins had three women students at the time. Advocates of extrasensory perception thrive on partial samples. They like to report cases of a gifted individual (Hubert Pearce, Basil Shakleton, or another) who has produced laboratory results for which the odds are 10,000,000 to 1 against chance being the explanation. Commonly, those who bother to question such claims discover that the individual cases were part of a longer series of tests and that the results of the entire experiment were not given.

IRRELEVANT NUMBERS

An argument can be bolstered with irrelevant statistics. Some years ago tobacco companies responded to evidence that smoking may cause cancer by counting filter traps. Viceroy boasted 20,000 filters ("twice as many as the other two largest-selling brands") until Parliament began claiming 30,000, and Hit Parade overwhelmed both with 400,000. (That was an average figure. The testing lab reported that one Hit Parade filter had 597,000 filter traps.) These are impressive figures, but they are totally meaningless. There was no evidence that *any* filter protected a person from the dangerous effects of smoking. And no one had defined "filter trap."

Many arguments assign numbers to undefined objects. When you're told that Americans reported 550 UFOs last month, you wonder what these people saw. When you face the sensational headline "Asthma Deaths in U.S. Double in Seven Years," you read on and see the reason: Authorities have changed the definition of "asthma."

Advertisers take the practice a step further and employ numbers without references. You see a travel ad for Martinique offering "Four times the pleasure" and one for Montreal boasting "It's four times better." Better than what? Don't ask.

Ads for pain relievers and cigarettes offer precise numbers and irrelevant comparisons. Anacin boasts 800 milligrams of pain reliever and observes that Tylenol, Bayer, and Bufferin have only 650. The ads present no evidence that the extra milligrams make any real difference to the consumer.

Kent Golden Lights are celebrated for having only 8 milligrams of tar ("as low as you can go and still get good taste") in an ad warning that Camel Lights and Raleighs have 9. In a rich area of comparison, Cambridge claims it has "the lowest tar *ever*," Carlton says it is "lowest," and Now insists it is "really the lowest." All are telling the truth because they are measuring different things. Cambridge refers to the 85s soft pack, Carlton to the 100s box, and Now to the 100s soft pack. Again, the ads never show how these figures make any difference to the average smoker.

Even when counting clearly defined items, speakers can offer irrelevant numbers. Responding to a demonstrated statistical relationship between cigarette smoking and an increased incidence of lung cancer, they can observe that the vast majority of smokers do not get cancer. As violent crimes increase, they can oppose gun control laws by establishing that only 0.0034 percent of American handguns are involved in homicides.

Equally creative computation goes into the unemployment figures produced by the U.S. Bureau of Labor Statistics. Because any administration can be faulted if unemployment is too high, the Bureau uses polling techniques that systematically underestimate the economic hardship within the labor force. A person is not "unemployed" unless he or she has actively looked for work in the preceding month. This method of counting eliminates people who have been sick, who have been forced into early retirement, and who have looked for months and have given up in despair.

However, a person can be looking regularly for work and still not be "unemployed." A dock worker who mows lawns two afternoons a month counts as being fully employed. Someone who helps out a brother in a family business and works for nothing counts as being fully employed. If his daughter works an hour a month as a baby-sitter, she is just as employed (in administration figures) as a chemist who works 60 hours a week at Monsanto.

In an inspired move, the Reagan administration chose to enlarge the work force to include people in military service. Because all those added had jobs, the percentage of Americans who were unemployed dropped significantly. One can visualize a future day when an administration decides that the only Americans truly unemployed are Puerto Rican teamsters out of work in Cleveland. Then it will celebrate a grand era of full employment.

A prime example of the use of an irrelevant statistic occurred in 1985 when corporate officers at the Coca-Cola Company changed the taste of Coke. They had nearly 200,000 tests demonstrating that the public preferred the taste of the new Coke to the old Coke and preferred it to Pepsi. Still, the change produced a nationwide protest that forced them to bring back the old Coke. Nobody cared about the 200,000 tests. As one critic said, "It's like they redesigned the flag."

There is a kind of irrelevance in statistics derived from a singular example. Hollywood Bread, for example, advertised that it had fewer calories per slice than other breads; this was true because its slices were thinner. Carlton cigarettes boasted that it had been tested as the lowest in "tar" of all filter kings; one reason was that it had a longer filter than other cigarettes of the same length and therefore contained less tobacco. Television personality Hugh Downs announced that he got 28.3 miles per gallon while driving a Mustang II from Phoenix to Los Angeles. The trip is largely downhill.

HOMEMADE STATISTICS

The preceding examples indicate that people do not have to make up statistics to create a misleading argument. But they can, of course, make up statistics if they want to. For example, the temperance advocate who built an analogy on the claim that there were 10,000 deaths from alcohol poisoning to 1 death from mad-dog bites was using figures that exist nowhere else.

Homemade statistics usually relate to things that have not been measured or are impossible to measure. Authorities can be suspiciously precise about events too trivial to have been counted. (Dr. Joyce Brothers reported that the "American girl kisses an average of seventy-nine men before getting married." A Lane cedar chest advertisement warned that moths destroy $400,000,000 worth of goods each year.) They can be glibly confident about obscure facts. (A *Nation* article said that there were 9,000,000 rats in New York City; Massachusetts Congressman Paul White, introducing a bill to make swearing illegal, announced that Americans curse 700,000 times a second.)

Imaginary numbers like these usually relate to areas in which it is impossible to get real figures. To make an impressive argument, advocates may want to specify the number of homosexuals in America today—or the number of pot smokers or adulterous wives. They may want to report how much money was spent on pornography last year—or on welfare fraud or illegal abortions. The writers can find some information in these areas, but because exact counts remain unavailable, they are strongly tempted to produce a number that supports the case they are trying to make. Many give in. Remember this the next time you see headlines announcing that a rail strike in Chicago is costing the city $2,000,000 a day.

Even in instances where a measure of scientific computation occurred, resulting statistics often seem singularly creative. Consider these examples, taken from recent news stories:

1. Seventeen percent of the babies born to near-affluent parents are unwanted.
2. Up to 30 percent of American coeds are harassed by their professors.
3. Five percent of Americans dream in color.
4. Men aged 35 to 50 average one sexual thought every 25 minutes.
5. Every five seconds a woman is beaten in the United States.
6. Humans have engaged in 452,783 wars since the beginning of recorded history.

Maybe you saw the Planned Parenthood ad that appeared in leading newspapers recently. It said, "They did it 9,000 times on television last year. How come nobody got pregnant?" Or maybe you saw the ad as it appeared later in *USA Today*. It began, "They did it 20,000 times on television last year."

With a little practice, you can identify homemade statistics with the naked eye.

ENHANCING A STATISTIC

With careful presentation, proponents can make any statistic seem bigger or smaller, as their argument requires. For example, many newspapers reported an Oberlin College poll that claimed that 40 percent of the unmarried coeds had engaged in sex, that 1 in 13 of these women became pregnant, and that 80 percent of the pregnancies were terminated by abortion. The "80 percent" figure seems startling until you ask, "80 percent of what?" Relatively modest statistics appear sensational when given as percentages of percentages of percentages.

More commonly, a person changes the character of a statistic by simple comparison. The speaker relates it to a smaller number to make it seem large or to a larger number to make it seem small. The contrasting number need have no relevance aside from offering an advantageous comparison.

In presidential primaries, candidates routinely predict weak results. They point out that the contest is not in their strongest state, that other duties have limited their public appearances, and that, all in all, they will do well to win 8 percent of the vote. Then when they win 11 percent, their followers announce, "He did well. His vote exceeded expectations." One reverses the process to dwarf a statistic. When Governor George Wallace—a law and order spokesman—had to face the fact that Alabama had the highest murder rate of any state in the nation (11.4 murders per 100,000 people), his office explained that this figure was not nearly so high as that for Detroit, Los Angeles, and other major cities.

In a summary statement on statistical manipulation, Darrell Huff (*How to Lie with Statistics,* New York, Norton, 1954) counseled the business community:

> There are often many ways of expressing any figure. You can, for instance, express exactly the same fact by calling it a one percent return on sales, a fifteen percent return on investment, a ten-million-dollar profit, an increase of profits of forty percent (compared with 1935–39 average), and a decrease of sixty percent from last year. The method is to choose which one sounds best for the purpose at hand and trust that few who read it will recognize how imperfectly it reflects the situation.

In a society subject to political controversy, social argument, and Madison Avenue rhetoric, such argument is common.

You should recognize examples of distorted statistics and avoid them as much as possible in your writing.

Of course you won't want to use specific numbers when they hurt the case you are making. Consider the diamond industry ad urging the purchase of an expensive engagement ring: "Is two months' salary too much to spend for something that will last forever?" (One might answer, "Is $4000 too much to spend on a marriage that will last two months?")

Even when numbers favor your case, do not use them too extensively.

A mass audience is rarely persuaded by a body of statistics. This explains why they are used so infrequently in the antismoking campaigns of the American Cancer Society and the American Heart Association.

You should remember, finally, that a number by itself means little or nothing. If in a particular year Montreal's baseball team leads the major leagues with 179 double plays, what does that mean? That it has a fine second baseman? That it has poor pitchers? That its home park has an Astroturf infield? Who knows? When 46 of 100 beer drinkers who "regularly drink Budweiser" preferred an unmarked mug of Schlitz (in a 1980 New Orleans test), what does that prove? Probably that most drinkers can't tell one beer from another. What can you conclude about an $18,000 annual salary, a 150-word poem, a $9.95 meal? Not much. An important quality of statistical argument was expressed in a scene in the film *Annie Hall:* The lovers, played by Diane Keaton and Woody Allen, are asked by their psychiatrists how often they have sex. She responds, "All the time. Three times a week." And he says, "Hardly at all. Three times a week."

EXERCISES

How reliable are these statistical arguments?

1. Studies of 22 states that maintained different drinking ages for beer show that fatal car crash rates were higher for 18- to 20-year-old drivers where the legal drinking age was 21.
2. If you begin having your hair styled, are people going to think you've gone soft? Half the Los Angeles Rams' line has their hair styled. If you want to laugh at them, go ahead. We don't.
3. Listening mistakes in the United States cost $10 billion a year.
4. Listerine Antiseptic stops bad breath four times better than toothpaste.
5. According to the Rodale Press, Inc., cigarette smoking costs Americans $50 billion a year.
6. On Solidarity Day (September 19, 1981), thousands of union workers massed in Washington to protest the Reagan administration's economic policies. United States park police estimated the crowd at 260,000. AFL-CIO sources called it half a million.
7. According to Rev. David S. Lundy's article in *Kiwanis Magazine,* in Las Vegas one in every eight women under 45 is a prostitute.
8. Using a simple cipher (A=6, B=12, C=18, etc.), the words KISSINGER and COMPUTER both total 666, the number of the Antichrist. Certainly, this proves something.
9. Leo Guild's book *What Are the Odds?* reports that a young man with a broken engagement behind him is "75 percent as happy" as one who has never been engaged.
10. It is estimated that each year some 10 million wise Americans spend $500 million on essential life-building food supplements and vitamin capsules. Can 10 million Americans be wrong?

11. "27 million Americans can't read a bedtime story to a child."
    —Coalition for Literacy
12. Sinners will burn in Hell, where the fire is 20,000 degrees Farenheit.
13. "Banging your head against a wall burns 150 calories an hour."
    —*National Enquirer* (July 15, 1986)
14. "Over 10 million men suffer impotence problems in the U.S. today."
    —Ken Druck
15. "It costs HEW $3 in overhead to deliver $1 to a needy person in this
    country."—Ronald Reagan
16. In her heyday, Clara Bow received more mail per week than the
    average town of 5000.
17. Studies show that therapy that includes an aspirin a day reduces
    heart attacks as much as 50 percent for some people. Aspirin,
    combined with exercise and the right foods, could save as many as
    50,000 lives a year.
18. "1 in 10 have psychic power."—Uri Geller
19. The Government Accounting Office, urged on by Senator William
    Proxmire, calculated that the 1985 presidential inaugural events cost
    the nation $15,512,339.59.
20. "The nuclear power industry has virtually stopped in the U.S. because
    of fear. This is true despite the fact that for more than 20 years the
    commercial nuclear industry has operated under unprecedented public
    health scrutiny and that to date there have been no radiation-related
    injuries (let alone deaths) suffered by any member of the public."
    —Robert L. DuPont

ESSAY ASSIGNMENTS

Write an essay either affirming or opposing one of these statements. The
material you encounter in your background reading will include statistical
argument, and so should your essay.

1. American industry *is* fighting pollution.
2. We need gun control laws to curtail crime.
3. Sex education leads to promiscuity, pregnancy, and disease.
4. It's proved: Cigarette smoking causes lung cancer.
5. IQ tests do not prove anything.
6. American income tax laws should be revised.
7. Laetrile is an effective treatment for cancer.
8. Statistics prove that X is a mistake. (Fill in the X.)

THE FEDERAL
DEFICIT

FRED SHAW

I guess everyone here today has seen the television show "The Six Million Dollar Man." In the tradition of prime-time TV, it is exciting and a lot of fun. Today, I'm going to give you my "Four Million Dollar Speech."

I hope it will excite your interest and concern, but I don't think you will find it to be a lot of fun.

You see, it will cost the federal government an estimated $100 billion simply to pay interest on the national debt this year. This is about $190,000 each and every minute of the year.

At that rate, in the time I will spend speaking today—a little over 20 minutes—the federal government will run up another $4 million or so in interest due.

Four million dollars.

Even to a banker, that's a lot of money.

As a banker, I view money and credit differently from the way most people do.

Because of my profession, I take the long view. To the banker, money is more than wealth—it is also the means to produce more wealth. Bankers always see money and credit as investments intended to pay off down the line.

Today, I want to take the opportunity to give you the commercial banker's perspective on the federal budget and on the deficits that it is producing.

Now we all know that federal budget deficits must somehow be financed. To do this the government can simply increase the amount of dollars in circulation or it can borrow money.

Pretend for a moment that I am the only banker in the country. Were the government to ask me as a banker for a loan to finance the entire federal deficit at the level it is forecast to run over the next few years, I would have to consider very closely whether to make the loan or not.

In making judgements about credit, a banker looks at five factors, which we call the five C's: character, capacity, capital, collateral, and condition.

Judging the government's application by these criteria, I as a banker would conclude that: the government doesn't default on its loans; therefore, it passes the test of character; as long as the government can tax, it has the capacity to repay; the capital and the collateral are there, because they are the nation itself, *but* both the long-term condition of the economy and the financial condition of the government would give me reason to pause.

Look at the results such a loan would have.

SOURCE: Reprinted by permission from *Vital Speeches of the Day, April 15, 1984.* From a speech delivered at the Downtown Lions Club, Memphis, Tennessee, February 22, 1984.

What are we trying to achieve with economic policy?

Ideally, we want a stable economy with low inflation, low unemployment, and strong growth. The last year has seen our economy develop nicely along these lines.

But I am afraid that if large federal budget deficits are allowed to continue, they would make the continued achievement and long-term maintenance of these goals difficult, if not altogether impossible.

Indeed, if these deficits are not soon curtailed, the chances increase that our economy will be plunged right back into recession; interest rates will soar; inflation will rise with a vengeance and double digit unemployment will return.

Quite simply, we must recognize and confront the federal budget problem *now*, or we may seriously jeopardize the standard of living for all of us in the long run.

According to preliminary forecasts by the non-partisan Congressional Budget Office, under the government's current taxing and spending policies the deficit will continue to grow for the foreseeable future. The deficit for 1984 is estimated at $185 billion; for 1986, it will be $197 billion; and by 1989, it is estimated at a staggering $280 billion.

Of course, deficit estimates depend on the economic assumptions used and are tricky to make. But the important point here is, no matter which assumptions one uses, the deficit is already too high, and it will continue to rise.

The deficit problem really has two parts—magnitude and time.

Our annual deficits and the total debt we have established are so enormous that they are difficult for most people to comprehend.

I would like to take a moment to try to put the amounts into perspective.

What's a billion?

To spend a billion dollars, a shopper would have to spend a hundred dollars a minute—each and every minute—for 19 years.

A billion seconds ago, America was still reeling from the surprise attack on Pearl Harbor.

A billion minutes ago, Christ was still living.

A billion hours ago, man had not appeared on earth.

A billion federal budget dollars ago was only yesterday.

We now use the figure of $200 billion as the benchmark for deficits. Just what is $200 billion?

Look at $200 billion in this way. If you had $200 billion worth of freshly printed $1 bills and you stacked these bills one on top of the other, your stack, when completed, would be more than 14,000 miles high and would weigh approximately 4 billion pounds.

So much for $200 billion.

Remember, this is just one year's worth of debt. We have amassed a *total* debt in excess of $1.3 trillion. Let's try to get a handle on this one-trillion-plus dollar national debt by looking at what a trillion is.

If you divided one trillion dollars among every man, woman and child in the U.S., every individual would get approximately $4,400.

One trillion dollars in single dollar bills would cover 3,931 square miles, an area almost four hundred times the size of Washington, D.C. Placed end to end, they would stretch around the world 1,800 times.

In 1982 prices, one trillion dollars would buy more than 172 million new automobiles and more than 18 million new homes.

Remember, though, that our national debt is actually 1.3 trillion dollars.

As for the time component, for the last 30 years Congress has consistently expanded the size of the federal budget.

Like an adolescent who has just discovered credit cards, the lawmakers have just as consistently spent beyond our means.

In 1970, the entire federal budget was $200 billion and that year we had a $2.8 billion deficit.

In 1983, the federal budget exceeded $800 billion and we had a deficit of about $200 billion. Our current deficit exceeds the total amount of money spent by the government just 13 years earlier!

If the government in Washington continues its present course, it is truly frightening to think what might happen in the next thirteen years.

It is also truly frightening to think of the people—our families, friends, colleagues, neighbors—who don't believe that the deficit is a problem. Besides the difficulty of comprehending the numbers involved, there are myths in this country that blind people to the threat the federal deficit represents.

John Kennedy once said, "The great enemy of the truth is very often not the lie—deliberate, contrived and dishonest—but the myth—persistent, persuasive and unrealistic."

The truth is that the federal deficits must be reduced or we will all suffer, but two pervasive myths concerning deficits must be dispelled before serious efforts can be made at reducing them.

The first myth is that the deficit is somehow a short-term glitch: that it has really only been with us for the last couple of years and can easily be eradicated by a robust economic recovery.

The fact is, however, that the deficits we are now faced with have been structurally embedded into the economy. Since 1961, the federal government has experienced 22 deficits and just one surplus. Even under the most optimistic of growth scenarios—unless major changes are made—we will be facing deficits at least until the end of this decade and probably beyond that.

The second budget myth is that the deficit really does not matter. While we know it is out there, it really does not touch on our everyday affairs. And besides, when figured as a percentage of the Gross National Product or the total amount of debt outstanding, the deficit doesn't look that large.

Such thinking is not only terribly misleading, it is downright dangerous.

Mammoth deficits do affect our everyday lives—they help determine how many Americans are working, how much the value of their dollar is eroded by inflation and how difficult it is for businesses and consumers to get credit.

As a banker accustomed to taking the long view—that is, looking at money and credit as an investment—allow me to explain how the deficit affects the everyday lives of every American.

The important question is not how large the deficit is compared to the Gross National Product or total outstanding debt. The important question is how much net new savings the federal government will absorb trying to finance the deficit and how much will be left over for private investment in plant and equipment, research, technology and consumer goods.

Investment, in other words, which is essential if our economy is to keep moving and our standard of living is to be maintained.

Traditionally, the federal government has used about one-quarter of our national savings pool.

If deficits continue at their current high level, this figure will be closer to one-half to two-thirds of that pool—year after year.

The obvious result of this course is that interest rates are pushed higher and higher, since there is greater competition for the same amount of capital. Think about that the next time you or someone you know wants to purchase a car or a home.

It has been said that our nation pays the debts of the last generation by issuing bonds payable to the next generation. This is like using a giant chain letter to pass along the day of reckoning from one generation to the next, thankful that we were able to avoid dealing with it. What we are really doing is staining future generations with a sea of red ink.

Furthermore, we not only owe our debt to future generations, we owe a substantial part of it—as much as 30 percent, according to some estimates—to overseas interests who purchase federal securities as an investment. I think it is all well and good for anyone who wants to invest in America to do so—but what happens if one morning they wake up and decide not to do so anymore? What happens then?

I do want to point out here that in modern economic theory, the budget does not have to be balanced every year.

In a recession, such as the one we just went through, a deficit may provide a cushioning effect—in part because slack production means there is less overall competition for funds.

But as the economy picks up, as it has this last year, demand for funds begins to rise and the deficit begins to have a negative drag. The greater the deficit, the greater the drag. Period.

As an alternative to borrowing, the federal government may decide to finance its deficit by creating more money. Then we will suffer from inflation. In the classic economic definition, we will have more dollars chasing the same amount of goods.

Take a moment to recall how bad our inflation was just four years ago.

In 1980, we had an inflation rate in excess of 20 percent. Twenty percent annual inflation means that in addition to the normal income tax you pay the government, you also pay a 20-cent-on-the-dollar "penalty tax."

When inflation is on the rise, no one has any incentive to save or invest. Industry becomes starved for capital, savers watch their nest eggs disappear and recession returns to the horizon. In addition, interest rates rise.

That's right. Whichever course the government takes to finance its deficit—borrowing, creating money or a mix of the two—interest rates rise.

And rising interest rates bring higher unemployment in their wake.

For example, high interest rates cause our dollar to gain value in comparison to foreign currencies. Since 1980, the dollar has appreciated by 50 percent against the money of other nations. As a result, American goods and services became extremely expensive in foreign markets. Exports were lost, and trade deficits resulted ($65 billion last year alone).

In the abstract, these figures may not seem all that important. You might think they are gathered simply to keep an economist busy or to fill the appendix of yet another government report.

But the fact is, every billion dollars worth of American exports creates 25,000 American jobs. And since 1978, more than 80 percent—or almost 5 million—new manufacturing jobs in the U.S. were export-related. Chances are good that the livelihood of someone you know depends in some fashion on American exports.

I have gone into such detail and depth today to underscore the fact that the only way we are going to extricate ourselves from this deficit mess is to significantly reduce overall government spending. Budget reductions must be made to maintain the four goals of economic policy: stability, growth, continued low inflation and low unemployment. All types of government spending should be candidates for reduction.

Federal spending falls into four general areas: defense, direct benefit payments for individuals, known as entitlements; interest on debt; and a mish-mash group called non-defense discretionary expenditures, which includes most federal departments, such as Treasury, Labor and Commerce. This last group makes up about 14 percent of the entire federal budget.

Of course, Congress appropriates the money that runs the government, but much of that money must first be requested by the federal bureaucracy.

The late Leonard Reed, a writer and former bureaucrat himself, has given probably the best description of how the bureaucracy views its role in the federal budget process.

"No activity in a government agency is given as high a priority as securing and enlarging its budget," he once wrote. "Bureaucrats almost invariably believe in the function their agency exists to perform, whether it is providing information to farmers or preserving the national forests. A new bureaucracy, the darling of the Administration that establishes it, has a missionary zeal about its function. As the bureaucracy ages, it loses glamour and finds itself expending an increasing share of its energy on obtaining funds.

"Since there is a certain logic to the proposition that without money an agency can't function," Reed concluded, "the bureaucrat . . . finds nothing wrong with spending more and more of his time and attention aiding the quest for more money, much of which is now added to support the large money-raising apparatus that has grown up in the agency."

One of the more notorious results of this evolution is Washington's end-of-the-year spending spree. In the weeks before the September 30 deadline, it is harvest time for consultants and contractors as each agency tries to use up all its appropriated funds so that it won't appear to have been overbudgeted.

I don't intend to go into the details of horror stories on federal agency expenditures. We've heard them so often that they have become familiar. I can only hope that this familiarity will breed contempt—contempt for the practice of putting narrow bureaucratic interest above the interest of the public.

Since defense and direct benefit payments for individuals made up about 71 percent of government expenditures last year, it is obvious that these areas must be examined closely. The entitlement programs—programs like Medicare and Medicaid, veterans' benefits and the like—can only be changed by changing the underlying laws which entitle people to benefits. Unless the laws are changed, this category will continue to make up almost half of the budget.

Fortunately, since we live in a democracy we can deal with the deficits—but it is going to take a large degree of unselfish discipline.

Democracies are deficit prone exactly because it is far more pleasant to raise spending than to reduce it. As can be expected, the Santa Clauses get re-elected and the Scrooges get rejected.

We all know how easy it is to add an extra item to our budget—to expand our wish list. But try to delete an item from the government budget—whether it be a dam or a highway, a military base or a new type of tank—and the special interests will cry out in wounded anguish.

But the funny thing is, you and I make up the special interests. Take a minute to think about whether you receive some sort of government benefit.

- Are you a farmer earning thousands of dollars for not planting a crop?
- Are you a small businessman taking advantage of government loans?
- Are you a parent with a child in college who receives a government subsidized loan?

The list could go on and on. The important point is that we have got to realize that we cannot reduce the deficit unless and until we ourselves as individuals make some sacrifice.

As a banker familiar with the political process, I fear that future attempts to deal with the entitlement problem will run the danger of ending up like the recent compromise on funding the largest entitlement of all—Social Security.

True, the compromise was a step in the right direction, but it did not go far enough and did not solve the problem of the long-run viability of the system. There was too much emphasis on increases in taxes rather than reductions in benefits. More work needs to be done on reducing the growth of benefits in the long run.

Since I've brought up that great bugaboo—taxes—I should explain how banking economists view the issue.

Taxation affects more than the balance sheet of a government—indeed it has long been recognized that taxes may have a negative effect on the long-run health of the economy. The power to tax is truly the power to destroy. Furthermore, in the context of the deficit, tax increases may fail to reduce the deficits by shifting the political focus away from the need to reduce expenditures.

Let me give you a recent example.

Not too many months ago, Congress approved a $98.3 billion tax hike bill. For every $1 of tax increase mandated by this bill, we were supposed to see $3 in corresponding spending reductions. The legislation was hailed as a great fiscal achievement.

But we have yet to see the spending reductions which we were promised, and, furthermore, economists tell us that this legislation had a negative impact on the prospects for long-term economic growth by decreasing incentives to invest.

Taxes are not the answer to the deficit crisis.

In conclusion, I would like to again stress that we cannot expect to solve the deficit crisis until we appreciate how it affects the quality of our lives.

More than 200 years ago, Alexander Hamilton wrote that a national debt, if it is not excessive, will be to us a national blessing. Riding his train of thought a little further down the line, *if* a national debt is excessive, it becomes a national curse. Our national debt threatens to be the cause of great harm to all Americans. It has already turned us all—you, me, every American alive plus all those who will be born for years to come—into history's largest debtor class.

When Hamilton was alive, individuals who could not pay their debts were thrown into debtors' prison.

Our accumulated deficits are slowly but surely incarcerating our entire population in what soon may become an inescapable debtors' prison. The walls of this prison are not made of brick, concrete and steel. Instead, they are composed of high interest rates, inflation, unemployment and sluggish investment.

Our key to escape may be found by reducing these deficits through discipline in the spending process.

For that key to work, however, we must start to turn it around now.

We must begin to make it clear to our elected representatives that we will no longer tolerate the buy-now-pay-whenever spending binges which got us into this deficit mess. And, we must begin to support and work for candidates who have pledged to put a lid on government spending wherever it originates.

But remember, this course will also require some degree of sacrifice from all of us. Each of us must be willing to forego some little "goodie" the government has provided—whether it be an increase in a benefit check, a tax loophole or whatever. We are the ones who are going to have to act if we ever hope to see the deficit logjam broken.

Let's do it now . . . before it is too late.

DISCUSSION QUESTIONS

1. Why does the author take so much time clarifying what a billion is and what a trillion is? Can't an audience of business people be expected to know that?
2. Except when making these clarifications, does the author use a great many statistics? Would it help him to use more?
3. What does the style of the essay tell you about the author?
4. What do his specific references to himself tell you?

5. Do his style and his personal references make him more persuasive or less persuasive?

6. "Take a minute to think about whether you receive some sort of government benefit." Identify the places in which the author refers to his audience. Do these references make him more persuasive?

7. "What we are really doing is staining future generations with a sea of red ink." Would his argument be more persuasive if the author took out this metaphor and substituted some statistics?

8. This is one of the longest essays in this book. When you read it, did it seem long? Why or why not?

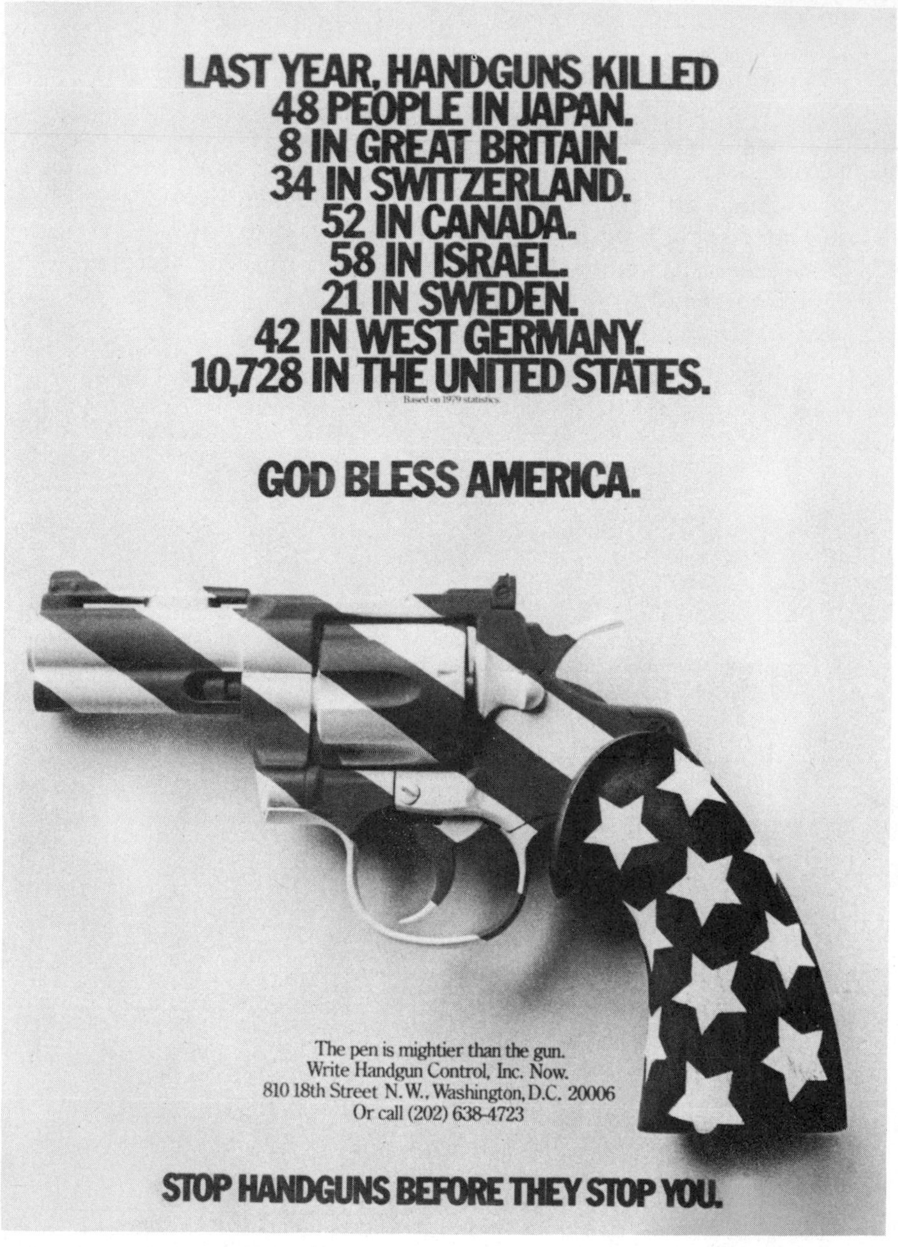

Courtesy of Handgun Control, Inc.

DISCUSSION QUESTIONS

1. What is the unstated conclusion of this ad? What is the author advocating?
2. Is the argument persuasive?
3. Would the argument be less persuasive if you were told the number of stabbings in Britain, the number of bombings in Ireland, the number of fatal beatings in West Germany, and so on?
4. If the sale of handguns was made illegal tomorrow, do you think the figures on the ad would be significantly different a year from now? Why or why not?

THE BALDNESS EXPERIMENT

GEORGE DELEON

The winos who hung around my Brooklyn neighborhood in 1950 were not funny. With their handout hands, reeking breaths, and weird, ugly injuries, they were so self-rejecting that you could bark them away even while you shoved them a nickel. My friends and I didn't think they were funny, but we observed one thing that always busted us up. Almost without exception, they had all their hair.

Seriously: we never saw a bald bum. Have you? When was the last time you remember a street alky stumbler with nothing on top?

Black, white, old, young, short, tall, all of them had a full mop. And hair that wouldn't quit. It leaped up as if it were electrified, or shagged down in complete asocial indifference, or zoomed back absurdly neat, gray-black and glued. Inexplicably, it seemed that boozing burned out the guts but grew hair.

Fifteen years later, I offered this observation to my undergraduate classes in the psychology of personality. Then, one semester, I decided to get past the laugh, integrate my present self with my past self, and actually test the hypothesis that booze grows hair.

I conceived a simple investigation, with the class participating as co-researchers. In the project, we'd get some real data on the density, or rather the incidence, of baldness in a random sample of rummies. The tactic was to beachhead ourselves on the Bowery in New York City, fan out in teams of two, and gradually move up from somewhere around Prince Street to 14th Street, the end of the bum region.

On two successive Saturday mornings, the whole research outfit—me, four men, and two women—met on the corner of Bowery and Houston to carry out the plan. Every other derelict who was not unconscious was approached, talked to, and looked at. Since no one usually walks up to a rummy except cops and other rummies, something seemed to happen when two pretty young students of mine would say, "Sir, I'd like to ask you a few questions." The winos would rock a bit and—no kidding—you could almost see a little ego emerging.

In planning the research, I decided that we should gather as much information as we could that might be relevant to the experiment. We decided to mark down answers to questions about age, race, ethnicity, marital status, family baldness, drinking life, etc. We even asked our subjects where they usually slept (in or out of doors), figuring that, too, might influence their hair growth.

While one team member interrogated, the other circled around the subject, studying the head, raised and lowered, to observe the pate. Subjects were evaluated on a four-point baldness scale as hairy, receding, bald pate, or totally bald.

Interesting problems developed from the beginning; what appeared to

SOURCE: Reprinted with permission from *Psychology Today* magazine. Copyright © 1977.

be simple was really complex. When do you call a guy bald? What does "receding" mean? (We dispensed with the use of rulers or vernier calipers, assuming that, bombed or not, the derelict would shuffle off as soon as we pulled out any kind of hardware. We felt grateful that he tolerated the paper, pencils, and questions.) So there was no quantification, no precision. We simply had to make quick judgments.

Our teams interviewed over 60 Bowery subjects, paying them a quarter a pop, all of which came out of my pocket. Back at the school, the data were tallied and, sure enough, the results confirmed my intuition. Only about 25 percent could be called receding or totally bald, with the remainder being pated or hirsute. I had been right all along, and we reported the results to the class.

But it turns out that the skepticism of annoyed youth may actually be the quintessence of good scientific research. After I enjoyed the laughs and took a few bows, a number of students, not on the teams, were quick to raise some sharp objections.

First, and most obvious, was that we needed to study baldness in a group of nonderelicts in order to make proper conclusions. Second, wasn't it possible that the teams had been influenced by my colorful classroom predictions about hairy bums and had tended to judge the subjects as nonbalding?

The criticism was first rate. I knew that because it threw me into an immediate depression. I hated the students who offered it. I also knew that we'd have to do the whole study again with new teams and new derelicts. This time, nonderelicts would have to be included, too, and I would offer no advance hypothesis that might bias, in my favor, the way kids looked at heads.

I waited a whole academic year, got a new personality class, and this time took no chances. During the lectures, it was necessary to arouse the interest of the class in the broad issue of bums and baldness. So I suggested that derelicts were a special group of people who seemed to lose their hair sooner and more completely than other men. In short, I lied. Morality aside, it was a tough one to tell because I feared that it would shape the kids' perception the other way. They might actually see receding hairlines and shiny heads where there really was only hair. But I had to take the risk of betting against myself to make the win more sure.

Out on the turf again a new and larger research squad of six men and six women worked over five straight Saturdays. They did the Bowery in pairs, interviewing about 80 derelicts.

We also went after a comparison group. Any man walking in or out of Bloomingdale's or cruising along 5th Avenue in the 50s was operationally defined as a nonderelict. These fine fellows we decided to call "sterlings." "Sterling" male shoppers in tweeds were stopped on a random basis in front of Bloomingdale's revolving doors. They were put through the whole routine of questions about drinking, age, etc., and their heads were carefully checked out. One difference was that we were too embarrassed to hand them quarters, so we didn't. Then, about a month later, to extend our control group, I sent five squads into a faculty meeting at Wagner College and got the same information on 49 college professors in one sweep.

Happily, the new set of derelict data turned out the same as the old, and the results of the three comparison groups were more striking than expected. When the information was presented simply as nonbald versus balding (which combined receding plus pated plus total), we found that 71 percent of the college professors were balding, 53 percent of the sterlings, and, of the derelicts (both years), only 36 percent (see Figure 1).

There were no ethnic or racial differences, nor were the other factors in the questionnaire very important. Still, age must matter, and it does.

Under age 25, we found 17 (21 percent) sterlings, but only one derelict and no professors. In fact, the average age of the sterlings was 37.5, while it was 47.5 for the other two groups. This makes sense, since it takes a lot of years to become either a derelict or a college professor.

Figure 2 shows the percentage of balding across several age levels. Naturally, the older men in all groups contain a greater proportion of hair losers. But after age 40, the differences among the groups are fascinating. The sterlings and professors reveal similar rising percentages, with the profs leading. The derelicts, however, in the years 41 to 55, actually show a slight decrease, and of the 50 guys on the Bowery past age 55, only 44 percent showed signs of balding as compared with about 80 percent of the oldies in the other groups. So the stereotype of the balding egghead professor is not contradicted by these data. For the Bowery bum, there's no doubt that he simply keeps his hair.

Now comes the hard part: what does it all mean? Though it did not show up in our data, I'm sure that genetics is relevant. Even so, what is the likelihood that only the bums have fewer bald daddies? Not much.

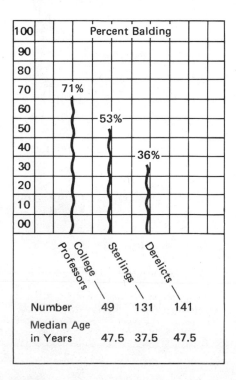

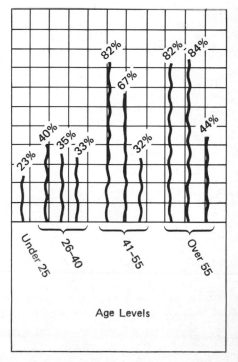

Figure 1   Figure 2

These results also rule out ethnic and racial factors. Hair and air didn't go together, since the derelicts who said they usually slept out were no less bald than those who snoozed in the dorms of the flophouse hotels.

Are the bums breezier and more carefree? Calm or numbed so that they don't feel the stress that most of us do? Is it the food they eat, or don't eat?

No. We concluded that it must be the alcohol and some resulting biochemical activity. It happens, since completing the study, that I've learned that medical literature does point to some interaction between liver damage, alcohol metabolism, the female hormone estrogen, hair growth and retention. Seems reasonable to me.

If so, I'm elated that our finds are valid. But, in a way, it doesn't matter. The whole trip started for me back in Brooklyn, as a joke. Later, my students and I really observed, recorded what we saw, and attempted to draw conclusions. Seeking the truth is always an adventure; the scientist is in all of us.

DISCUSSION QUESTIONS

1. The author reports three separate readings of the derelict–baldness issue: his observations as a youth, the first study he and his class made, and the final study. Since they all came to the same conclusion, why is the final study more significant than the others?
2. Why did the teams ask questions about age, race, ethnicity, marital status, family baldness, drinking habits, sleeping place, and so on? Why didn't they just check hair?
3. Explain the following:
   a. why the first research team interviewed only every other derelict
   b. why they made no precise measurements of the derelicts' hair
   c. why the author lied to the second research team about what he expected to prove
   d. why the derelicts were compared to men around Bloomingdale's and to professors
   e. why the author offered an age analysis at the end
4. "Black, white, old, young, short, tall, all of them had a full mop. And hair that wouldn't quit." What is the tone of this essay? Does the tone add to the author's case?
5. Baldness is usually considered a genetic factor. How does the author explain this away? Is he persuasive?
6. What is amusing about defining male Bloomingdale's shoppers as "nonderelict"?
7. "Now comes the hard part: what does it all mean?" What does this sentence tell you about statistics?
8. How effective is the author's writing style?

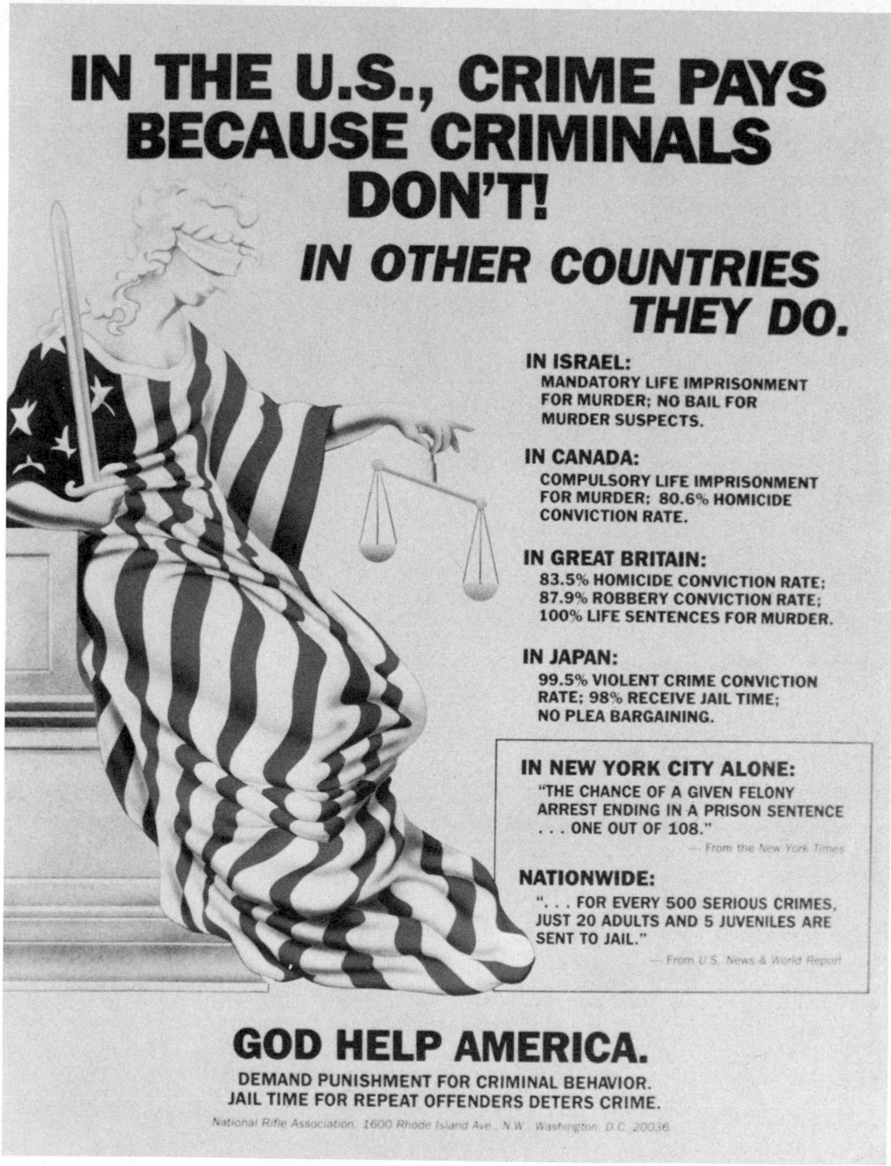

Courtesy of the National Rifle Association of America.

DISCUSSION QUESTIONS

1. This ad was written to answer the argument on page 135. Is this an effective response?
2. What does this ad say about the sale of handguns in the United States?
3. What did the argument on page 135 say about high and low conviction rates and about compulsory sentences?
4. Name the fallacy illustrated by this argument.
5. Why should the National Rifle Association be so concerned about conviction rates and compulsory sentences?

THE TRAIL
OF 666

The number 666 is rapidly becoming man's favorite number. Dr. Mary Stewart Relfe, in her book *When Your Money Fails,* made the following observations:

- World Bank code number is "666."
- Australia's national bank cards have on them "666."
- New credit cards in U.S. are now being assigned the prefix "666."
- Central computers for Sears, Belks, Penneys, and Montgomery Wards around the world have all their transactions prefixed with "666."
- Shoes made in European Common Market Countries have stamped on inside label "666."
- Computers made by Lear Siegler have a seal on the side on which is stamped the number "666."
- IRS Instructions for Non-profit Corporation Employee 1979, W-2 Form requires the prefix "666."
- IRS began to require the prefix "666" on some forms; for example, W-2P, disability is 666.3; death is 666.4, etc., as early as 1977.
- Tanks built by Chrysler Corporation . . . have on their sides "666."
- South Central Bell's new Telco Credit Union Cards require the prefix "666," then the person's social security number.
- Metric rulers distributed in 1979 throughout the U.S. have in the center the number "666."
- ID tags on 1979 GM cars produced in Flint, Michigan contain the number "666."
- United States Selective Cards have on them "666."
- Overseas telephone operator number from Israel is "666."
- Arab-owned vehicles in Jerusalem have license plates prefixed with "666."
- Record album released by a rock group, Black Sabbath, is named "666."
- The films *Omen I* and *II* concern themselves with a world dictator and the number "666."
- Some IBM supermarket equipment is prefixed with the number 3—"666."
- JC Penney began prefixing account numbers in August, 1980, with "666."
- MasterCard began using on their August, 1980 statements "66."
- Formula for NCR Model 304 Supermarket Computer System is 6 60 6, "666."

Dr. Relfe relied considerably on information in Southern Radio Church publications, and we ourselves are able to document many items relating to the increasing appearance of the number "666." For example, a listener forwarded a shirt to Pastor Webber that was made in China with

SOURCE: Reprinted by permission of the Southwest Radio Church of the Air. Reprinted from *The Gospel Truth,* May 1981.

the trademark number 666. In Israel we have personally seen and photographed hundreds of vehicles with 666 prefixes in the license plate numbers. We have an IRS form in our possession with information requested under a 666 code numbering system. The November 25, 1980 edition of *The Jerusalem Post* carried a large ad announcing a national 666 contest.

It can be argued that with the great increases in the use of numbers in the modern world of commerce that the number 666 actually appears with no greater frequency than the combination of any other number, i.e., 222, 333 or 444. Nevertheless, it is our opinion that the affinity for the use of 666 is growing, and it is preferred over any other number especially in the areas of governmental control, finance, and computer technology. This does not mean that we should label anything or everything that displays the number 666 as bearing the "mark of the beast," but it does indicate that the world is being psychologically prepared to accept 666 as the *all encompassing* number of the future. There is coming a day when a world governmental system will demand that everyone in the world take a mark and the number 666 in order to work, buy or sell. This fact is clearly set forth in God's Word:

"And he causeth all, both small and great, rich and poor, free and bond, to receive a mark in their right hand, or in their foreheads: And that no man might buy or sell, save he that had the mark, or the name of the beast, or the number of his name. Here is wisdom. Let him that hath understanding count the number of the beast: for it is the number of a man; and his number is Six hundred threescore and six." (Rev. 13:16–18).

DISCUSSION QUESTIONS

1. Are some of these "666" appearances more easily explained than others? Why might the number be used in *The Omen* and as a Black Sabbath record title?
2. In the given examples, does the number always appear as a simple, isolated "666"? When is this not the case?
3. What is the advantage of including "66," "6 60 6," and configurations like 470066671 as examples of the recurring number?
4. If the number recurs to prepare the world psychologically for the coming of the Antichrist, who is writing this number all over?
5. What does "psychologically prepared" mean?
6. What advantages does a person have who seeks to find a significant, recurring number in modern usage?

PART TWO

ARGUMENT
FOR ANALYSIS

*Do not despise prophesying,
but test everything; hold fast
what is good.*

—*St. Paul,* I Thessalonians

Courtesy of Steve Kelly and Copley News Service.

THE HUNDREDTH
MONKEY PHENOMENON

RON AMUNDSON

Claims of the paranormal are supported in many ways. Personal reports ("I was kidnapped by extraterrestrials"), appeals to puzzling everyday experiences ("Did you ever get a phone call from someone you had just dreamed about?"), and references to "ancient wisdom" are a few. Citations of actual scientific results are usually limited to ESP experiments and a few attempts to mystify further the already bizarre discoveries of modern physics. But the New Age is upon us (we're told) and New Age authors like Rupert Sheldrake (1981) and Lyall Watson (1979) support their new visions of reality with scientific documentation. Sheldrake has a bibliography of about 200 listings, and Watson lists exactly 600 sources. The sources cited are mostly respectable academic and scientific publications. The days of "[unnamed] scientists say" and "Fred Jones, while walking alone in the woods one day. . ." are gone. Or are they?

I teach college courses in epistemology, in the philosophy of science, and in pseudoscience and the occult. Students in these courses naturally bring to class examples of remarkable and paranormal claims. During the past few years one such claim has become especially popular, the "Hundredth Monkey Phenomenon." This phenomenon was baptized by Lyall Watson, who documents the case with references to five highly respectable articles by Japanese primatologists (Imanishi 1963; Kawai 1963 and 1965; Kawamura 1963; and Tsumori 1967). Watson's discussion of this phenomenon covers less than two pages. (Except where noted, all references to Watson are to pages 147 and 148.) But this brief report has inspired much attention. Following Watson, a book (Keyes 1982), a newsletter article (*Brain/Mind Bulletin* 1982), and a film (Hartley 1983) have each been created with the title "The Hundredth Monkey." In addition we find a journal article entitled "The 'Hundredth Monkey' and Humanity's Quest for Survival" (Stein 1983) and an article called "The Quantum Monkey" in a popular magazine (*Science Digest* 1981). Each relies on Watson as the sole source of information on the remarkable and supernatural behavior of primates.

The monkeys referred to are indeed remarkable. They are Japanese macaques *(Macaca fuscata),* which live in wild troops on several islands in Japan. They have been under observation for years. During 1952 and 1953 the primatologists began "provisioning" the troops—providing them with such foods as sweet potatoes and wheat. This kept the monkeys from raiding farms and also made them easier to observe. The food was left in open areas, often on beaches. As a result of this new economy, the monkeys developed several innovative forms of behavior. One of these was invented in 1953 by an 18-month-old female that the observers named "Imo." Imo was a member of the troop on Koshima island. She discovered that sand and grit could be removed from the sweet potatoes

SOURCE: Reprinted with permission from *The Skeptical Inquirer,* Summer 1985.

by washing them in a stream or in the ocean. Imo's playmates and her mother learned this trick from Imo, and it soon spread to other members of the troop. Unlike most food customs, this innovation was learned by older monkeys from younger ones. In most other matters the children learn from their parents. The potato-washing habit spread gradually, according to Watson, up until 1958. But in the fall of 1958 a remarkable event occurred on Koshima. This event formed the basis of the "Hundredth Monkey Phenomenon."

THE MIRACLE ON KOSHIMA

According to Watson, all of the juveniles on Koshima were washing their potatoes by early 1958, but the only adult washers were those who had learned from the children. In the fall of that year something astounding happened. The exact nature of the event is unclear. Watson says:

> . . . One has to gather the rest of the story from personal anecdotes and bits of folklore among primate researchers, because most of them are still not quite sure what happened. And those who do suspect the truth are reluctant to publish it for fear of ridicule. So I am forced to improvise the details, but as near as I can tell, this is what seems to have happened. In the autumn of that year an unspecified number of monkeys on Koshima were washing sweet potatoes in the sea. . . . Let us say, for argument's sake, that the number was ninety-nine and that at eleven o'clock on a Tuesday morning, one further convert was added to the fold in the usual way. But the addition of the hundredth monkey apparently carried the number across some sort of threshold, pushing it through a kind of critical mass, because by that evening almost everyone was doing it. Not only that, but the habit seems to have jumped natural barriers and to have appeared spontaneously, like glycerine crystals in sealed laboratory jars, in colonies on other islands and on the mainland in a troop at Takasakiyama.

A sort of group consciousness had developed among the monkeys, Watson tells us. It had developed suddenly, as a result of one last monkey's learning potato washing by conventional means. The sudden learning of the rest of the Koshima troop was not attributable to the normal one-monkey-at-a-time method of previous years. The new phenomenon of group consciousness was responsible not only for the sudden learning on Koshima but for the equally sudden acquisition of the habit by monkeys across the sea. Watson admits that he was forced to "improvise" some of the details—the time of the day, the day of the week, and the exact number of monkeys required for the "critical mass" were not specified in the scientific literature. But by evening (or at least in a very short period of time) almost everyone (or at least a large number of the remaining monkeys) in the colony had suddenly acquired the custom. This is remarkable in part because of the slow and gradual mode of acquisition that had typified the first five years after Imo's innovation. Even more remarkable was the sudden jumping of natural boundaries, apparently caused by the Koshima miracle.

DOCUMENTATION

In this section I investigate the relations between Watson's description of the Hundredth Monkey Phenomenon and the scientific sources by which he validates it. To be sure, we must not expect too much from the sources. Watson has warned us that the complete story was not told and that he was "forced to improvise the details." But we should expect to find some evidence of the mysteriousness of the Koshima event of 1958. In particular, we should expect to find evidence of an episode of sudden learning within the troop at this time (though perhaps not in one afternoon) and evidence of the sudden appearance of potato washing in other troops sometime soon after the Koshima event. We also have a negative expectation of the literature; it should *fail* to report certain important details. It will not (we expect) tell us the exact number of monkeys washing potatoes prior to or after the event of 1958, nor will it provide us with an explanation of how the post-event Koshima learners were able to acquire their knowledge. After all, it is Watson's claim that the event produced *paranormal* learning of potato washing. These three expectations will be tested against the literature. Was there a sudden event at Koshima? Did acquisition at other colonies follow closely the Koshima event? Does Watson improvise details *only* when the cited literature fails to provide adequate information? The following comments will be restricted to the literature on macaques actually cited by Watson.

Almost all of the information about the Koshima troop appears in a journal article by Masao Kawai (1965); the other articles are secondary on this topic. Kawai's article is remarkably detailed in its description of the Koshima events. The troop numbered 20 in 1952 and grew to 59 by 1962. (At least in the numerical sense, there was never a "hundredth monkey" on Koshima.) Watson states that "an unspecified number" of monkeys on Koshima had acquired the potato-washing habit by 1958. Actually this number was far from unspecified. Kawai's data allowed the reader to determine the dates of acquisition of potato washing (and two other food behaviors), as well as the dates of birth and geneological relationships, *of every monkey in the Koshima troop from 1949 to 1962* (Figure 1, pp. 2–3, and elsewhere in the paper). In March 1958, exactly 2 of 11 monkeys over 7 years old had learned potato washing, while exactly 15 of 19 monkeys between 2 and 7 had the habit (p. 3) This amounts to 17 of 30 noninfant monkeys. There is no mention in this paper (or in any other) of a sudden learning event in the fall of 1958. However, it is noted that by 1962, 36 of the 49 monkeys had acquired the habit. So both the population and the number of potato washers had increased by 19 during this four-year period. Perhaps this is what suggested to Watson that a sudden event occurred in the fall of 1958. And perhaps (since one can only surmise) this idea was reinforced in Watson's mind by the following statement by Kawai: "The acquisition of [potato washing] behavior can be divided into two periods; before and after 1958" (p. 5).

So Kawai does not give a time of year, a day of the week, or even the season for any sudden event in 1958. But he does at least identify the year. And is Kawai mystified about the difference between pre- and post-1958 acquisition? Is he "not quite sure what happened"? Is he reluctant to publish details "for fear of ridicule?" No. He publishes the whole story, in gothic detail. The post-1958 learning period was remarkable only for its normalcy. The period from 1953 to 1958 had been a period of exciting innovation. The troop encountered new food sources, and the juveniles invented ways of dealing with these sources. But by 1958 the innovative youths had become status quo adults; macaques mature faster than humans. The unusual juvenile-to-adult teaching methods reverted to the more traditional process of learning one's food manners at one's mother's knee. Imo's first child, a male named "Ika," was born in 1957 (pp. 5, 7). Imo and her former playmates brought up their children as good little potato-washers. One can only hope that Ika has been less trouble to his Mom than Imo was to hers. Kawai speaks of the innovative period from 1953 to 1958 as "individual propagation" (p. 5) and the period after 1958 as "pre-cultural propagation" (p. 8). (This latter term does not indicate anything unusual for the monkey troops. The troops under normal circumstances have behavioral idiosyncrasies and customs that are passed along within the group by "pre-cultural" means. The expression only indicates a reluctance to refer to monkey behavior as genuinely "cultural.")

So there was nothing left unsaid in Kawai's description. There was nothing mysterious, or even sudden, in the events of 1958. Nineteen fifty-eight and 1959 were the years of maturation of a group of innovative youngsters. The human hippies of the 1960s now know that feeling. In fact 1958 was a singularly poor year for habit acquisition on Koshima. Only two monkeys learned to wash potatoes during that year, young females named Zabon and Nogi. An average of three a year had learned potato washing during the previous five years. There is no evidence that Zabon and Nogi were psychic or in any other way unusual.

Let us try to take Watson seriously for a moment longer. Since only two monkeys learned potato washing during 1958 (according to Watson's own citation), one of them must have been the "Hundredth Monkey." Watson leaves "unspecified" which monkey it was, so I am "forced to improvise" and "say, for argument's sake" that it was Zabon. This means that poor little Nogi carries the trim metaphysical burden of being the "almost everyone in the colony" who, according to Watson, suddenly and miraculously began to wash her potatoes on that autumn afternoon.

Watson claims that the potato-washing habit "spontaneously" leaped natural barriers. Is there evidence of this? Well, two sources report that the behavior was observed off Koshima, in at least five different colonies (Kawai 1965, 23; Tsumori 1967, 219). These reports specifically state that the behavior was observed only among a few individual monkeys and that it had not spread throughout a colony. There is no report of when these behaviors occurred. They must have been observed sometime between 1953 and 1967. But there is nothing to indicate that they followed closely upon some supposed miraculous event on Koshima during the autumn of 1958, or that they occurred suddenly at any other time, or that they were in any other way remarkable.

In fact there is absolutely no reason to believe in the 1958 miracle on Koshima. There is every reason to deny it. Watson's description of the event is refuted *in great detail* by the very sources he cites to validate it. In contrast to Watson's claims of a sudden and inexplicable event, "Such behavior patterns seem to be smoothly transmitted among individuals in the troop and handed down to the next generation" (Tsumori 1967, 207).

METHODOLOGY OF PSEUDOSCIENCE

The factual issue ends here. Watson's claim of a "Hundredth Monkey Phenomenon" is conclusively refuted by the very sources he cites in its support. He either failed to read or misreported the information in these scientific articles. But Watson's own mode of reasoning and reporting, as well as the responses he has inspired in the popular literature, deserve attention. They exemplify the pseudoscientific tradition. Consider the following:

1. *Hidden sources of information:* Watson informs us that the scientific reports leave important data "unspecified." This is simply false. But, more subtly, he tells us that most of the researchers are still unsure of what happened and that those who "do suspect the truth are reluctant to publish it for fear of ridicule." In one fell swoop Watson brands himself as courageous, explains why no one else has dared report this miraculous phenomenon, and discourages us from checking the cited literature for corroboration. Watson got the real story from "personal anecdotes and bits of folklore among primate researchers. . . ." Those of us who don't hobnob with such folks must trust Watson. The technique was effective. Of the commentaries I have found on the Hundredth Monkey Phenomenon, not one shows evidence of having consulted the scientific sources cited by Watson. Nonetheless, each presents Watson's fantasy as a scientifically authenticated fact. Nor is additional information available from Watson. I have written both to Watson and to his publishers requesting such information and have received no reply.

2. *Aversion to naturalistic explanations:* The fact is that potato washing was observed on different islands. Watson infers that it had traveled in some paranormal way from one location to another. Like other aficionados of the paranormal, Watson ignores two plausible explanations of the concurrence of potato washing. First, it could well have been an independent innovation—different monkeys inventing the same solution to a common problem. This process is anathema to the pseudoscientist. The natives of the Americas simply *could not have* invented the pyramid independent of the Egyptians—they just didn't have the smarts. In more extreme cases (von Däniken, for example) a *human being* is just too dumb to invent certain clever things—extraterrestrials must have done it.

Watson assumes that Imo was the only monkey capable of recognizing the usefulness of washing potatoes. In his words, Imo was "a monkey genius" and potato washing is "comparable almost to the invention of the wheel." Monkeys on other islands were too dumb for this sort of innovation. But keep in mind that these monkeys didn't even *have* potatoes to wash before 1952 or 1953, when provisioning began. Monkeys in at least five locations had learned potato washing by 1962. This suggests to me that these monkeys are clever creatures. It suggests to Watson that *one* monkey was clever and that the paranormal took care of the rest. A second neglected explanation is natural diffusion. And indeed Kawai reports that in 1960 a potato washer named "Jugo" swam from Koshima to the island on which the Takasakiyama troop lives. Jugo returned in 1964 (Kawai 1965, 17). Watson does not mention this. The Japanese monkeys are known to be both clever and mobile, and either characteristic might explain the interisland spread of potato washing. Watson ignores both explanations, preferring to invent a new paranormal power.

3. *Inflation of the miracle:* As myths get passed along, everyone puffs them up a bit. The following two examples come from second-generation commentaries that quote extensively from Watson. Nevertheless, even

Watson's claims are beginning to bulge. First, the primatologists' reports had mentioned that only a few isolated cases of off-Koshima potato-washing were observed. Watson reports this as the habit's having "appeared spontaneously . . . in colonies on other islands. . . ." Not actually false, since the few individuals were indeed *in* other colonies (though only individuals and not whole colonies adopted the behavior). Following Watson, Ken Keyes reports that, after the hundredth Koshima monkey, "colonies of monkeys on other islands . . . began washing their sweet potatoes"! (Keyes 1982, p. 16). From Keyes, one gets the image of spontaneous mass orgies of spud-dunking. A second example: Regarding the primatologists' attitudes toward the events of 1958, Watson reports only that they are "still not quite sure what happened." But the primatological confusion quickly grows, for *Science Digest* (1981) reports "a mystery which has stumped scientists for nearly a quarter of a century." In these two particular cases, Watson's own statements are at least modest. They're not what one would call accurate, but not exorbitantly false either. By the second generation we find that "not quite sure what happened" becomes "stumped for nearly a quarter of a century," and the habit that *appeared in* individuals within colonies of monkeys becomes a habit *of* colonies of monkeys. Please keep in mind that the second generation relies *only* on Watson for its information; even Watson's none-too-accurate report has been distorted—and not, needless to say, in the direction of accuracy.

    4. *The paranormal validates the paranormal:* The validity of one supernatural report is strengthened by its consistency with other such reports. Watson's commentators show how this works. Keyes supports the Hundredth Monkey Phenomenon by its consistency with J. B. Rhine's work at Duke, which "demonstrated" telepathy between individual humans. "We now know that the strength of this extrasensory communication can be amplified to a powerfully effective level when the consciousness of the 'hundredth person' is added" (Keyes 1982, 18). Elda Hartley's film "The Hundredth Monkey" invokes Edgar Cayce. And in a remarkable feat of group consciousness, *four of the five* secondary sources emphasize the similarities between Watson's Hundredth Monkey Phenomenon and Rupert Sheldrake's notion of the "morphogenetic field." The spontaneous recognition of the similarities between Watson and Sheldrake seems to have leaped the natural boundaries between the four publications! Now *there's* a miracle! (Surely independent invention or natural diffusion couldn't account for such a coincidence.)

CONCLUSIONS

I must admit sympathy for some of the secondary sources on the Hundredth Monkey Phenomenon. This feeling comes from the purpose for which the phenomenon was cited. Ken Keyes's book uses the phenomenon as a theme, but the real topic of the book is nuclear disarmament. Arthur Stein's article and (to a lesser extent) the Hartley film are inspired by Keyes's hope that the Hundredth Monkey Phenomenon may help prevent nuclear war. The message is that "you may be the Hundredth Monkey" whose contribution to the collective consciousness turns the world away from nuclear holocaust. It is hard to find fault in this motive. For these very same reasons, one couldn't fault the motives of a child who wrote to Santa Claus requesting world nuclear disarmament as a Christmas present. We can only hope that Santa Claus and the Hundredth Monkey are not our best chances to avoid nuclear war.

Watson's primary concern is not prevention of war but sheer love of the paranormal. His book begins with a description of a child who, before Watson's own eyes, and with a "short implosive sound, very soft, like a cork being drawn in the dark," psychically turned a tennis ball inside out—fuzz side in, rubber side out—without losing air pressure (p. 18). Just after the Hundredth Monkey discussion, Watson makes a revealing point. He quotes with approval a statement attributed to Lawrence Blair: "When a myth is shared by large numbers of people, it becomes a reality" (p. 148). This sort of relativist epistemology is not unusual in New Age thought. I would express Blair's thought somewhat differently: "Convince enough people of a lie, and it becomes the truth." I suggest that someone who accepts this view of truth is not to be trusted as a source of knowledge. He may, of course, be a marvelous source of fantasy, rumor, and pseudoscientific best-sellers.

I prefer epistemological realism to this sort of relativism. Truth is not dependent on the numbers of believers or on the frequency of published repetition. My preferred epistemology can be expressed simply: Facts are facts. There is no Hundredth Monkey Phenomenon.

REFERENCES

Brain/Mind Bulletin. 1982. The hundredth monkey. In "Updated Special Issue: 'A New Science of Life.'"

Hartley, Elda (producer). *The Hundredth Monkey* (film and videotape). Hartley Film Foundation, Inc. Cos Cob, Conn.

Imanishi, Kinji. 1963. Social behavior in Japanese monkeys. In *Primate Social Behavior,* Charles A. Southwick, ed. Toronto: Van Nostrand.

Kawai, Masao. 1963. On the newly-acquired behaviors of the natural troop of Japanese monkeys on Koshima island. *Primates,* 4:113–115.

———. 1965. On the newly-acquired pre-cultural behavior of the natural troop of Japanese monkeys on Koshima Islet. *Primates,* 6:1–30.

Kawamura, Syunzo. 1963. Subcultural propagation among Japanese macaques. In *Primate Social Behavior,* Charles A. Southwick, ed. Toronto: Van Nostrand.

Keyes, Ken, Jr. 1982. *The Hundredth Monkey.* Coos Bay, Ore.: Vision Books.

Science Digest. 1981. The quantum monkey. Vol. 8:57.

Sheldrake, Rupert. 1981. *A New Science Life,* Los Angeles: J. P. Tarcher.

Stein, Arthur. 1983. The "hundredth monkey" and humanity's quest for survival. *Phoenix Journal of Transpersonal Anthropology,* 7: 29–40.

Tsumori, Atsuo. 1967. Newly acquired behavior and social interactions of Japanese monkeys. In *Social Communication Among Primates.* Stuart Altman, ed. Chicago: University of Chicago Press.

Watson, Lyall. 1979. *Lifetide.* New York: Simon and Schuster.

These are the facts. Since 1982, according to confirmed eyewitness reports, the contras have raped, tortured, kidnapped, blown up, gunned down, maimed, mutilated and burned more than 10,000 Nicaraguan civilians. Now, in the middle of viable peace negotiations in Central America,

NO MORE KILLING, NO MORE LIES.

Congress is calmly deliberating whether to send these terrorists millions of dollars more for road mines, rockets and bullets... or merely confine our assistance to "humanitarian" aid. Three hundred prominent American religious leaders, and thousands of private U.S. citizens who have seen for themselves what's happening in Nicaragua, protest this atrocity. Tell the man or woman who represents you in Washington to cut off the contras once and for all. Call your senators at (202) 224-3121; your representative at (202) 225-3121. Or send an urgent mailgram. Call toll-free (800) 257-4900 and ask for Western Union Operator 9321.

For a copy of corroborated eyewitness accounts of civilian victims of the U.S. contra war, covering the first eight months of this year, send $5 to Witness for Peace, PO Box 29497, Washington, D.C. 20017. Contributions to our U.S.-based nonprofit program bringing people of conscience to Nicaragua to observe first-hand are tax deductible and profoundly appreciated.

Produced by Public Media Center.

Courtesy of the Public Media Center (San Francisco) and Witness for Peace.

VARSITY
RACISM?

KENNETH S. KANTZER

Recently, university presidents have made some decisions aimed at
cracking down on colleges and universities that hire athletes to play ball
but do not also give them an education. Many black leaders have hotly
protested these decisions. The charge: racism, pure and simple. Jesse N.
Stone, Jr., president of the Southern University system of Louisiana, says,
"The end result of all this is the black athlete has been too good. . . .
White schools no longer want black athletes."

The opposition from the black community is nearly unanimous and
includes the ablest black leaders—such as the Reverend Jesse Jackson,
president of People United to Serve Humanity (PUSH), and the Reverend
Benjamin Hooks, executive director of the National Association for the
Advancement of Colored People.

What is this ruling that has set off the most heated race relations
controversy in sports for more than a quarter century? It is NCAA Rule
48, requiring that, beginning in the fall of 1986, freshmen who wish to
participate in sports events of our major colleges and universities must
have earned a 2.0 average in 11 standard college preparatory courses
while in high school, and attained a minimum score of 700 on the
Scholastic Aptitude Test (SAT). Students who do not make the grade can
still be admitted, but will not be able to play until their sophomore year,
assuming they have achieved satisfactory academic progress during their
freshman year.

The original rule passed in 1983 does, however, contain many
provisions to give low scoring students a better chance of making the
grade. The rule is now being weakened, due to black protests.

How can stricter academic requirements be interpreted as racist?
Because 55 percent of all black students score lower than 700 as
compared with only 14 percent of white students. Many blacks,
moreover, are convinced that such tests reflect a cultural bias favoring
white students.

Not for one moment do we deny that racial discrimination plays an
active role in American sports and in the American educational system. It
is to the everlasting shame of our elementary and secondary programs
that such a disproportionate percentage of blacks cannot make a 2.0
average or attain acceptable SAT scores. But this is not primarily because
the tests are discriminatory, but because the education blacks receive is
discriminatory. Harry Edwards, who is black, is professor of sociology at
the University of California, Berkeley. He says, "The evidence is
overwhelming that such tests discriminate principally on the basis of class
rather than race." The difference is not between blacks and whites but
between students from well-off families and students from poor families.

Why not then give poor blacks a chance for a college education on the basis of their superior athletic ability? Because the present arrangement *does not give them an education!* It encourages them—in fact, it provides overwhelming rewards for them—to ignore their education through high school and college and devote themselves exclusively to excellence in sports. This is precisely what our college and university athletic programs are teaching our young people—especially black young people, and more especially still, financially impoverished black youngsters. So Edwards notes that the charge against Rule 48 "is both factually contestable and *strategically regrettable*" (emphasis added).

The problem is not rooted in sports, but in American culture and in our system of schooling.

OPPORTUNITY

But the presidents of our major institutions and the world of college sports now have a marvelous opportunity to improve the system radically, and especially aid disadvantaged blacks.

Professor Edwards argues: "The standards are too low." So the presidents must set even higher standards than Rule 48's 2.0 average or 700 SAT score. This may seem strange at first, but close inspection shows it to be necessary. Few students making those scores are prepared to do successful college work. Freshmen with borderline scores must remain ineligible for sports programs so they can adjust to college-level study and prove they are capable of a college education. Most important, athletes should be required to maintain a satisfactory grade level through their college career and take enough solid courses to enable them to make steady progress toward graduation in the normal four years.

As it stands now, the recipients of athletic scholarships are not getting an education. Studies prove that nearly three-quarters never graduate from college, and three-quarters of those who do, graduate with physical education degrees or majors specially concocted for athletes so they can get by without doing regular college work. If these figures are valid, less than 10 percent of all college and university athletes on athletic scholarships are actually receiving a college education.

The vast majority of these athletes will secure no educational preparation to help them make an effective contribution to society or to secure a job when they drop out of college.

So Penn State's Joe Paterno, named 1982 "Coach of the Year," declared: "We have raped a generation and a half of young black athletes. We have taken kids and sold them on bouncing a ball, running around a track and catching a football—that being able to do certain things athletically is an end in itself. We cannot afford to do that to another generation."

But will it work? Will laying down more stringent *academic* requirements for college athletes make for better education? Two years ago, an entire Los Angeles school system passed a rule requiring of all high school athletes a C average with no failing grade. Immediately, 6,000 students became ineligible to compete in inter-school activities. But one year later, 3,000 of those youngsters had improved their grades enough to become eligible.

A college requirement that, to remain eligible, all athletes must make normal progress toward graduation in standard programs would guarantee that most black athletes who now never graduate would secure an education. And that would be a great gain for blacks in American culture. Particularly because of the status of athletics among black youth, tens of thousands of blacks, who at present are not getting an education, would immediately be motivated to secure a basic high school and college education.

Blacks have everything to gain and nothing worthwhile to lose by stricter academic standards for athletes in high schools and colleges. As Edwards says, "The standards are too low."

HOLDING HUMAN
HEALTH HOSTAGE

MICHAEL E. DeBAKEY, M.D.

Chancellor; Chairman, Department of Surgery; and Director, The DeBakey Heart Center, Baylor College of Medicine, Houston, Texas

As a patient-advocate, both in and out of the operating room, I feel a responsibility to protect the rights of patients to medical advances resulting from animal research. Had the animal legislation now pending in Congress been enacted when I began my career, it would have prevented me from developing a number of lifesaving procedures in my research laboratory. Instead of restoring thousands of patients to a normal life and a return to productive work, my colleagues and I would have been helpless to offer many of our patients any real hope at all. This legislation, known as the Mrazek bill, seeks to ban the use of pound animals for any research supported by the National Institutes of Health, the chief source of funds for biomedical research in this country. Are we now to hold human health hostage to the rights of abandoned animals to be killed in pounds?

Even with today's technology, I could not have developed on a computer the roller pump that made open-heart surgery possible or the artificial artery that restored to health previously doomed patients with aneurysms. Nor could we have attempted the first successful coronary artery bypass or implanted the first temporary mechanical heart with which we saved a patient's life two decades ago. Would animal-rights activists have objected to the first kidney, heart, or liver transplant? Would they forego the protection humanity enjoys today against poliomyelitis, tetanus, diphtheria, and whooping cough or the treatment for strep throat, ear infections, bronchitis, and pneumonia—all the products of animal research? Would they have denied the 11 million diabetics the right to life that insulin has given them—or victims of cancer the help they have received from radiation and chemotherapy? It was in monkeys that the deadly AIDS virus was isolated, and that isolation is the initial step in the ultimate development of a vaccine. Would the animal-rights activists halt that research and allow an epidemic to rage unopposed? The truth is that there are no satisfactory insentient models at present for certain types of biomedical research and testing. A computer is not a living system and would not have produced the dramatic medical advances of the past few decades.

Only about 1% of abandoned dogs are released for research. If pounds are such a meager source of research animals, you may ask, why am I concerned about losing that source? My reasons are well-founded, I believe: not only are pound animals of particular value in research on heart and kidney disease, brain injury, stroke, blindness, and deafness, but a ban on their use could have grave and far-reaching consequences

SOURCE: Reprinted by permission of the author.

for human and animal health. In addition, such a ban would impose an extra burden on taxpayers and could price many important research projects out of existence. Each dog and cat bred specifically for research costs hundreds of dollars more than a pound animal. The Mrazek bill makes no accommodation in appropriations for this substantial rise in cost. For many of our most productive researchers, the additional expense would shut down their laboratories. Critical work on inducing tolerance in organ grafts, for example, and on minimizing damage to cardiac muscles after heart attacks has been halted in some research laboratories because of soaring costs of dogs.

Moreover, eliminating the use of pound animals in research would, paradoxically, cause even more animals to die. According to the American Humane Society, 7 million pet dogs are abandoned to pounds or shelters each year, 5 million of which are killed—600 "trusting pets" killed hourly. Yet some would have you believe that killing animals in a pound is more virtuous than having them help to advance medical knowledge and ultimately benefit human and animal health. I don't like to see life taken from any species unnecessarily, and that would happen if this law is enacted. Every year we would have to breed an additional 138,000 dogs and 50,000 cats for research to replace the pound animals, which would then be put to death anyway because no one wants them. With the current overpopulation of dogs and cats, the logic of such a policy escapes me.

It was humane concerns that led me into medicine. I strongly disapprove of cruelty to animals as well as humans. Medical scientists are not engaged in cockfighting, bullfighting, bull-dogging, calf-roping, or any other "sport" imposing stress or violence on animals. Rather, they are searching for ways to relieve suffering and preserve life. Unquestionably, every precaution should be taken, and enforced, to ensure that laboratory animals are treated humanely. Responsible scientists observe humane guidelines, not only because their search for new medical knowledge is motivated by compassion for the suffering, but because they know that improper treatment adversely affects the quality of their research. Scientists are also obligated to use insentient models when these are satisfactory, but, again, no responsible scientist would incur the substantial expense and devote the considerable space required for housing and caring for animals when other equally satisfactory models were available.

If scientists abandon cat and dog experiments for other models that are not as suitable or as well understood, many potential medical breakthroughs may be severely crippled or halted. Grave diseases such as AIDS, cancer, heart disease, muscular dystrophy, Alzheimer's disease, and other serious conditions will, however, continue to plague our families, friends, and fellow citizens, and those patients will properly expect to receive effective treatments and cures.

Remember, too, that pets have also profited from animal research. It is doubtful that animals could be treated today for heart or kidney disease, leukemia, or other serious disorders if animal research had been prohibited previously. If an animal is seriously ill or injured, would the animal-rights activists deny him a form of treatment potentially beneficial but never used before—and therefore experimental? Until one is faced with a life-threatening condition of a loved one—human or animal—it is difficult to answer that question truthfully.

We have aggressive advocates of the rights of trees, sharks, bats, whales, seals, and other mammals, but what about the rights of ailing humans? Shrill attacks against speciesism are difficult to defend when one observes pit bulldogs mauling and killing children, wolves killing deer, cats consuming rats and birds, and birds consuming worms. And even vegetarians destroy living plants for consumption. Self-preservation is a primary instinct of all members of the animal kingdom, and patients with that instinct deserve our compassion, protection, and assistance as much as other species.

Some animal-rights zealots have been quoted as regarding "the right to human life as a perversion," meat-eating as "primitive, barbaric, and arrogant," and pet ownership as an "absolutely abysmal situation brought about by human manipulation." It is difficult to believe that many animal lovers would embrace such an extreme position. There is a difference, moreover, between animal welfare and antisciencism. Infiltrating laboratories surreptitiously by posing as volunteer workers, destroying research records, vandalizing research facilities, bombing, and threatening scientists are all irrational methods of persuasion. At one research institution, damages amounted to more than a half million dollars when computers were destroyed, blood was poured on files, and liberationist slogans were painted on laboratory walls. Research on infant blindness was halted for eight months while claims of animal abuse were investigated, only to be found baseless. Such harassment, demoralization, and interference divert funds from productive research to security and discourage bright young people from entering research. Once the manpower chain is broken, it will not be easily restored. And where will we then turn for answers to devastating human diseases? Guerilla tactics, lurid pictures, and sensational headlines may inflame emotions, but they do not lead to rational judgments. More important, should we condone harassment, terrorism, and violence masquerading as concern for animal rights?

As a physician, my greatest concern is, of course, for the suffering human beings who will be denied effective treatment because we took action that seems superficially humane but may ultimately render us powerless against certain diseases. What do I tell dying patients who are waiting for the medical advances that these threatened investigations may produce—that there is no hope because we have been prevented from acquiring the new knowledge needed to correct their conditions? As a human being and physician, I cannot conceive of telling parents their sick child is doomed because we cannot use all the tools at our disposal. Surely those who object to animals in research laboratories must be equally distressed at seeing sick children hooked up to tubes. How will those parents feel about a society that legislates the rights of animals above those of humans?

Through research, we have made remarkable advances in medicine, but we still do not have all the answers. If the animal-rights activists could witness the heartbreaking suffering of patients and families that I encounter daily, I doubt that they would deliberately pose a direct threat to human and animal health by demanding that we abandon some of our most fruitful methods of medical investigation. The American public must decide: Shall we tell hundreds of thousands of victims of heart attacks, cancer, AIDS, and numerous other dread diseases that the right of abandoned animals to die in a pound supersedes the patients' rights to relief from suffering and premature death? In making that decision, let us use not anger and hatred but reason and good will.

A recent graduate of the Bernhard Goetz school of self-defense

*1985 Copley News Service ST. PETERSBURG TIMES Bennett

Courtesy of H. Clay Bennett and Copley News Service.

ANSWERS TO THE MOST ASKED
QUESTIONS ABOUT CIGARETTES

TOBACCO INSTITUTE

Does cigarette smoke endanger nonsmokers? What's the latest research?

Some people who want smoking banned or restricted say that smoke in the indoor air can cause disease in nonsmokers. However, scientists who have examined the relevant research say it just doesn't add up. Meanwhile, studies by indoor air experts show other increasing problems with radon, formaldehyde, fungi, bacteria and other substances.

Three scientific conferences in 1983 and 1984, involving more than 50 eminent scientists from around the world, have reviewed the evidence about environmental tobacco smoke (ETS). Each concluded that ETS has not been proven to have adverse health effects.

At the first, medical researchers from nine countries at the University of Geneva concluded: "An overall evaluation based upon available scientific data leads to the conclusion that an increased risk [in lung cancer] for nonsmokers from ETS exposure has not been established."

Another, convened by the National Institutes of Health, U.S. Department of Health and Human Services, determined that the possible effect of ETS on the respiratory system "varies from negligible to quite small."

The third, organized in Vienna by Ernst Wynder of the American Health Foundation and H. Valentin of the Bavarian Academy for Occupational and Social Medicine, in cooperation with the World Health Organization and the International Green Cross, concluded:

"Should lawmakers wish to take legislative measures with regard to passive smoking, they will, for the present, not be able to base their efforts on a demonstrated health hazard from passive smoking."

A February, 1985, *Consumer Reports* article reviewed nonsmoker concerns about ETS, concluding that "the evidence of risk from passive exposure is sparse and often conflicting."

The issue is emotional. That may cloud the perception and humor of those who dislike cigarette smoke. Meanwhile, scientific studies on the nonsmoker question continue, as they should.

What happens to cigarette smoke in the air? Is it true that smoke that drifts off the end of a cigarette contains far greater quantities of "tar," nicotine and carbon monoxide than smoke drawn from the cigarette by a smoker?

Yes, if one measures directly at the burning end. But the smoke is immediately *diluted* by the surrounding air, to the point that its contribution to the air we breathe is minimal.

One widely studied component of tobacco smoke has been carbon

SOURCE: Reprinted by permission of the Tobacco Institute.

monoxide (CO). Its main sources are motor vehicles, industrial processes and nature itself—not environmental tobacco smoke. Indoor levels are affected by outside levels and by cooking and heating, among other factors.

Searching for nicotine in the air, because its only source is tobacco smoke, Harvard University researchers found only tiny amounts in the atmosphere of cocktail lounges, restaurants, bus stations and airline terminals. This suggested to one scientist that a nonsmoker would have to spend 100 hours straight in the smokiest bar to inhale the equivalent of a single filtertip cigarette.

What happens when a law restricts smoking?

Ask the people who must enforce it. Law enforcement agencies across the country have criticized the stretching of their limited resources to include enforcement of smoking laws.

For example: The Los Angeles County sheriff said, "Police should spend their time patrolling our streets for burglars, not prowling office buildings searching for illegal smokers."

In Dade County, Fla., the Police Benevolent Association declared, "We don't have enough police to handle the crime we have. We don't need a new crime to contend with."

The *Law Officer,* journal of the International Conference of Police Associations, editorialized that "If there was ever an occasion when a law officer could agree with an 'offender' who declares, 'You should be out catching criminals,' this must certainly be it."

The chairman of the National Black Police Association told the New York senate that "the limited amount of personnel that we do have could better spend their time in making our neighborhoods safe."

What good is an unnecessary law that is unenforceable, that creates expenses, inconveniences and confrontations? It breeds disrespect for *all* law. It causes all of us—smokers and nonsmokers alike—to lose a little bit of freedom.

WHY
SPANISH TRANSLATIONS?

MAURICIO MOLINA

I was naive 20 years ago. I say this because I came here from Central America and readily accepted what my parents told me. What they told me was that if I wanted to thrive here I had better learn English. English, it seems, was the language that people spoke in this country. In my innocence and naivete, however, it never occurred to me that I really didn't have to. I can see now that I could have refused.

Yes, English is the language of the United States. But if it is, why can I take the written part of my driver's license test in Spanish? If it is, why are businesses forced to provide Spanish translations of practically every blank credit application or contract agreement? And not just businesses—government offices must also have quite a number of Spanish translations for those who want them.

Clearly, my old language did not get left behind. Don't misunderstand; this is real nice. It allows me to luxuriate in the knowledge, sweet indeed, that I am privileged. Without a doubt this is the land of opportunity. And I know it. But for those of us whom people call "Hispanics," it's a little bit more. It's the land where opportunity itself is served and seasoned as if this were the old country.

How stupid you must think me for complaining! Should we not simply take the opportunity and run? Why complain? Complaining may only spoil the fun for those among us who don't want to learn English.

But I choose to complain. I do it because questions nag at me. For instance, just who are those people for whom the Spanish translations are provided? It's a good guess that they're not Chinese, or French, or Serbo-Croatian. Of course, we know them already as "Hispanics." But what in the world does this mean?

A Hispanic is someone who came, or whose ancestors came, from a region where Spanish is the only language spoken. Nothing more. Racially, a Hispanic may be anything. It's a mistake to say "Hispanic" and mean by the term a black Cuban just as much as it would puzzle a Chilean named O'Hara.

As to who precisely among Hispanics has a need for the Spanish translations, I can't tell yet for sure. If you'll follow me a bit, though, we may together unravel this puzzle and learn something.

I would divide Hispanics living in the United States into two groups: those who were born in this country and those who came from elsewhere. It is easy to see that a number of individuals in the latter group, people who perhaps knew no English when they arrived, may have linguistic problems here. Logically, some among them may have need of Spanish translations.

The first group I mentioned, made up of people born and reared here, should have no need of any translations, right? Well, not exactly. I'm told that many among them know English very poorly, if at all. So of course they need the help. But here I hope you'll forgive me if I pause to say that I think this is a very strange thing. I mean, isn't it odd in this day and age that people born right here in the United States may not somehow have mastered English?

Who, then, are the translations meant for? Ah, you probably guessed it by now. They're meant for a goodly cross section of Hispanics—average, reasonably healthy and intelligent children and adults.

I regard these translations as a waste of effort and money. To me they constitute a largesse of opportunity totally lacking a logical foundation. And what is the "logic" behind them? The answer I get is that these people are favored so that they may not suffer, because of their handicap, a diminution of their constitutional rights. The thing isn't done out of kindness, but simply out of a sense of fair play.

Fair play? I think not. Unfairness would be to deny these people the opportunity to learn English. But the question is, are they being denied? From where I live I couldn't throw a rock out the window without risking severe injury to a number of English teachers. And at various places nearby—YMCAs, colleges, high schools, grammar schools, convention halls—English courses are available for the foreign-born or anyone else who needs them. That, ladies and gentlemen, is opportunity. It's there, but it won't pull you by the nose.

This country has been, is and, I pray, will continue to be, the land of opportunity. It has never been a place where the lazy came to be coddled. It has never been a haven for those who would not look out for their needs.

What do I think should be done? I think that no Spanish translations should be made of anything. Except for one. Spanish translations should be made, and these distributed widely, detailing the availability of English courses throughout Hispanic communities.

What if people don't bother to attend? Well, it's a free country.

IF THEY'RE OLD ENOUGH TO GET PREGNANT, THEY'RE OLD ENOUGH NOT TO.

There's a forty percent chance she'll get pregnant before she's nineteen. One of the million teens who get pregnant each year.

That's the highest teen pregnancy rate in the industrialized world. And you don't have to look far for the reason: two-thirds of sexually-active teens in America use no method of birth control or fail to use it consistently.

The personal consequences of teen pregnancy are tragic and the social costs are staggering. Over $16 billion each year. That's the price we pay for misinformation and ignorance about the facts of life.

We need to equip our children with basic information about the risks of pregnancy and about contraception.

Most teens know less about such things than you might think. Few people realize that only two states and the District of Columbia require sex education programs in schools. And the mass media, marketing sex with no mention of precautions, only make matters worse.

Even parents who care the most may fail to make sure their children are informed—fearing they might appear to condone behavior they wish to discourage. But research shows that when parents hesitate, teens tend not to.

Studies also find that teens who've been thoroughly informed about the facts of life are much more likely to say no to peer pressure. And to start later.

That's why Planned Parenthood encourages better parent-child communication. Works to improve sex education. And maintains that all sexually-active people, including teens, should be able to get the birth control help they need and want.

Given the facts, teens can make responsible decisions. Denied the facts, all they can make are mistakes.

Biologically, after all, any teenage girl *can* get pregnant. The only question is whether she won't.

You can help. Write us for more information. Use the coupon.

The soaring teen pregnancy rate is everybody's problem. I want to help:

☐ Please send me information about Planned Parenthood's POWER (Parents Organized to Win Educational Rights) Campaign so I can make a difference where I live.

☐ Send me a copy of the booklet, "How to Talk with Your Child about Sexuality" (one dollar enclosed).

☐ Here's my tax-deductible contribution to support all of Planned Parenthood's programs encouraging responsible decisions by teens and adults: ☐ $25 ☐ $35 ☐ $50 ☐ $75 ☐ $150 ☐ $500 or: $_____.
Send your check to 810 Seventh Avenue, New York, NY 10019

NAME _____

STREET/CITY/ZIP _____

Planned Parenthood®
Federation of America

This ad was paid for with private contributions. © Copyright 1986

Reprinted with permission of Planned Parenthood Federation of America, Inc.

TIME RESORTS TO HOKUM

JAMES J. KILPATRICK

In a dull week not long ago, when hard news was dawdling at an ebb tide, Time magazine put together the kind of cover story that is known in the trade as a thumbsucker. Such articles, the desperate resort of editorial writers everywhere, also are known as evergreens and think pieces. Time's contribution to the art of omphaloskepsis had to do with "America's search for its moral bearings."

Concluded Time's Walter Shapiro: "Hypocrisy, betrayal and greed unsettle the nation's soul. . . . America finds itself wallowing in a moral morass."

That reference to "the nation's soul" identified the piece instantly as a thumbsucker, but this was something more. What it was, was mostly hokum.

"Once again it is morning in America," the elegy began. But in this scandal-scarred spring, it is a bitter and despondent morning: "Lamentation is in the air, and clay feet litter the ground." At every hand Time sees moral laxity and uncontrolled avarice. The Reagan administration holds the view that "wealth is the measure of all men." A sleaze factor has infected society. Time paints "a portrait of impropriety on a grand scale." In brief, the nation has lost its moral compass and is headed for the ultimate bowwows. Farewell to all that has been honorable, virtuous and wholesome! Degradation abounds! Let us hand Mr. Shapiro a towel.

Sure, plenty of things are wrong in the United States today. There never has been a time in our history when a litany of woes could not be sung. One would have to be deaf, dumb and blind not to be concerned today about drug abuse, teen-age pregnancy, persistent poverty, racial tensions and the shortcomings in American education. Conservatives especially are disappointed and disgusted by the sorry behavior of many Reagan appointees. As the Prayer Book used to say, we bewail our manifold sins and wickedness, and there is no health in us.

But Time's perception of a "moral morass" needs to be put in perspective. None of our contemporary failings approaches those offenses that have stained the American past. As Justice Thurgood Marshall recently reminded us, the very Constitution that we are venerating this summer gave its explicit sanction to human slavery. A century and a half ago, Americans engaged in the systematic slaughter and forced expulsion of the Indian tribes.

Moral morass? For decades after the Civil War, states both North and South maintained public systems of racial segregation. Legislators and public officials conspired to deny black people a right to vote.

Time cites examples of contemporary venality and supposes that these are measures of radically declining values. Bosh! The greed of an Ivan Boesky differs only in degree, not in kind, from the greed of the Vanderbilts and Morgans. Theodore Roosevelt long ago warned against a life of "swollen, slothful ease." He condemned "malefactors of great wealth" and denounced "government by plutocracy." What can be said for the nation's soul in an era of sweat shops and child labor?

Yes, there is some empirical evidence of changes in some moral values. During the '60s and '70s, the Census Bureau found a fourfold increase in the number of common-law marriages. Bastardy has soared, and the bearing of illegitimate children has lost its stigma. Chastity and fidelity seem no longer to be widely revered. But it is a fair inquiry to ask if adultery is more prevalent today than it was in the time of Grover Cleveland. There is reason to believe that the more things change, the more they stay the same.

As a newspaperman, I have been worrying over the nation's soul for nearly 50 years. Believe me, I know no more than I knew as a cub reporter. What I do know is that America is blessed by millions of good people, honorable officials, kind neighbors and loving parents. This is a better America than the America I was born in, and the best is yet to come.

UNION
SOLIDARITY

JOHN CLAUDE BRU

In response to Robert Wade and his endorsement of the union-busting tactics of International Paper—all in the name of free enterprise:

It is obvious that he and IP have little regard for the key element in our free enterprise system—our workers.

Be assured, most of us do believe in God. We're going to stand tall; we're going to continue to fight for our rights as American citizens. We are not going back to the sweat shops of yesterday. Not to worry, IP won't take this one to Japan or Mexico; they need our trees.

Granted, they could win this battle and replace these workers—but they won't win the war. If need be, we will work to organize the new employees to protect themselves from a company that seems to think that people, their livelihoods, their very life and limb, are as expendable as the trees from which they make their precious paper and enormous profits.

We don't have to beg. We make our supplications to God; we evoke our constitutional rights; and we share with and support our brothers and sisters. We won't stop fighting until the American creed of life, liberty and the pursuit of happiness is the reality for all people, not just a few at the top.

The wisdom of most corporate heads is born of carnality and it is presumptuous and decadent. The fallible yet often idolized computer will not be our savior; neither will the cunning investors and stockbrokers of Wall Street. Ultimately, it will be the American workers, as we grow stronger, more principled, and more committed to God—the giver of life eternal—that quells the rise and threat of communism and makes this old world a decent and beautiful place to live.

We know we're not perfect. We sin and have to repent repeatedly; and we know we have to work diligently and seek morality and justice. But we who have acknowledged Him have our faith, our confidence, not in the frail and carnal wisdom of man, but in God our Savior and His infinite wisdom.

I strongly support and stand in firm solidarity with my brothers and sisters, the locked-out workers at IP.

SOURCE: Reprinted from the *Mobile Register,* November 24, 1987. Reprinted by permission of the author.

Courtesy of Revlon, Inc.

EVOLUTION AS
FACT AND THEORY

STEPHEN JAY GOULD

Kirtley Mather, who died last year at age 89, was a pillar of both science and the Christian religion in America and one of my dearest friends. The difference of half a century in our ages evaporated before our common interests. The most curious thing we shared was a battle we each fought at the same age. For Kirtley had gone to Tennessee with Clarence Darrow to testify for evolution at the Scopes trial of 1925. When I think that we are enmeshed again in the same struggle for one of the best documented, most compelling and exciting concepts in all of science, I don't know whether to laugh or cry.

According to idealized principles of scientific discourse, the arousal of dormant issues should reflect fresh data that give renewed life to abandoned notions. Those outside the current debate may therefore be excused for suspecting that creationists have come up with something new, or that evolutionists have generated some serious internal trouble. But nothing has changed; the creationists have not a single new fact or argument. Darrow and Bryan were at least more entertaining than we lesser antagonists today. The rise of creationism is politics, pure and simple; it represents one issue (and by no means the major concern) of the resurgent evangelical right. Arguments that seemed kooky just a decade ago have re-entered the mainstream.

CREATIONISM IS NOT SCIENCE

The basic attack of the creationists falls apart on two general counts before we even reach the supposed factual details of their complaints against evolution. First, they play upon a vernacular misunderstanding of the word "theory" to convey the false impression that we evolutionists are covering up the rotten core of our edifice. Second, they misuse a popular philosophy of science to argue that they are behaving scientifically in attacking evolution. Yet the same philosophy demonstrates that their own belief is not science, and that "scientific creationism" is therefore meaningless and self-contradictory, a superb example of what Orwell called "newspeak."

In the American vernacular, "theory" often means "imperfect fact"—part of a hierarchy of confidence running downhill from fact to theory to hypothesis to guess. Thus the power of the creationist argument: evolution is "only" a theory, and intense debate now rages about many aspects of the theory. If evolution is less than a fact, and scientists can't even make up their minds about the theory, then what confidence can we have in it? Indeed, President Reagan echoed this argument before an evangelical group in Dallas when he said (in what I devoutly hope was campaign rhetoric): "Well, it is a theory. It is a scientific theory only, and it has in recent years been challenged in the world of science—that is, not believed in the scientific community to be as infallible as it once was."

Well, evolution *is* a theory. It is also a fact. And facts and theories are different things, not rungs in a hierarchy of increasing certainty. Facts are the world's data. Theories are structures of ideas that explain and interpret facts. Facts do not go away when scientists debate rival theories to explain them. Einstein's theory of gravitation replaced Newton's, but apples did not suspend themselves in mid-air pending the outcome. And human beings evolved from apelike ancestors whether they did so by Darwin's proposed mechanism or by some other, yet to be discovered.

Moreover, "fact" does not mean "absolute certainty." The final proofs of logic and mathematics flow deductively from stated premises and achieve certainty only because they are *not* about the empirical world. Evolutionists make no claim for perpetual truth, though creationists often do (and then attack us for a style of argument that they themselves favor). In science, "fact" can only mean "confirmed to such a degree that it would be perverse to withhold provisional assent." I suppose that apples might start to rise tomorrow, but the possibility does not merit equal time in physics classrooms.

Evolutionists have been clear about this distinction between fact and theory from the very beginning, if only because we have always acknowledged how far we are from completely understanding the mechanisms (theory) by which evolution (fact) occurred. Darwin continually emphasized the difference between his two great and separate accomplishments: establishing the fact of evolution, and proposing a theory—natural selection—to explain the mechanism of evolution. He wrote in *The Descent of Man:* "I had two distinct objects in view; firstly, to show that species had not been separately created, and secondly, that natural selection had been the chief agent of change. . . . Hence if I have erred in . . . having exaggerated its [natural selection's] power . . . I have at least, as I hope, done good service in aiding to overthrow the dogma of separate creations."

Thus Darwin acknowledged the provisional nature of natural selection while affirming the fact of evolution. The fruitful theoretical debate that Darwin initiated has never ceased. From the 1940s through the 1960s, Darwin's own theory of natural selection did achieve a temporary hegemony that it never enjoyed in his lifetime. But renewed debate characterizes our decade, and, while no biologist questions the importance of natural selection, many now doubt its ubiquity. In particular, many evolutionists argue that substantial amounts of genetic change may not be subject to natural selection and may spread through populations at random. Others are challenging Darwin's linking of natural selection with gradual, imperceptible change through all intermediary degrees; they are arguing that most evolutionary events may occur far more rapidly than Darwin envisioned.

Scientists regard debates on fundamental issues of theory as a sign of intellectual health and a source of excitement. Science is—and how else can I say it?—most fun when it plays with interesting ideas, examines their implications, and recognizes that old information may be explained in surprisingly new ways. Evolutionary theory is now enjoying this uncommon vigor. Yet amidst all this turmoil no biologist has been led to doubt the fact that evolution occurred; we are debating *how* it happened. We are all trying to explain the same thing: the tree of evolutionary descent linking all organisms by ties of genealogy. Creationists pervert and caricature this debate by conveniently neglecting the common conviction that underlies it, and by falsely suggesting that we now doubt the very phenomenon we are struggling to understand.

Using another invalid argument, creationists claim that "the dogma of separate creations," as Darwin characterized it a century ago, is a scientific theory meriting equal time with evolution in high school biology curricula. But a prevailing viewpoint among philosophers of science belies this creationist argument. Philosopher Karl Popper has argued for decades that the primary criterion of science is the falsifiability of its theories. We can never prove absolutely, but we can falsify. A set of ideas that cannot, in principle, be falsified is not science.

The entire creationist argument involves little more than a rhetorical attempt to falsify evolution by presenting supposed contradictions among its supporters. Their brand of creationism, they claim, is "scientific" because it follows the Popperian model in trying to demolish evolution. Yet Popper's argument must apply in both directions. One does not become a scientist by the simple act of trying to falsify another scientific system; one has to present an alternative system that also meets Popper's criterion—it too must be falsifiable in principle.

"Scientific creationism" is a self-contradictory, nonsense phrase precisely because it cannot be falsified. I can envision observations and experiments that would disprove any evolutionary theory I know, but I cannot imagine what potential data could lead creationists to abandon their beliefs. Unbeatable systems are dogma, not science. Lest I seem harsh or rhetorical, I quote creationism's leading intellectual, Duane Gish, Ph.D., from his recent (1978) book *Evolution? The Fossils Say No!* "By creation we mean the bringing into being by a supernatural Creator of the basic kinds of plants and animals by the process of sudden, or fiat, creation. We do not know how the Creator created, what processes He used, *for He used processes which are not now operating anywhere in the natural universe* [Gish's italics]. This is why we refer to creation as special creation. We cannot discover by scientific investigations anything about the creative processes used by the Creator." Pray tell, Dr. Gish, in the light of your last sentence, what then is "scientific" creationism?

THE FACT OF EVOLUTION

Our confidence that evolution occurred centers upon three general arguments. First, we have abundant, direct, observational evidence of evolution in action, from both the field and the laboratory. It ranges from countless experiments on change in nearly everything about fruit flies subjected to artificial selection in the laboratory to the famous British moths that turned black when industrial soot darkened the trees upon which they rest. (The moths gain protection from sharp-sighted bird predators by blending into the background.) Creationists do not deny these observations; how could they? Creationists have tightened their act.

They now argue that God only created "basic kinds," and allowed for limited evolutionary meandering within them. Thus toy poodles and Great Danes come from the dog kind and moths can change color, but nature cannot convert a dog to a cat or a monkey to a man.

The second and third arguments for evolution—the case for major changes—do not involve direct observation of evolution in action. They rest upon inference, but are no less secure for that reason. Major evolutionary change requires too much time for direct observation on the scale of recorded human history. All historical sciences rest upon inference, and evolution is no different from geology, cosmology, or human history in this respect. In principle, we cannot observe processes that operated in the past. We must infer them from results that still survive: living and fossil organisms for evolution, documents and artifacts for human history, strata and topography for geology.

The second argument—that the imperfection of nature reveals evolution—strikes many people as ironic, for they feel that evolution should be most elegantly displayed in the nearly perfect adaptation expressed by some organisms—the chamber of a gull's wing, or butterflies that cannot be seen in ground litter because they mimic leaves so precisely. But perfection could be imposed by a wise creator or evolved by natural selection. Perfection covers the tracks of past history. And past history—the evidence of descent—is our mark of evolution.

Evolution lies exposed in the *imperfections* that record a history of descent. Why should a rat run, a bat fly, a porpoise swim, and I type this essay with structures built of the same bones unless we all inherited them from a common ancestor? An engineer, starting from scratch, could design better limbs in each case. Why should all the large native mammals of Australia be marsupials, unless they descended from a common ancestor isolated on this island continent? Marsupials are not "better," or ideally suited for Australia; many have been wiped out by placental mammals imported by man from other continents. This principle of imperfection extends to all historical sciences. When we recognize the etymology of September, October, November, and December (seventh, eighth, ninth, and tenth, from the Latin), we know that two additional items (January and February) must have been added to an original calendar of ten months.

The third argument is more direct: transitions are often found in the fossil record. Preserved transitions are not common—and should not be, according to our understanding of evolution (see next section)—but they are not entirely wanting, as creationists often claim. The lower jaw of reptiles contains several bones, that of mammals only one. The non-mammalian jawbones are reduced, step by step, in mammalian ancestors until they become tiny nubbins located at the back of the jaw. The "hammer" and "anvil" bones of the mammalian ear are descendants of these nubbins. How could such a transition be accomplished? the creationists ask. Surely a bone is either entirely in the jaw or in the ear. Yet paleontologists have discovered two transitional lineages of therapsids (the so-called mammal-like reptiles) with a double jaw joint—one composed of the old quadrate and articular bones (soon to become the hammer and anvil), the other of the squamosal and dentary bones (as in modern mammals). For that matter, what better transitional form could we desire than the oldest human, *Australopithecus afarensis,* with its apelike palate, its human upright stance, and a cranial capacity larger than any ape's of the same body size but a full 1,000 cubic centimeters below ours? If God made each of the half dozen human species discovered in ancient rocks, why did he create in an unbroken temporal sequence of progressively more modern features—increasing cranial capacity, reduced face and teeth, larger body size? Did he create to mimic evolution and test our faith thereby?

AN EXAMPLE OF CREATIONIST ARGUMENT

Faced with these facts of evolution and the philosophical bankruptcy of their own position, creationists rely upon distortion and innuendo to buttress their rhetorical claim. If I sound sharp or bitter, indeed I am—for I have become a major target of these practices.

I count myself among the evolutionists who argue for a jerky, or episodic, rather than a smoothly gradual, pace of change. In 1972 my colleague Niles Eldredge and I developed the theory of punctuated equilibrium [*Discover,* October]. We argued that two outstanding facts of the fossil record—geologically "sudden" origin of new species and failure to change thereafter (stasis)—reflect the predictions of evolutionary theory, not the imperfections of the fossil record. In most theories, small isolated populations are the source of new species, and the process of speciation takes thousands or tens of thousands of years. This amount of time, so long when measured against our lives, is a geological microsecond. It represents much less than 1 per cent of the average life span for a fossil invertebrate species—more than 10 million years. Large, widespread, and well-established species, on the other hand, are not expected to change very much. We believe that the inertia of large populations explains the stasis of most fossil species over millions of years.

We proposed the theory of punctuated equilibrium largely to provide a different explanation for pervasive trends in the fossil record. Trends, we argued, cannot be attributed to gradual transformation within lineages, but must arise from the differential success of certain kinds of species. A trend, we argued, is more like climbing a flight of stairs (punctuations and stasis) than rolling up an inclined plane.

Since we proposed punctuated equilibria to explain trends, it is infuriating to be quoted again and again by creationists—whether through design or stupidity, I do not know—as admitting that the fossil record includes no transitional forms. Transitional forms are generally lacking at the species level, but are abundant between larger groups. The evolution from reptiles to mammals, as mentioned earlier, is well documented. Yet a pamphlet entitled "Harvard Scientists Agree Evolution Is a Hoax" states: "The facts of punctuated equilibrium which Gould and Eldredge . . . are forcing Darwinists to swallow fit the picture that Bryan insisted on, and which God has revealed to us in the Bible."

Continuing the distortion, several creationists have equated the theory of punctuated equilibrium with a caricature of the beliefs of Richard Goldschmidt, a great early geneticist. Goldschmidt argued, in a famous book published in 1940, that new groups can arise all at once through major mutations. He referred to these suddenly transformed creatures as "hopeful monsters." (I am attracted to some aspects of the non-caricatured version, but Goldschmidt's theory still has nothing to do with punctuated equilibrium.) Creationist Luther Sunderland talks of the "punctuated equilibrium hopeful monster theory" and tells his hopeful readers that "it amounts to tacit admission that anti-evolutionists are correct in asserting there is no fossil evidence supporting the theory that all life is connected to a common ancestor." Duane Gish writes, "According to Goldschmidt, and now apparently according to Gould, a reptile laid an egg from which the first bird, feathers and all, was produced." Any evolutionist who believed such nonsense would rightly be laughed off the intellectual stage; yet the only theory that could ever envision such a scenario for the evolution of birds is creationism—God acts in the egg.

CONCLUSION

I am both angry at and amused by the creationists; but mostly I am deeply sad. Sad for many reasons. Sad because so many people who respond to creationist appeals are troubled for the right reason, but venting their anger at the wrong target. It is true that scientists have often been dogmatic and elitist. It is true that we have often allowed the white-coated, advertising image to represent us—"Scientists say that Brand X cures bunions ten times faster than . . ." We have not fought it adequately because we derive benefits from appearing as a new priesthood. It is also true that faceless bureaucratic state power intrudes more and more into our lives and removes choices that should belong to individuals and communities. I can understand that requiring that evolution be taught in the schools might be seen as one more insult on all these grounds. But the culprit is not, and cannot be, evolution or any other fact of the natural world. Identify and fight your legitimate enemies by all means, but we are not among them.

I am sad because the practical result of this brouhaha will not be expanded coverage to include creationism (that would also make me sad), but the reduction or excision of evolution from high school curricula. Evolution is one of the half dozen "great ideas" developed by science. It speaks to the profound issues of genealogy that fascinate all of us—the "roots" phenomenon writ large. Where did we come from? Where did life arise? How did it develop? How are organisms related? It forces us to think, ponder, and wonder. Shall we deprive millions of this knowledge and once again teach biology as a set of dull and unconnected facts, without the thread that weaves diverse material into a supple unity?

But most of all I am saddened by a trend I am just beginning to discern among my colleagues. I sense that some now wish to mute the healthy debate about theory that has brought new life to evolutionary biology. It provides grist for creationist mills, they say, even if only by distortion. Perhaps we should lie low and rally round the flag of strict Darwinism, at least for the moment—a kind of old-time religion on our part.

But we should borrow another metaphor and recognize that we too have to tread a straight and narrow path, surrounded by roads to perdition. For if we ever begin to suppress our search to understand nature, to quench our own intellectual excitement in a misguided effort to present a united front where it does not and should not exist, then we are truly lost.

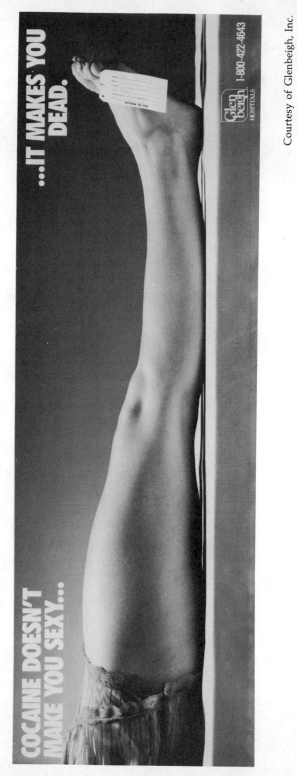

PORN DOESN'T CAUSE VIOLENCE, BUT A FEAR OF NEW IDEAS DOES

RUTH MCGAFFEY

I must respond to the Meese Commission's Report on Pornography as well as several comments that have appeared in these pages regarding pornography and censorship. My purpose is not to defend pornography, but if my commitment to the First Amendment makes that necessary, I am willing to do so.

I find much pornography disgusting as well as demeaning to women. The same is true of much commercial advertising, including the ring-around-the-collar commercial. Both depict a woman I do not like.

I also find racist stereotypes offensive. I think uninformed people, ignorant students and religious bigots are offensive. When I taught at Northwestern University last semester and had to live in Chicago, I found Chicago Bear fans repulsive. Neither the First Amendment nor any other part of the Constitution, however, guarantees me a right to live without being offended. Those who would ban sexually explicit material are no different from those who would censor Huckleberry Finn because of racist stereotypes, those who criticize other books because of sexist stereotypes and still others who object to curriculum materials because of offensive ideas on religion or values.

Americans are scared stiff of ideas and people with whom they disagree. We have persecuted all sorts of religious and political groups. We are afraid that these strange groups will influence us and, worst of all, will influence our children.

Those who fear sexually explicit material rejoice in the Meese Commission's report because it agrees with their intuitive fear of pornography. They believe that it has established a link between pornography and violent crimes against women. Yet no respectable social scientist would agree.

Fear of pornography or any other sort of message is based on the theory that messages can magically make people do things they wouldn't otherwise do. That theory is not true. People don't change their behavior very easily. After 30 years of research, scholars have not been able to prove that even subliminal persuasion works. Nor has research on brainwashing shown that to be effective. Modern communication research indicates that the response of any audience to a message depends more upon the predisposition of the audience than upon the power of the speaker, writer, or film-maker. People generally search out information that supports what they already believe. The danger is much more acute when people are not exposed to all kinds of ideas. Then, without experience in questioning ideas, without a "critical mind," they may be more easily persuaded. Researchers believe, for example, that the apparent

SOURCE: Reprinted from the *Milwaukee Journal,* September 28, 1986. Reprinted by permission of the author.

success of some totalitarian propaganda results not from some magic techniques but from a monopoly control over information.

What kind of ideas do rapists and child abusers and wife beaters already have? What we might find by looking at their testimony is that this society really believes that men have the right to make decisions for women. Analysis of the background of wife beaters does not reveal pornography, but rather parents who considered women's role to be appropriately subordinate to men. I have met very well-educated women who don't work or go to school because "My husband won't let me." Grown women who think they have to have permission to do something for themselves are sick, and the men who assert that dominance are sicker. It is not much of a jump from that attitude to believing that men have a right to control women sexually. An amazing number of men admit that they would rape if they could get away with it. Date and marital rape are common. It is highly simplistic to say that pornography either caused this widespread cultural attitude or that it causes acts of violence.

Furthermore, that claim is counterproductive. It allows men to excuse their actions. We laugh when we hear "the devil made me do it," but saying that "pornography made me do it" is exactly the same thing.

Instead of worrying about all the dangerous ideas and pictures and films in the world, we should be worrying about developing minds that are comfortable with uncertainty and complexity, not obedient minds. We must teach our children to question what they are told even when it comes from us. In this society we have rejected the elitist notion that some should make choices for others. That at least is the theory of the First Amendment.

Our Founding Fathers did not envision a nation of cowards. Freedom of expression was put in a primary position in the Bill of Rights because a self-governing people must be able to discuss all ideas regardless of how repulsive they might be. Anti-Jewish, anti-black or anti-Catholic statements offend most decent Americans. Swastikas as well as the white sheets of the KKK and the pornography of *Hustler* are not only offensive but also frightening to the majority of our people. These ideas we hate, however, must be protected if the marketplace of ideas is to survive for those ideas we love.

LEFT-HANDERS (THOSE SICKOS) GOT NO REASON TO LIVE!

ROGER L. GUFFEY

If you ask me, the U.S. Supreme Court ruling concerning certain sexual acts between consenting adults in the privacy of their own homes heralds a much welcome return to the right, rather than an invasion of privacy and individual rights. To further this admirable goal of moving to the right, I want to encourage the court now to go after one of the most despicable and un-American actions that threatens our great country today: left-handed people.

Ha, ha, you say. Most people do not realize how truly malevolent these subversive little perverts are. Look up the word "sinister" in the dictionary and you find two meanings: evil or left-handed. Still not convinced, eh? Historically, the U.S. government has fought leftists worldwide, so let's do it in this country before we take on those in Nicaragua. In this century, every other English speaking nation makes its citizens drive on the left (i.e., wrong) side of the road. If that doesn't prove how un-American left-handers are, I don't know what does.

Besides, left-handers are not normal. They are so unnatural that I can pick them out of a crowd a mile away. Our society has no use for their sick, twisted kind. Just think of all the things we have designed exclusively for the right-handers: scissors, shirt pockets, phone dials, wrist watches, toilet flush handles, books, etc. Have you ever seen a car with the ignition switch on the left side of the steering column? No, and you won't, because that's not the way God told Henry Ford to make them. You can even turn right against a red light, but if you try to make a left-hand turn against the light, you will find yourself going against society because it is not natural.

Oh, sure, the bleeding hearts will say that we need compassion for these sickos because they were born that way. Hogwash. It's a choice they make. If every mother would give her children a swift rap in the chops at the first sign of this filthy, disgusting left-handed behavior, this degenerate psychosis would vanish. Now, I am all for respecting everybody's rights to be different as long as I agree with what they are doing, but you have to draw the line somewhere. There won't be any left-handers in heaven, you can count on that.

The solution is not just social ostracism. We should all band together and pray fervently that God will strike these little perverts dead. Once this society returns to the moral character and justice that made this country great and prosecutes these deviant miscreants and genetic mistakes to the fullest extent of the law, everything will be all right. Act now before we all go out and buy left-handed bicycles. Take heart. God is on our side.

SOURCE: Reprinted from the *Lexington Herald-Leader*, July 10, 1987. Reprinted by permission of the author.

An all-electric home? I think I'll pass!

It doesn't take a Vince Lombardi to figure out that buying an all-electric home is like running your fullback off tackle when it's third and 13. Neither of 'em makes any sense.

Get on the ball. Tackle the high cost of electricity with natural gas.

KnoWhatImean?

LOUISIANA GAS SERVICE COMPANY

LGS is an independent utility and not affiliated with any other utility.

Courtesy of Louisiana Gas Service Company.

THE LITTLE RED SCHOOL HOUSE

EDWARD PATTERSON

The little red school house perched like a miniature ruby on a sea of emerald green that was the remote and verdant farming valley in some distant region of America.

The decree of man's law against the word of God in schools had travelled with devilish speed unmolested through the heavens, hopscotching from one ice cold and indifferent antenna to another till it reached this tiny village tucked away in some forgotten cranny of the nation. The school principal got his Government's under God decree, however contradictory sounding, to forthwith cease and desist from any kind of worship in his little red school house. He would obey the letter of the law of man.

All his pupils were under his incessant surveillance so seriously did he take his obligation to man over God. He monitored them in study and at play lest they lapse into prayer for any reason. God would be expelled from school from the time the bell ushered in a new day until it exited a finished one.

In his home, the principal had a son of his own, the age of his youngest pupils. He was a hopeless cripple, that terrible sentence in fate's court of justice that has no mercy, that constant reminder of the miracle of birth and its attendant peril. Thoughts of his poor boy at home in prison tortured him remorselessly. God was his adversary, a truant, too, perforce.

In all kinds of weather during recreation periods, the principal meandered down to the creek behind the school. This way he would oversee his pupils lest they seemed to pray. It was an opportunity as well for him to meditate and let loose still another deluge of bitter emotions that ceaselessly assaulted him.

This eventful day, the earliest winter snow had blanketed the good earth. It was especially painful to hear the laughter of children at play like joyful notes from a flute happily pirouetting skyward then dancing as if in a chorus line below a curtain of clouds. He thought of his injured son and sank weeping to his knees. He looked up to heaven as if in prayer but there was only a curse on his lips.

It was then he noticed another little boy kneeling right beside him. The principal, rubbing his eyes with his sleeves in disbelief, jumped up, indignant. But the look on the lad's face stopped him short.

He told him he was sorry to break the rules but that he was praying for the principal himself and his own crippled little boy. Then he took his hand and gently said, "Let school out early. Go home now and greet your son."

The principal went back to the little red school house, rang the bell

SOURCE: Reprinted from the *New York Times,* October 9, 1987. Reprinted by permission of the author.

and dismissed his pupils. Down by the creek, the reverent little boy had vanished.

The principal dashed home. As he reached the gate to the path leading to the front door, a bundle of winter clothes tumbled towards him and leaping, cuddled in his arms.

His crippled son cried out, "Look, Daddy, I'm whole," and then he ran and jumped and somersaulted in a kind of halo around his father, the principal.

From that time on, the schoolday started with a prayer of hope and ended with a prayer of thanks. The loudest voice of all was the principal's. The biggest smile of all was his son's.

But the greatest lesson of all was that the mention of God was as much a blessing and no more a threat in the little red school house than ever it had been in church or temple.

IS THIS THAT OLD-TIME RELIGION?

The latest absurd distortion of religious freedom to emerge from the "Scopes II" trial in Greeneville, Tenn., is U.S. District Judge Thomas G. Hill's decision that the local school board must pay $50,521 to a group of fundamentalist parents for, among other things, the cost of enrolling their children in private schools.

In a lawsuit that went to trial last July, the parents asserted that their children were being forced to read books that, in one way or another, offended their fundamentalist religious beliefs. *The Wizard of Oz* was objectionable because, among other things, it has good witches in it. *The Diary of Ann Frank* was a problem because the young diarist expresses a tolerance of all religions. Even *Goldilocks and the Three Bears* was unfit because Goldilocks evades punishment for the crime of breaking and entering.

Judge Hill found in the parents' favor last October, giving them the option to remove their children from classes using materials to which they objected. This week he ordered school officials to reimburse the parents for the cost of sending their children to Christian academies during the time that the reading of the objectionable books was mandatory, and certain other costs.

The judgment is dangerous in many ways as a legal precedent. One can imagine a yuppie couple bringing suit against a school board in this area, claiming that the curriculum in the public schools contains anti-Anglican references—perhaps an unflattering reference to Henry VIII in a history textbook—that offended them as Episcopalians. The way would seem to be open for them then to enroll their children at Episcopal Academy and later demand that the school board pay the tuition to the private school.

Perhaps that's somewhat farfetched. Far more likely, and far more pernicious, is the effect that this kind of litigation—and judgment—can have on education generally. In a situation where any book in which a woman has a career of her own can be a cause of legal action (and this was another complaint of the Greeneville parents), there's an inevitable chilling effect on school administrators and even individual teachers that leads them to avoid challenging, thought-provoking instruction.

SOURCE: Reprinted with permission from *The Philadelphia Inquirer,* December 20, 1986.

You don't have to be a man to appreciate a great beer.

Coors LIGHT.

There's no slowing down with The Silver Bullet.®

Courtesy of the Adolph Coors Company.

FOR
THE BIRDS

LILLIAN R. JACKSON

Bird-watching is an old fascination to many, but new to me. As the recipient of a large bird feeder, I hung it high enough to avoid the pussy cats and bought a bag of seed. In a short time, it attracted a variety of birds. I bought a bigger bag. Each morning I put out more. Sure enough, the birds increased. The more seed, the more birds. They now come from all directions and fight each other.

Only a week ago, these birds lived harmoniously and fed themselves. There were no starving birds in my yard. There were no birds screeching and attacking each other.

It is obvious that if I continue to put out seed, I shall destroy their ability to ever provide for themselves. Will they know to go farther south for the winter, or will I be obligated to house them? What about their self-esteem? Having removed their pride and incentive, will a bird-brainologist be necessary to convince them that, although they no longer have to dig for worms or feed their babies, they are still worthwhile birds?

My lawyer has advised me that any attempt to take the feeder down or decrease the feed will result in an attack by a number of bird-minded groups.

Nature having endowed each species with the ability to provide for itself, I stand guilty of violating nature's laws. My punishment has been swift and sure. The benefactors of my so-called charity squat all over everything with impunity and, as usual, the worms are the winners.

What is the solution? Shall I increase the seed until they get too fat to fly? Will I then be liable for their health care? In attempting to rehabilitate them, I brought in a self-sufficient bird but he was soon seduced by the open trough. After all, the most seductive and addictive of all drugs is "free."

Under laws enacted by a coalition of cuckoos, dodos, whooping cranes, vultures, et al, it appears that under threat of imprisonment, I shall be forced to keep increasing the seed until the feeder collapses and the patiently waiting predators take over.

This is for the birds.

SOURCE: Reprinted from the *Mobile Register,* July 13, 1987. Reprinted by permission of the author.

SHOULD U.S. WOMEN
GO MINI AGAIN?

ALAN MILLSTEIN

Ramon Navarro and Francis X. Bushman wore it first. We have the
Romans and MGM's Louis B. Mayer to thank for it.

The look that swept the world in 1925 and is now the sensation of
the fall collections in Paris and New York shall forever be known not as
the "miniskirt" but rather the "Ben Hur."

The fashion cabal has been herded once more into a virtual stampede
to a fall season filled with the possibility of financial disaster.

The chief "Bull" who has caused this rush to the short skirts is none
other than John B. Fairchild, the "Jeane Dixon" of the fashion industry
and publisher of "Women's Wear Daily."

This preposterous look, which appeared on runways and in
newspapers during March and April, first turned up as a fashion idea in
the mid-'60s when a Frenchman named Courreges and an Englishwoman
named Mary Quant made hemlines into headlines.

The "look" was perfectly timed for the times: The "Ben Hur" look
(circa 1925): Ramon Navarro and Francis X. Bushman wearing the latest
look in "hot hides" and stretch minis.

The '60s was the era of sexual permissiveness. It became OK for the
lady from Dubuque to be showing some thigh when the first lady from
Washington, Jackie Onassis, was on TV and in newsprint wearing the
Courreges suit.

The '60s were a time of the three p's: Permissiveness, penicillin and
the pill. The women organized for their "equal rights," the blacks won
their civil liberties, and the college kids demonstrated against a war they
didn't want to fight.

The short skirt fit the times and fulfilled a fantasy that every woman
was Brigitte Bardot or Marilyn Monroe.

Today the newsweeklies have made "safe sex" and the AIDS crisis
their special province, and the newsstand sales of these magazines have
demonstrated that sex is still a paying proposition as long as it's safely
written about by doctors, researchers, ministers or politicians.

The White House is preaching "abstinence" and the preachers are
suggesting a return to "chastity" before marriage. The new look is out of
step with the times.

The fashion industry has a real dilemma that it must confront. Short
skirts are great on young bodies and the athletically fit. The population in
this country is aging and the conspicuous consumers are now approaching
their 40s.

The reality of the marketplace is that most women over 40 need to
cover up, not uncover, the thigh. What the short skirts need are great
knees and incredible thighs.

SOURCE: Reprinted from the *Mobile Register,* September 2, 1987 (reprinted from the *Fashion Network Report,* Vol. 1, No. 1, 1987.) Reprinted by permission of the author.

This fall season will cause new wrinkles and consternation for the fashion consumer. She is aware that the mores of the '80s call for a return to conservatism. Her mirror tells her that time has not been kind to her legs. The tailor tells her that alterations on her skirts are outrageously expensive if available at all.

What will the fashion customer do: buy pants!

The message for the fashion customer is clear: find the look that fits the lifestyle needs of your life.

Today's women are dramatically different from the women of the '60s. There is a woman on the Supreme Court; there was a woman nominee for the vice president of the country; women now occupy half the seats in law schools; and more than 60 percent of women are in the work force.

The fallout from the "Ben Hur" madness will be seen in stores this fall. You can register your pleasure or displeasure for this fashion change at the cash register.

The mini madness that has caught up the New York design community has no more reality to the times than the blimp does to jet age travel. They both have something in common: A lot of hot air!

DO YOU HAVE THE RIGHT NAME?

"If You Don't, You May Never Be Happy"

Millions of people are misnamed at birth, causing them problems and unhappiness throughout their lives.

Many of us realize we do not fit our names, but few people do anything about it. This is unfortunate because it has been scientifically proven than an individual's life can turnaround dramatically when given the right name.

Just think about it. Don't you have a different feeling about a person because of his or her name? Some names have a strong, happy, confident sound while others make you feel lethargic, sad, lacking in energy.

If you've ever wished you had a different name and if you would like to feel better about yourself, Krishna Ram-Davi will meditate in your behalf and determine your **true** name.

These are some of the warning signs that indicate you are going through life with the wrong first name:

1. Do you feel sluggish, lacking energy much of the time?

2. Do events usually work against you rather than with you?

3. Do you care more about people than they care about you?

4. Do you sometimes lack confidence and wonder how others feel about you?

Please be aware that you do not have to change your present name in any way. When you receive your **true** first name, you will immediately feel and experience the difference, the improvement. Your true name will affect you internally, and it is not necessary for anyone else to learn of your name. Your new aura will radiate inner confidence and happiness, and those around you will soon recognize the "new" you!

Send $16.00 + 50¢ postage to Krishna Ram-Davi and ask him to send you your **true** name.

SOURCE: Reprinted from *Astrology and Psychic News*, Vol. LXVI. Courtesy of Krishna Ram-Davi and the California Astrology Assn.

ACCESS TO PUBLIC LANDS:
A NATIONAL NECESSITY

CYNTHIA RIGGS

Quick! Name America's largest landowner. No, not the King Ranch. No, not the Bank of America. No, Exxon isn't even in the running. The answer is the federal government. Of America's 2,271 million acres, 720 million belong to Uncle Sam. Add another 966 million underwater acres of the country's continental shelf, and you've got an impressive bit of real estate there.

In terms of the nation's resources, that vast range of public property represents enormous volumes of timber, grass, and minerals. Copper, zinc, gold, vanadium, tantalum, iron, and silver are among dozens of metallic minerals mined on federal lands. In energy minerals alone, government land may contain more than half the nation's remaining resources. According to the Department of Energy, this includes 85 percent of the nation's crude oil, 40 percent of natural gas, 40 percent of uranium, 35 percent of coal, 80 percent of oil shale, 85 percent of tar sands, and 50 percent of geothermal resources.

What does this mean to those of us who don't even own a 50- by 100-foot lot? Like others who visit national parks and camp in national forests and photograph national monuments, we consider these lands our heritage. Divide it among us, and we'd each have something like three acres apiece. Like all landowners, we'd like those three acres cared for, protected, preserved. It's nice to be a landowner. But there's the rub. Each of us also needs farmland for crops, rangeland for grazing, timber for homes, metals for machines, and energy for heat and fuel. For these, we must turn increasingly to those same public lands of ours where such resources are still to be found.

"No one can feel happy about intrusions upon the wilderness," writes Dr. Charles F. Parks, professor of geology at Stanford University, in his book, *Earthbound.* "It is justified only by the urgency of the need."

The need is urgent, and getting more so. Yet tens of millions of acres of public lands have been closed to mineral development by law or administrative actions. As of early 1983, only 162 million acres of federal onshore land and 13 million acres of offshore land were under lease for oil and natural gas exploration and production.

And the trend is away from development and toward preservation. In many cases the economic use of land is prohibited in favor of a single-purpose use, such as preserving an area where a species of bird may nest, setting aside territory for grizzly bears, reestablishing a prairie ecosystem, or saving a historic site. From this clear need to protect a specific site, the drive for preservation has overwhelmed the concept of multiple use until today vast acreages of federal lands are permanently closed without reason or need, often without an evaluation of the land's aesthetic, biological, recreational, and economic resources. Would-be users—miners, skiers, cattle and sheep ranchers, farmers, campers, timber harvesters, energy firms—are affected.

Groups opposed to the multiple use of federal lands defend their stand in strong language: ". . . the industrial juggernaut must not further degrade the environment . . ." says an official of the Wilderness Society. Authors of the original law governing mineral extraction on federal lands are called a "rapacious gaggle of politicos" motivated by "cupidity and corruption." Under the appealing slogan, "Preserve the Wilderness," the Society fights to keep federal lands out of the hands of the "destroyers."

Who are the destroyers?

"Anyone who uses a sheet of paper, who drives an automobile, who has a telephone, a radio, a refrigerator," Dr. Parks says. "Anyone who owns a television set or uses artificial light. Anyone who heats a home, who applies paint, hammers a nail, or flushes a toilet. Even the staunchest of preservationists is such a destroyer."

Are environmentalists hypocritical, then?

Not really. Most hold their convictions with the best of intentions and genuine good will. They fear that without the strongest of safeguards, all public lands would be subject to indiscriminate development. They see bulldozers coming over every horizon. Yet most federal lands have no potential for mining or oil. Mineral lodes and oil-and-gas-bearing structures are not common. Their very rarity is what gives their development such high priority. The U.S. Geological Survey has identified 260 million of its on-shore acres in the lower 48 states as worth exploring for petroleum, which is a small percentage of the total acreage of federal lands. Of that, oil or gas deposits might lie beneath no more than one out of 10 of those acres. Were oil exploration encouraged to the fullest, few Americans would ever see signs of it. Nor would development, as conducted under today's environmental regulations, result in more than temporary change to the land.

Nonetheless, some environmental professionals continue to insist that more land should be set aside as wilderness. Robert Cahn, Washington editor for *Audubon Magazine,* writing of land within Alaska Wildlife Refuges, says that "the national interest might be served better by wilderness than by development." Cahn praises the Alaska National Interest Lands Conservation Act (which added 10 new national parks, 44 million acres to the National Park, and 56 million acres to the National Wilderness Preservation System) as "the greatest land-protection law in modern history."

And so it is. Yet land withdrawals of such magnitude must inevitably have serious implications for the American economy. "Civilized people want and must have raw materials, especially energy, at moderate prices," emphasizes Dr. Parks. "Nations have gone to the extreme of war to obtain them. For this reason, if for no other, those who advocate the preservation of large wilderness areas known to contain valuable and necessary raw materials are not going to prevail."

Other scientists confirm this view. Dr. William Conway, director of the New York Zoological Society and Bronx Zoo, advises, "It is absolutely impractical to imagine that the human race will not develop the undeveloped lands that remain on this earth." And he calls for a collaborative effort for development and conservation.

Similarly, public officials worried for America's welfare deplore extremes in the name of the environment. John B. Crowell, Jr., Assistant Secretary of Agriculture for Natural Resources and Environment, speaking at an Audubon Society meeting on pressures on the land, told his audience, "We are concerned that additions to the wilderness system be made with careful consideration of the costs . . . of foregoing the long-term availability of resources such as timber, minerals, oil and gas, geothermal power, developed recreation, and forest production."

The wilderness of which he speaks is one of several categories of the federal land system, which includes national parks and national monuments. The former now encompasses 68 million acres of land of exceptional natural, historic, or recreational value; the latter, a much smaller volume, covering the smallest area compatible with proper care or management. National monuments may be single buildings, such as Ford's Theatre in Washington, D.C., or an area of special geologic interest, such as the 211,000-acre Dinosaur National Monument in Utah and Colorado.

Mineral extraction is prohibited in national parks and national monuments.

Wildlife preserves account for almost 90 million acres of federal lands. Almost 54 million acres were added in 1980, all in Alaska. Petroleum exploration and production is permitted by law on wildlife refuges, provided proper environmental precautions are taken. In practice, however, few leases have been granted for such activities in these areas.

Wild and scenic rivers comprise another one million acres in the 49 states other than Alaska, and five million acres in Alaska. This relatively small percentage of federal land has a large impact on energy development because it limits access to other lands. Seismic or exploration crews cannot work across or near scenic rivers, and pipeline rights of way are restricted. Another federal land designation that limits economic use is that of National Grasslands and Wetlands. Petroleum operations are permitted legally, but administrative delays in granting leases drag on for months and even years. Military reservations make up another 30 million acres, and on these lands, public use of all kinds is tightly restricted. Indian lands generally have not presented an access problem, and tribal councils have worked with oil companies to make oil exploration and production compatible with Indian use—and economically desirable.

Two land programs particularly inhibiting to economic development are the Wilderness Preservation System, set up in 1964, and the Endangered Species Act. Together, these programs present a tangle of confusing and sometimes contradictory regulations.

The Wilderness Act defines wilderness as "an area where the earth and its community of life are untrammeled by man, where man himself is a visitor who does not remain." A wilderness area must be at least 5,000 acres in area, roadless, and unimproved. The wilderness program has grown from nine million acres to 80 million acres. If land now under study is added to the system, the wilderness area could be doubled to 167 million acres. The wilderness designation puts land off limits to all but a few users, such as backpackers. Motorized vehicles are prohibited, and road and permanent facilities are not allowed.

Some groups feel this is the way it should be. "Just because (land) is there, it's important, whether you or I or anyone else can get at it or not," says Stephen Chapman, of Minnesota's Clean Air, Clean Water Unlimited. "Perhaps (the land) is even better because we can't get to it."

Of wilderness, an article in *Harper's* magazine explains that "The wilderness concept appears valid if it is recognized for what it is—an attempt to create what are essentially 'ecological museums' in scenic and biologically significant areas of the lands. But 'wilderness' in the hands of environmentalists has become an all-purpose tool for stopping economic activity as well."

Conveniently ignored in all of this is the fact that most government land is not suitable for the "wilderness" category proposed for it. It has little aesthetic or recreational value. It has nothing in common with those spectacular parks such as Yellowstone, Yosemite, the Grand Canyon, or the Grand Teton. When land of scientific and recreational value is subtracted from the total, hundreds of millions of acres remain that can and should contribute to the national welfare through practical use. Its value as a source of raw materials far exceeds its value for recreation or science. Yet these lands, too, are often locked up with the rest.

Ignored, too, is the fact that the environmental impact of such economic activities as oil and gas extraction is slight, temporary, and carried out under strict guidelines that allow the land to revert eventually to its natural state. Yet it continues to be an article of faith among environmental activists that oil and gas activities equate with wholesale and permanent destruction which can be prevented only by prohibiting access to areas where the presence of hydrocarbons is suspected.

The Endangered Species Act is another law that has been widely used to stop economic activity. The story of the snail darter is well known. This small, minnow-sized fish, found in an area about to be inundated by construction of the Tellico Dam, a part of the TVA system, was pronounced an endangered species. As a result, construction of the multimillion-dollar dam was delayed for years at immense cost while scientists studied the possibility of relocating the fish to a new habitat. Eventually, it was discovered that snail darters are not all that uncommon, and the species was removed from the endangered list. But not until millions of dollars and valuable time had been lost.

Even private land is not exempt from the government's land policies. According to the Chase Manhattan Bank, about 30 percent of private land in the lower 48 states "has been effectively withdrawn by the need to comply with mind-boggling environmental laws and regulations. All this without any explicit analysis of the energy loss associated with alternate land uses."

Should Americans worry about the loss of energy resources? Some say no. We have enough oil and gas now, goes the argument. Let's lock up the land until we need its raw materials.

Yet the argument collapses in the face of the facts:

- America imports one-third of its oil at a cost of $50 billion a year.
- America consumes two barrels of oil from its reserves for each barrel of new oil found.
- On today's oil search, tomorrow's energy security depends.

Oil development is a long-range proposition. From the time a decision is made to prospect for oil, some 10 years may be needed to go through the lengthy process of looking for, finding, testing, developing, and producing oil into the nation's supply system. If the oil search is not pressed today, there won't be enough to go around tomorrow.

This reality lends a sense of urgency to the need to resolve a growing impasse over access to public lands. Arbitrary barriers to exploration and development of minerals on most public lands are neither wise nor necessary. A policy of careful, orderly, and steady development is preferable to one of nothing today followed by a crash program tomorrow when the awful truth sinks in.

Isn't that what you would prefer for your three acres? Should you be among the few to claim three acres in the Grand Canyon, you would certainly vote to protect it. But if you are among the many with three parched acres of sagebrush, tumbleweed, and alkali dust in Nevada's Basin and Range Province, or in the frozen bleak and barren tundra of North Alaska, your decision might well be, "Let's see if there isn't some badly needed oil under that land."

WHAT JESUS SAID ABOUT HOMOSEXUALITY:

WHAT THE VATICAN HAS TO SAY:
"INTRINSIC MORAL EVIL...
AN OBJECTIVE DISORDER...BEHAVIOR TO WHICH
NO ONE HAS ANY CONCEIVABLE RIGHT"[1]

WHAT IN THE WORLD IS GOING ON HERE?

What Dignity/USA says about homosexuality: After serious study of our spiritual heritage, we believe that lesbian and gay Catholics are numbered among the People of God, and that they can express their sexuality in a manner that is responsible, loving and consonant with Christ's message.[2]

For nearly 20 years, Dignity has been the national organization fighting for equal rights for lesbians and gay men in the Catholic Church. In over 100 chapters across America, Dignity sponsors the Mass and Sacraments, along with educational and social programs, and a Biennial Convention.

But now, Dignity chapters are under attack. Ultraconservative forces in the Vatican and in America are seeking to turn the clock back to pre-Vatican II days. They are forbidding us to worship on Church property. Priests are prohibited from ministering to us. A whole group of the faithful is being ignored, discarded and despised—because of its sexual orientation.

But the Church is more than a building or a small group of men. The Church is black and white, women and men, gay and straight. The Church is the whole People of God.

When an institution as powerful as the Catholic Church discriminates, all people suffer. You know someone who is gay or lesbian. We are your brothers and sisters, your sons and daughters. We are lay people and clergy. We, too, are the People of God.

Dignity calls on the National Conference of Catholic Bishops to speak out against the expulsion of Dignity chapters, and to dialogue with us on the pastoral care of lesbian and gay Catholics.

Oppressive measures strengthen Dignity. We will continue our struggle. We invite you to join us.

Please use the coupon below or write: Dignity/USA, Suite 11-T, 1500 Massachusetts Avenue, N.W., Washington, D.C. 20005. Help support our work by making a tax-deductible contribution or request more information. Make checks payable to Dignity/USA. Our mailing list and all inquiries are held in strict confidence.

[1] Vatican Congregation for the Doctrine of the Faith, "Letter to the Bishops of the Catholic Church on the Pastoral Care of Homosexual Persons," October 1, 1986.
[2] See Dignity/USA, "Statement of Position and Purpose."

☐ **YES!** I want to help Dignity. Here is my tax-deductible contribution:
  ☐ $15 ☐ $25 ☐ $50 ☐ $100 ☐ $500 ☐ Other: $_____
☐ Please send me more information.
☐ I want information about the Eighth Biennial Dignity Convention to be held in Miami, Florida, July 23–26, 1987.

Name _____

Address _____

City _____ State _____ Zip _____

Send to: Dignity/USA, Suite 11-T, 1500 Massachusetts Avenue, N.W., Washington, D.C. 20005. Make checks payable to Dignity/USA. Our mailing list and all inquiries are held in strict confidence.

Courtesy of Dignity/USA.

SOUTH AFRICA
PULLOUT IS UNPRINCIPLED

CAL THOMAS

The call by the Rev. Leon Sullivan for a complete pullout of U.S. businesses from South Africa is a new twist on the old story about the doctor who said the operation was a success, but the patient died.

Sullivan's principles, which called for integration of corporate facilities, establishment of equal and fair employment practices, and an increase in the number of black managers, had begun to work.

Now, Sullivan wants to pull the plug on his patient by removing its life-support system.

U.S. corporations have, in many cases, been on the front line of social change in South Africa, cajoling the government to follow their lead in hiring, promotion, and pay of nonwhites. Of the 200 U.S. companies in South Africa, more than 170 have signed the Sullivan Principles.

In fact, the promotion of blacks over whites to managerial positions was against South African law at the time the practice began. It was the presence and financial clout of U.S. companies that persuaded the South African government not to enforce its own laws.

U.S. companies have confronted the Group Areas Act and persuaded the European Economic Community to formulate its own code for doing business in the country.

General Motors, before it caved in to domestic pressures, forced a change in the whites-only law at the beach in Port Elizabeth. Since GM sold out to South African managers, workers can expect a 30 percent drop in pay, according to South Africa policy analyst William Pascoe of the Heritage Foundation. U.S. companies, says Pascoe, pay the best wages in South Africa.

It is one thing to fulminate against U.S. companies in South Africa from the security of a domestic platform. It is quite another to be on the receiving end of lower wages in South Africa. Leon Sullivan does not have to worry about where his next meal is coming from.

The most articulate nonwhite voice in South Africa is Zulu chief Mangosuthu G. Buthelezi, who wrote more than two years ago in *The Wall Street Journal,* "To stand on American indignant principles by withdrawing diplomatically and economically from South Africa would only demonstrate the moral ineptitude of a great nation."

Why do some prefer the voice of a U.S. minister to that of a South African leader who speaks with authority about his own country?

In the matter of principles, it appears that Chief Buthelezi has more than others.

SOURCE: Reprinted from *USA Today,* June 8, 1987. Reprinted by permission of the author.

MARRIAGE AND
CATHOLIC DOCTRINE

JAMES COUNCIL

EDITORS:

Neither your article "Synod Secret Poll" (NCR, Nov. 28) nor the family synod itself speaks to my problem.

I am a divorced Catholic who has remarried. Joan and I are active members of Holy Family parish. I have petitioned the diocesan marriage tribunal for an annulment. Laura, my former wife, is cooperating with me in seeking this. She too is remarried to a Catholic.

During the long annulment proceedings, I have met the various biblical and ecclesiastical statements relating to my case. And I am confused.

1. Under the Old Testament law, I could put Laura away for any cause I thought sufficient. (Hillel, the Jewish scholar, listed as an adequate cause "burning the bread.")

2. Of course, under the law, I wouldn't have to put Laura away in order to wed Joan. I could keep any number of legal wives.

3. Jesus (in Matthew) suggested I could put Laura away if she were guilty of fornication.

4. Jesus (in Mark) said I could not put Laura away for any cause.

5. He said specifically that divorced persons living in subsequent marriages are guilty of fornication.

6. The new family synod has ruled that Joan and I can be full sacramental members of the church if there is no sex in our new marriage.

7. The Vatican has approved only one form of birth control: celibacy (either total or periodic). St. Augustine held out for total celibacy.

8. And finally, there is Pope John Paul's recent statement that it is sinful for any man to look after his wife with lust in his heart.

I don't know how I'm supposed to respond to this maze of doctrine, but it does make me yearn for those Old Testament days.

Still, it seems to me if I stick with the Gospels, I'm all right.

Following Jesus (in Matthew), I can put Laura away if she is guilty of fornication. Following Jesus (in Mark), she *is* guilty of fornication because she's living in a new marriage. Consequently, I should be able to put her away and wed my present spouse. (Laura can do the same with me.)

The problem is the Church, which keeps putting these prohibitions on sex in marriage. I can't look after my wife in lust. I must use celibacy to achieve birth control. I can keep my new marriage only if it is totally sexless.

Well, if I can't have sex in my new marriage (and Laura can't in hers), how can we commit the fornication necessary for us to put each

SOURCE: Reprinted by permission of the *National Catholic Reporter*, P.O. Box 419281, Kansas City, MO 64141. From the January 9, 1981 issue.

other away and validate our new marriages and become once again full members of the Church? This is Catch-22 morality.

I will appreciate any clarification one of your writers might give me in this situation. He might begin by advising me if it is lawful to lust after my ex wife. I have to meet Laura every other Wednesday at the marriage tribunal, and she's looking good.

■ **Don Addis**

THE EPISCOPAL CHURCH MEETS THE SEXUAL REVOLUTION

RAYMOND J. LAWRENCE

Recent events in the Episcopal Church belie scattered claims of late that the sexual revolution is over. On the contrary, it seems to be just getting underway in the Episcopal Church.

The Episcopal Bishop of Newark, John Spong, has now stated publicly what many bishops admit privately, that the church should acknowledge and perhaps even give its blessing to certain sexual relationships between unmarried persons. Spong makes a very sensible proposal: he merely asks the institutional church to come clean publicly on the issue and "admit the inadequacy of [its] accepted notions of sex ethics."

The reaction to the Newark statement in some places is as if the cornerstone of the Christian religion had been kicked away. In Texas there was a firestorm of reaction. The Episcopal Bishop of Texas (Houston), Maurice Benitez, said the Newark statement was "totally contrary to Judeo-Christian morality and contrary to Holy Scriptures." He added that apart from marriage, sexual abstinence was the rule for all Christian people. One of the Bishop's lieutenants, the Rev. Larry Hall, further sounded the alarm: "There is great confusion . . . about how Christian people are to relate sexually to each other. . . . It's frightening."

Benitez of Texas made this issue the centerpiece of his address to the convention. "Chastity," he said, "means faithfulness in marriage and abstinence apart from marriage ." He declared that chastity was the teaching of the church for 2,000 years, that it was the will of God, and that it was "necessary for a blessed and happy life." This is the moral norm that the church should set for society, he said, and at that point the convention gave him a standing ovation.

The frenzy of reaction is a puzzling one. The sight of several hundred mostly affluent, urbane Episcopalians rising to a standing ovation at the call for no sex outside marriage was a surrealistic performance piece. Houston is as erotic as it is affluent, and there is still plenty of wealth in Houston, in spite of the oil recession. The largest Episcopal parishes, nestled in Houston's affluent west side, sport far more than their per capita share of Mercedes and BMWs. These churches are just like upper-strata parishes all over urban America. If a parish cleric in one of these churches attempted seriously to make a case for premarital virginity, he would be laughed at, or at best ignored. Episcopal clergy are not known for making fools of themselves.

Does any Houstonian actually think the typical bride who proceeds down the aisle of St. John the Divine of St. Martin's (George Bush's home parish) is actually a virgin waiting for marriage before participating in sexual intercourse? Any such maiden would be the exception, not the rule. She would also likely be thought a social retard.

SOURCE: Reprinted with permission from *The Churchman,* June–July 1987.

Then there is the large gay community in Houston, which flocks to the Episcopal Church in large numbers. Since Vance Packard, everyone knows that Episcopalians claim the highest rung in the social ladder. They also offer generally a more artistic liturgy. Whatever else the burgeoning gay community may be known for, gays have a reputation for taste—good taste. The affluent Episcopal parishes in Houston have a significant share of the gay community. Since the AIDS epidemic they may be generally more conservative in their style, but no one thinks for a minute that they practice chastity as defined by the Bishop of Texas.

Even among the ranks of the Texas clergy there are a number of single persons, some gay, both men and women, who by common knowledge reject in belief as well as practice the obligations of chastity as defined by the Bishop.

If the clergy know full well how people are living, and that very few people actually believe any longer that sexual expression belongs strictly within the bounds of marriage, why then this frenzy of reaction?

History provides a clue to the riddle. Sexual purity, abstinence, was adopted by the church in the 4th century as its badge of identity and instrument of control. Chastity was not a biblical concern, either of the Old or New Testaments, the Bishop of Texas to the contrary notwithstanding. Nor was chastity a concern of the early church. It was established in the 4th century, reinforced in the Middle Ages, and to some extent undermined by the Reformation.

When Luther, the Augustinian monk, married Katy, the nun, he meant to strike a blow for sexual self-actualization and undermine the medieval valuation of chastity. Luther was only partially successful. Chastity has to some extent remained, though limping, an instrument of identity and control in both Catholic and Protestant traditions. The sexual revolution has reasserted Luther's challenge, though in a more radical and secular manner. Some, like the Bishop of Texas, are trying to restore that control and reestablish that badge of identity. But it is a badge that looks funny on Episcopalians.

When Constantine adopted the church in the 4th century, its critical gadfly relationship with the state was compromised. The identity of Christians was endangered. If every member of the body politic is a Christian, then no one is a Christian. Sexual purity was at that point claimed as the new badge of identity for Christians and remained so from thenceforth.

If the Bishop of Newark has his way, sexual purity, chastity, will be deep-sixed as an irrelevant issue in the modern world. The church might then have its hands freed truly to serve the modern world around issues that really matter to us all.

The church might even recover its original adversarial relationship to the state, and might find itself commenting on the frightening militaristic bent of the modern state before we destroy ourselves and our environment along with our enemies. That is something to be frightened about. That is a mortal concern far more deserving of our fear than the prevalence of persons cohabiting without benefit of clergy.

ONLY A TOUGH LAW CAN
FIX TRADE PROBLEMS

LANE KIRKLAND
President of the AFL-CIO

Trade has dominated the agenda of the 100th Congress for one simple reason: the massive U.S. trade deficit. It reached an astonishing $170 billion last year. In the last six years, the trade deficit more than quadrupled.

In agriculture, a healthy $23 billion surplus in 1980 fell to just $4 billion last year. In manufacturing, a $13 billion surplus in 1980 became a $145 billion deficit in 1986. For high technology products, a $27 billion surplus in 1980 has become a $4 billion deficit.

These unprecedented shifts have cost millions of jobs and devastated scores of communities. To finance purchases from abroad, the USA has become the world's largest debtor nation, surpassing Brazil. By the early 1990s, our foreign debt may reach $1 trillion. At that point, interest payments alone will consume at least $50 billion a year. Left unchecked, these imbalances threaten our future economic security and the stability of the international trading system.

The AFL-CIO recognizes that the USA's rapid decline in world trade is the result of many factors, including unstable exchange rates, the Third World debt crisis, and national mismanagement. But an equally important factor is the unfair and discriminatory trade practices of the USA's trading partners and the inability of current law and practice to guarantee fair and equal treatment for U.S. products and services in the international market. All too frequently, foreign markets remain closed to U.S. goods while those same countries enjoy unfettered access to the U.S. market. To ignore this reality is the height of folly.

Nearly everyone agrees the trade deficit is a problem. Years of negotiations and agreements have neither opened foreign markets to U.S. products nor made a dent in the deficit. Other countries are not going to abandon mercantilistic trade policies that have proven successful just because the USA asks them.

The trade deficit reduction amendments introduced by Rep. Richard Gephardt, D-Mo., and Sen. Donald Riegle Jr., D-Mich., address this serious problem in a responsible way. Both proposals would identify countries that use unfair and discriminatory trade practices to amass huge trade surpluses with us. They provide for a period of negotiations with those countries to eliminate the unfair practices, thereby increasing U.S. exports and reducing the trade deficit. If the negotiations fail, the president must act to reduce bilateral trade imbalances by 10 percent a year beginning in 1989, if the president has not waived these provisions subject to congressional procedures.

SOURCE: Reprinted from *USA Today*, April 30, 1987. Reprinted with permission of the AFL-CIO.

The USA needs a powerful lever to pry open foreign markets, and the biggest lever is access to the U.S. market. Unless our trading partners know what is expected of them, they will conduct business as usual—at the expense of U.S. producers and workers.

Any trade legislation that doesn't deal directly with the trade deficit simply isn't addressing the central issue.

WHEN THEY TELL YOU THAT ABORTION IS A MATTER JUST BETWEEN A WOMAN AND HER DOCTOR

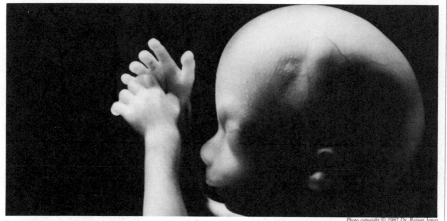

Photo copyright © 1982 Dr. Rainer Jonas

The incredible photograph above by Dr. Rainer Jonas shows what a healthy, active intrauterine child looks like at 19 weeks. Like the bud of a flower, beautiful. But, unfortunately still a candidate for elective abortion.

THEY'RE FORGETTING SOMEONE

Courtesy of Media: Right to Life of Michigan Educational Fund.

PRIVACY-INVADING PRESS
DOESN'T SERVE ANYONE

HOWARD L. REITER

What did Gary Hart do, and with whom did he do it? And should anybody care?

The answers to the first two questions are still up in the air, but the answer to the third should be a resounding "no."

Most people would probably agree that the media should not invade a presidential candidate's privacy unless the issue affected what kind of president he or she would be, and it is impossible to demonstrate that a person's sex life has a clear link to performance in office.

Some of the most revered names in U.S. public life—Franklin D. Roosevelt, John F. Kennedy, and Martin Luther King Jr.—apparently engaged in marital infidelity, but where is the evidence that it had any impact on the effectiveness of their leadership?

Perhaps the only serious issue that might be involved here is the question of integrity. A person whose private life is full of deception, some will argue, is the kind of person who will lie to the public as well. This, too, is questionable. The one president for whom lack of integrity became a career-ending issue, Richard Nixon, was relatively free of speculation about his private life.

Much more fundamental than the question of a public official's private life is the proper role of the news media.

When journalists stake out a candidate's town house or, in the case of Henry Kissinger a few years ago, go through a public official's garbage, they are demonstrating the seamy side of their preoccupation with political personalities rather than issues.

Through the years, we are told more than we need to know about our presidents' personal lives and less than we need to know about their policies—what the social critic Sidney Lens has called "politics by psychoanalysis."

In a parody of Gresham's Law, this trivial news drives the serious news about public issues out of the paper and off the air.

We may end up this campaign knowing a great deal about whether we would want Gary Hart—or any other candidate—as a neighbor or brother-in-law, and very little about what he would do in the Oval Office.

Obviously there are certain personal qualities we should know about candidates: Are the policies they advocate in public the same as those they favor in private? Are their tax returns honest? Can they work well with other politicians? Beyond such questions, journalists should stick to the state houses and legislative houses rather than the town houses, and educate the public about who is going to do what in the White House.

SOURCE: Reprinted from *USA Today*, May 5, 1987. Reprinted by permission of the author.

ET TU, PENNZOIL?

MICHAEL KINSLEY

The *Wall Street Journal* editorial page is red-in-the-face livid that some pissant Texas court wants to make Texaco pay Pennzoil more than $10 billion in reparations for thwarting a merger with Getty Oil Company three years ago. "Texas Common Law Massacre," the *Journal* has been calling it. "Ten-Gallon Outrage," the paper headlined April 14 after Texaco declared bankruptcy to avoid ponying up $12 billion to preserve its right to appeal.

The American business establishment is in general agreement (except for Pennzoil, of course) that this is a helluva way to run an economy. It's a "national embarrassment," says the *Journal,* that "local but utterly destructive legal pitfalls" can bring to ruin a multinational corporation. Will no "serious court" rid us of this turbulent judgment?

On the merits of this case, the business establishment is right to be angry. Pennzoil thought it had a deal to buy 43 percent of Getty for something between $3.5 billion and $5 billion, depending on how you figure. Texaco swooped in and bought the whole company for $10.1 billion. That's about $4.3 billion for the share Pennzoil wanted. It's not at all clear whether Pennzoil and Getty had a done deal that Getty ratted on, or a mere non-binding agreement to agree. But that's arguable. (And, believe me, they're arguing about it.) What's beyond reasonable argument is that Pennzoil didn't lose anything like $10 billion when the deal fell through.

Pennzoil's loss is the difference between what it was about to pay for a chunk of Getty and what that chunk was really worth. Judging from what Texaco paid two days later, that difference is a few hundred million at most—an amount undoubtedly surpassed by the legal bills. Snookered by a lot of malarkey about drilling costs, a Texas jury decided that Pennzoil's loss was actually $7.5 billion, and added $3 billion of punitive damages for good measure. An appeals court reduced the punitive damages to a neat billion, but meanwhile interest charges are swelling the whole pile.

The idea that 43 percent of Getty Oil was worth $7.5 billion more than Pennzoil had agreed to pay is self-evidently absurd. If the figure is correct, it means that the owners of Getty, with lots of expensive expert advice, sold their company—not once, but twice in three days—for about a third of its true value as determined by 12 lay people. If it's correct, then Texaco made a profit of $16 billion on its purchase of the whole company and should be able to pay off the judgment with billions to spare—in which case the stock market has lost its mind and Texaco's depressed shares are now the greatest bargain in Wall Street history. If the judgment is correct, why has Pennzoil rejected Texaco's offer to hand back that 43 percent chunk of Getty for less than Pennzoil's original price? Answer: The judgment is not correct. It's insane.

SOURCE: Reprinted by permission of *The New Republic,* © 1987, The New Republic, Inc. From the May 4, 1987, issue.

"If you concentrate on my accomplishments and abilities as a professional, in time you'll be able to overlook the fact that I'm a woman."

PRO/CON:
RESTRICT SMOKING IN PUBLIC PLACES?

JOSEPH CALIFANO AND PAUL SCREVANE

PRO

Interview with Joseph Califano, former Secretary of Health, Education and Welfare

Q Mr. Califano, why do you favor restricting smoking in public?

People—whether they're children, workers or pregnant women—should not be forced to breathe other people's smoke. Maybe you can drink alone or eat alone, but it is not possible to smoke alone in an enclosed space with other people.

Studies show that 5,000 Americans die each year because of secondhand smoke. A Japanese report concluded that nonsmoking wives of heavy smokers had an 80 percent higher risk of lung cancer than women married to nonsmokers. Study after study has associated involuntary smoking and lung cancer, pneumonia, asthma and bronchitis. A recent study has linked secondhand smoke to heart disease.

Q Where do you think smoking should be banned?

In schools, hospitals, sports arenas and convention halls, theaters, banks or other public places where people have to stand and wait. Sections of theater lobbies and other areas could be set aside for smokers. Smoking should not be permitted in stores. Restaurants should be required to provide smoke-free space. Employers should provide a smoke-free workplace for employees who wish it. I support the efforts to restrict smoking to designated areas in federal buildings. Virtually all assembly lines now prohibit smoking, and most large companies with large workroom areas have restrictions. Businesses that permit smoking at work can provide a room for smoking or segregate smokers in one part of a room with proper ventilation.

The commission I worked with to propose a New York City antismoking law recommended no restrictions for bars, private residences, hotel and motel rooms or tobacco stores.

Q Many restaurants already have no-smoking areas. Why should merchants and employers be forced to separate smokers?

Because the last five surgeons general have concluded that this is a public-health problem with heavy costs to our society. Why should the nonsmoker have to protect himself against breathing smoke any more than a customer should have to inspect the kitchen of a restaurant to see if it is sanitary?

Q Businesses argue that such measures are costly—

It costs no more than a sign that says "No-Smoking Section."

SOURCE: Copyright © 1986, *U.S. News & World Report.* Reprinted from issue of July 21, 1986.

Employers will save money in terms of reduced illness and absenteeism and increased productivity.

Q Is the real goal to force people to stop smoking altogether?

Not at all. That is their choice. I'm only trying to protect nonsmokers. But I do support employers who fund programs to help workers quit smoking if they want to. Smoking is slow-motion suicide. The point here is to prevent secondhand smoking from becoming slow-motion murder.

CON

Interview with Paul Screvane, former president, New York City Council

Q Mr. Screvane, why do you oppose banning or restricting smoking in public places?

Because such laws would set up two classes of citizens—smokers and nonsmokers—and would be very confrontational. They give the nonsmoker virtual dictatorial power to determine where smoking may not be permitted.

And such laws are unenforceable. Health departments and the police are already overworked.

Q What about studies that link smoke-filled rooms to lung cancer in nonsmokers?

I can find no evidence that secondary smoke is a danger. At three separate workshops on this very issue, scientists concluded that health hazards to nonsmokers could not be established.

Q Why then are cancer doctors among those pressing to ban smoking in public places?

Passive smoke is a subterfuge. They are really trying to make it difficult to smoke in public. They think many young people will say: "Well, if it's that inconvenient, why even get started on it? Forget it." They can't point to any scientific danger to nonsmokers. It's a sham, a fraud.

Q Don't you think restaurant patrons, for instance, have the right to dine without smoke if they wish?

If enough people came into a restaurant and said, "We will not patronize your place because you don't have a no-smoking section," they'd have one. Restaurants aren't required by law to provide sugar substitutes, but because of the pressures of the marketplace, most do.

Q What about the workplace? Shouldn't all workers have the right to a smoke-free environment?

The workplace is not always a big room in which you can segregate smokers and nonsmokers. What if 10 people work in a section and two are smokers? Can you put a wall around them? If they need to communicate with their fellow workers, I think you're depriving them of their livelihood.

Also, segregating smokers costs money. An AFL-CIO study estimated that an antismoking law would cost $265 million a year in New York City.

Q How would such laws cost employers money?

Besides reorganizing the office and putting up partitions, a company would suffer from time lost.

I smoke three packs a day, which means I smoke three or four cigarettes an hour. As president of Federal Metal Maintenance, Inc., I have my own office. But if I did not, I would have to absent myself from my workplace and go to a designated area to smoke. That's time—and time is money.

SOURCE: From the *Mobile Register,* August 5, 1987. By David Wiley Miller, *The San Francisco Examiner.* Copyright © by and permission of North America Syndicate, 1987.

RAISING THE MINIMUM WAGE
WILL PUT PEOPLE OUT OF WORK

SENATOR ORRIN G. HATCH

As Congress endeavors to reform our welfare system in a way that will provide individuals and families with a route to economic security and independence, it seems counter-productive to consider also increasing the minimum wage—a move that will inevitably put more people out of work.

Advocates say an increase will ease the burden of the working poor. But logic, experience and common sense suggest otherwise.

Sen. Edward Kennedy, D-Mass., and Rep. Augustus Hawkins, D-Calif., have introduced legislation that would force the minimum wage up nearly 40 percent during the next three years to $4.65. After 1990, the minimum wage would be indexed to half the average non-supervisory American worker's wage. That means automatic increases in the minimum wage—increases without further public comment or legislative action.

There are several key reasons to question the advisability of enacting such legislation.

First, economists are virtually unanimous on the fact that jobs will be lost if the minimum wage is increased. The Minimum Wage Study Commission concluded in 1981 that every 10 percent increase in the minimum wage could eliminate 70,000 to 200,000 jobs for teen-agers alone. Total job loss could be substantially higher.

Given a nearly 40 percent increase, the legislation proposed by Kennedy and Hawkins would jeopardize an additional 400,000 to 800,000 jobs, denying opportunities to thousands more.

Simply put, the minimum wage won't mean a thing—whatever the rate is—if people are forced out of their jobs. A higher wage is little consolation for someone who doesn't have a job.

Furthermore, by eliminating entry-level jobs that provide chances to acquire skills and job experience, the proposed legislation would make it even more difficult for unskilled or inexperienced individuals to obtain the training and work references they need to move up the employment ladder.

This bill not only cuts off people's employment and incomes, it also cuts off their opportunities for the future.

On the surface, it might seem that raising the minimum wage is a good idea. After all, inflation has drastically reduced the purchasing power of the minimum wage since 1981.

There is no question that families earning only minimum-wage incomes have a very rough time making ends meet. But an increase in the minimum wage is an ineffective weapon in the war on poverty.

A Congressional Budget Office study shows that only one in five minimum-wage earners fits the traditional working poor profile. In reality,

SOURCE: Reprinted from the *Mobile Press,* July 13, 1987. Reprinted by permission of the author.

the typical minimum wage employee is young, single and works part-time—but is not poor.

Since the minimum-wage law applies to the labor force across-the-board, the benefits of an increase are not directed to those families who need a raise the most.

On the contrary, minimum-wage boosts have increased, rather than reduced, pressures on the working poor, many of whom do not have the skills to compete for jobs at higher wage levels. As employers adjust to the higher federally mandated labor costs, workers without skills will be priced out of the market.

In short, a higher minimum wage may increase the incomes of some workers, but only at the expense of others.

Supporters of minimum-wage legislation are ignoring the real reasons some individuals remain employed at low wages. Today's jobs require a more highly skilled and more highly adaptable workforce.

Of the net new jobs created since 1983, 12.5 million have paid $10 an hour or more, and 3.2 million have paid between $6 and $10 an hour. About 4.3 million jobs paying $6 or less an hour have actually been lost.

The primary barriers to better jobs for those stuck at the minimum wage are poor reading and math skills, limited English proficiency and few job skills.

The way to break down these barriers is not through a federally imposed wage increase, but through more vigorous outreach to low-income heads of households by our training and educational programs. More than $13 billion has been requested for these programs next year.

The solution, as the proverb says, is to "teach a man to fish."

If we are serious about helping people in need, we must help them acquire the skills which will enable them to be independent and self-sufficient—and free of the minimum wage as the determinant of how far they can go.

COME HOME
FOR CHRISTMAS

ARCHBISHOP OSCAR LIPSCOMB

We cannot have a better theme to start the Season of Advent than the words of St. Paul to the Romans from the second reading of this weekend's Masses: "You know the time in which we are living. It is now the hour for you to wake from sleep, for our salvation is closer than when we first accepted the faith." (Rom. 13, 11) The beginning of a new year of grace in the Church reminds us that we do not have forever to live our lives. Each moment is special and none should be wasted.

Now the time we might spend at odds with one another, or with the Lord, even the time when we ignore each other, or the Lord is a terrible waste of one of our most precious gifts. That is why once again I invite those who share this holy time at Christmas with each other and the Lord to "come home." St. Matthew in our Gospel begs us not to be "totally unconcerned" at such an estrangement. It is so important that I beg you who hear or read these words to take them to heart yourselves, and pass them on as a personal invitation to others who might not otherwise hear the invitation, "Please, come home for Christmas."

Why such persons might have left is not really so important as the fact that they are missed and we truly want them back with us. Remember the prodigal son—God is like the father who rejoiced at the return of his child. We who are Church are no less anxious for those who have left.

Sometimes people need help in coming home—I ask all to lend a hand. The sacrament of reconciliation is a door opened wide at Christmas. The invitation to enter depends on all of us who are challenged to share the gifts of redemption with those who are not receiving them. We do this by attitude, example and joy. Your priest will help. He will never refuse a sympathetic ear and helping hand to anyone who seeks to turn to the Lord.

If you are away and feel that the Church has hurt or misunderstood you, as bishop I apologize for any wrong suffered, and ask all of the family of faith to help us heal and become one again. If it is sin that stands between you and the Lord, come back so that you do not stand alone. In unity there is strength you haven't even imagined—and especially from those who love you. If it is a situation or status such as a non-sacramental marriage, please do not be discouraged. Come home and let's talk about it. What can be done will be done. What can't will at least be placed in God's hands, and the bottom line is that He loves us beyond all imagining if we only keep faith, and keep trying.

SOURCE: Reprinted from *The Catholic Week,* November 28, 1986. Reprinted by permission of the author.

Cocaine lies.

After nearly a decade of being America's glamour drug, researchers are starting to uncover the truth about cocaine.

It's emerging as a very dangerous substance.

No one thinks the things described here will ever happen to them. But you can never be certain. Whenever and however you use cocaine, you're playing Russian roulette.

You can't get addicted to cocaine

Cocaine was once thought to be non-addictive, because users don't have the severe *physical* withdrawal symptoms of heroin—delirium, muscle-cramps, and convulsions.

However, cocaine is intensely addicting *psychologically*.

In animal studies, monkeys with unlimited access to cocaine self-administer until they die. One monkey pressed a bar 12,800 times to obtain a single dose of cocaine. Rhesus monkeys won't smoke tobacco or marijuana, but 100% will smoke cocaine, preferring it to sex and to food—even when starving.

Like monkey, like man.

If you take cocaine, you run a 10% chance of addiction. The risk is higher the younger you are, and may be as high as 50% for those who smoke cocaine. (Some crack users say they felt addicted from the *first time* they smoked.)

When you're addicted, all you think about is getting and using cocaine. Family, friends, job, home, possessions, and health become unimportant.

Because cocaine is expensive, you end up doing what all addicts do. You steal, cheat, lie, deal, sell anything and everything, including yourself. All the while you risk imprisonment. Because, never forget, cocaine is illegal.

There's no way to tell who'll become addicted. But one thing is certain.

No one who is an addict, set out to become one.

C'mon, just once can't hurt you.

Cocaine hits your heart before it hits your head. Your pulse rate rockets and your blood pressure soars. Even if you're only 15, you become a prime candidate for a heart attack, a stroke, or an epileptic-type fit.

In the brain, cocaine mainly affects a primitive part where the emotions are seated. Unfortunately, this part of the brain also controls your heart and lungs.

A big hit or a cumulative overdose may interrupt the electrical signal to your heart and lungs. They simply stop.

That's how basketball player Len Bias died.

If you're unlucky the first time you do coke, your body will lack a chemical that breaks down the drug. In which case, you'll be a first time O.D. Two lines will kill you.

Sex with coke is amazing.

Cocaine's powers as a sexual stimulant have never been proved or disproved. However, the evidence seems to suggest that the drug's reputation alone serves to heighten sexual feelings. (The same thing happens in Africa, where natives swear by powdered rhinoceros horn as an aphrodisiac.)

What is certain is that continued use of cocaine leads to impotence and finally complete loss of interest in sex.

It'll make you feel great.

Cocaine makes you feel like a new man, the joke goes. The only trouble is, the first thing the new man wants is more cocaine.

It's true. After the high wears off, you may feel a little anxious, irritable, or depressed. You've got the coke blues. But fortunately, they're easy to fix, with a few more lines or another hit on the pipe.

Of course, sooner or later you have to stop. Then—for days at a time—you may feel lethargic, depressed, even suicidal.

Says Dr. Arnold Washton, one of the country's leading cocaine experts: "It's impossible for the nonuser to imagine the deep, vicious depression that a cocaine addict suffers from."

Partnership for a Drug-Free America

Courtesy of DDB Needham Worldwide, Inc.

THE PRICE
OF FREEDOM

HARLON B. CARTER

There are many reflections on gun control, but the most compelling among them is that statement in our Declaration of Independence that men "are endowed by their Creator with certain unalienable rights."

Observe that our Founding Fathers were talking about rights which existed prior to governments or laws of men. Here is clear recognition that the Creator endowed men with certain rights with which governments should not tamper.

It follows, that if governments may not tamper with a right, neither may governments properly tamper with the reasonably expected means for making it effective.

The first of the rights identified by our Founding Fathers as an "unalienable right" was that of life. The other two were liberty and the pursuit of happiness. These are not things given by government. They are things from God, and the first of them is a man's right to protect his life, the right of defense from mortal attack.

John Adams said that men have rights "antecedent to all earthly governments—rights that cannot be repealed or restrained by human laws—rights derived from the great Legislator of the universe."

Nowhere is it said that we may not pay a high price for these rights. It is popularly said that the right to protect one's life, the right to keep and bear arms, costs lives. This is said without an adequate measure that more lives are saved by arms in good hands than are lost by arms in evil hands.

Moreover, as to a man's right to protect life or property, rarely is anything said about freedom of choice, without which, by definition, there is no freedom at all. Freedom of choice is not separable from judgment, and judgment is denied the essence of its character and usefulness where purged of risk.

The freedom of the press is envisioned here in these considerations. A free press is costly in terms of public and moral confusion, social disturbances, the causes of war, and the regular reporting on our national defense—and this even to the aid and comfort of our enemies. Yes, we know the price is high, but we deem a free press worth the price. Some disagree.

The paramount point to be made is that our "unalienable rights" may not be infringed by government merely because they suggest difficulties or because they are socially or politically inconvenient or even because they may at times be painful. Millions of men have given their lives in the last two thousand years in order to afford us recognition of, and guarantees contained in, the few simple phrases surrounding all our liberties—the most important of which might well lie within the quoted words of old John Adams.

SOURCE: Reprinted by permission of the National Rifle Association.

Our opponents in the areas of gun control find themselves in the unhappy position of arguing that the common man should be deprived of the means for possibly committing a crime, even if he has never committed one and there is no demonstrable intent he will do so. The common man? Yes. No government today, not even the most despotic, denies arms to the economically or politically privileged classes. Will the gun prohibitionists now say it was egalitarianism which is causing the purported gun problem? I predict they wouldn't dare.

Crimes are numerous and the means for committing them abound in so many forms that it is manifestly impossible for government to use prior restraints to prevent them. Any significant effort to do so presupposes smothering police presence.

Crime prevention, beyond educational persuasion and individual and community prudence, is impossible. An elementary example is the crime of arson. Any man with matches possesses the means to commit arson, but the experience of the ages tells us that there will never be a successful effort to curb the means for committing this crime by prohibiting people from possessing matches. It is not the usefulness of matches which calls for staying the hand of government in the face of their possession, but the abhorrence of prior restraint assuming guilt in the face of possible innocence.

To comport with our sense of justice, it is not the means for committing a crime which is a legitimate subject of restraint. There must also be, aside from arguments on intent, a presumption that a suspected individual is innocent until guilt is established in a fair trial.

In a society marked by greed and malice, depriving a man of the choice to have arms is to infringe upon his "unalienable right" to life, and perhaps even to destroy our basic concept of a government based on individual freedom, justice for all, and the presumption of innocence.

Today's concepts of gun control seem based on the premise that the people cannot be trusted and must be controlled; that they must be restrained prior to an offense, even in the absence of evidence of evil intent. I submit that a majority of Americans believe this is a premise which neither liberals nor conservatives can endure if we are to have a free society.

TOO MANY SEX EXPERTS
TEACHING THE SUBJECT

S. L. VARNADO

The American bishops' recent decision to institute a sex training program in Catholic schools makes me wonder if the bishops have suffered a collective stroke of amnesia in regard to their own childhood. If, instead of consulting with a group of supposed "sex experts," the bishops had taken a few minutes to recall their own playground and schoolroom experiences, they might have come to a far different conclusion. We are told on the highest authority that we should "become as little children." I strongly recommend this advice to our ecclesiastical superiors.

If we take the time to recollect our childhood experiences regarding sex, most of us will remember that we were, indeed, intensely interested in the subject. But we were intensely interested in a million other subjects. A child's mind is an abyss of unanswered questions on all possible (and a few impossible) subjects, including God, frogs, shadows, bugs, electricity and where babies come from. Children are obsessed with sex because they are obsessed with everything.

The belief that they have some special interest in sex—over and above other interests—is Freudian. The Freudian child is a little sexual psychopath who falls in love with his mother and yearns to do away with his father. A Freudian child (if one ever existed) would be extremely boring. His conversation would be as limited as that of a middle-aged lecher.

Real experience with real children provides a different picture. When my youngest son was six years old, my wife took him aside and explained the facts of life to him. The following year she consulted him again on the subject to see if he had any new questions, and she discovered that during the intervening time he had *forgotten the facts of life.* This is not exactly what I would call a burning interest in the subject.

Of course, it must never be supposed that those of us who oppose classroom sex instruction are necessarily opposed to sex instruction itself. On this question, as on others, children need proper answers, but whether the answers are best supplied by supposed "experts" (who have obtained their expertise in the laboratory) or by parents (who obtained theirs in the nursery) is another matter. By and large, I would put my money on parents. I have seen enough of "experts" to know that they are often people who have all the right answers to all the wrong questions.

In a field such as psychology, for instance, the expert is often a person who has spent a great deal of time in a laboratory studying the way mice run through a maze. This is unquestionably useful knowledge, but whether it would help the expert catch mice in his or her home is

SOURCE: Reprinted by permission of the *National Catholic Reporter,* P.O. Box 419281, Kansas City, MO 64141. Reprinted from the December 11, 1981, issue with the permission of the author.

uncertain. A cat would probably know a lot more about it than the expert.

Or in a field such as childhood nutrition, the expert may know all about the proper foods that make for proper health, but be incapable of getting a child to eat its spinach. For that task, what is needed is not an expert, but a mother. In fact, none of the more intimate aspects of life are entrusted to "experts." Why, then, should we take one of the most intimate aspects we know of—the training of children in this all important matter of sex—and hand it over to "experts"?

It would be a matter of some interest to learn where the U.S. bishops got their sex instruction as children. Did they learn it from their parents, or from experts—or did they learn it in that great and awesome place we hear so much about—the gutter? Are we to conclude that their own experience in this matter was so traumatic that they are determined to save the rest of us from a similar fate? If that is the case, how on earth did they ever become bishops?

If classroom sex instruction is so overwhelmingly crucial (as the bishops imply), how did the saints ever become saints without it? We are reasonably sure that Ss. Peter, Paul, Cosmas, Damien, Thomas Aquinas and Jerome never received classroom sex training. And we are absolutely certain that St. Simon Stylites did not. He, after all, spent most of his adult life seated ascetically on a column in the middle of the desert—not exactly an optimal environment for a Masters and Johnson course.

Moreover, the fact that Christendom became Christendom without benefit of sex training in the schools throws a dubious light upon the bishops' entire project. The Roman empire was probably the most sex-saturated entity before *Playboy* magazine, yet Christianity prevailed and grew strong without classroom sex training. Can our "sex experts" hope to accomplish more?

Despite any arguments advanced against this project, we will be told that "special conditions" of modern life demand sex training for our children. And there may be some slight truth to this argument. There can be little doubt that classroom sex courses will help children to enter more fully into a Johnny Carson monologue or the subtleties of a Bo Derek movie. If this is what our bishops want, I can only wish them well. But I will ask them to keep their hands off *my* children.

#3 in a Series on Civil Justice Reform

Life without risk

What would it be like to live in a country where the penalty for taking risks becomes so astronomical and unpredictable that people stop taking them? It isn't hard to imagine. We Americans are dangerously close to being there already.

A manufacturer of health care equipment recently abandoned its development of a home kidney dialysis unit. "The size of the damage claims and the probable costs of defending ourselves would make the whole project uneconomical," reported its chairman.

Since 1961, the number of all U.S. companies making measles vaccine has dropped from six to one; those making oral polio vaccine, from three to one. Their reasons for withdrawing? Fear of being sued. One manufacturer alone faces $3 billion in liability claims.

And there are even lawsuits pending against the clergy—suits alleging that this or that priest, minister or rabbi has been "negligent" in his private counsel.

It may shock you that even the clergy are within reach of this long legal arm, but in a way it's inevitable. Wherever there is risk, today there are lawsuits.

Directors resign from boards in response to expensive lawsuits from shareholders. Publishers consider dropping important stories as the fear of libel suits grows. YMCAs cut back gymnastics and diving programs. Schools abandon sports.

What if there were no risk? We might avoid lawsuits, but without risk there would be no innovation, no challenge of new ideas, no development of new products. There would be fewer jobs. And there would be no progress.

I don't want to live in a world where a minister, priest or rabbi is afraid to help the suffering. Nor one in which a doctor takes an extra test or X-ray—not for medical reasons—but for file-building against a possible lawsuit.

I want to see genuine fault restored to our concept of liability. We need to crack down on frivolous, harassing lawsuits. And we need to accept some risk and responsibility for ourselves.

I welcome your thoughts and ideas on how we can work together to restore balance and fairness to our civil justice system. And I would be pleased to send you information about some of the efforts that already are under way.

"I don't want to live in a world where a minister, priest or rabbi is afraid to help the suffering."

William O. Bailey
Vice Chairman
Ætna Life & Casualty
Hartford, CT 06156

William O. Bailey

FIGHT URBAN CRIMINALS, NOT INNOCENT VICTIMS

JESSE HILL FORD

New York City is, by definition, the place where absolutely nothing can be done about any number of horrible things. And a New Yorker, by definition, is someone who accepts this idiotic outlook as the greatest single, immutable fact of life. Thus, New Yorkers accept with equanimity mugging, maiming, and crimes *ad infinitum.*

Being a victim is regarded as reasonable tuition for living in the Big Apple. Self-defense is unthinkable. As we have just seen, anyone committing self-defense in New York City will be severely taken to task.

Thus, Bernhard Goetz was indicted and tried on 13 counts in a process that has taken his indefatigable prosecutors 2½ years, and they are not yet through. While acquitted of 12 charges, he was found guilty of "criminal possession of a weapon" by a jury that needed 32 hours to make up its mind. He could get seven years.

What is more outrageous is that although one grand jury refused to indict for attempted murder, his prosecutors, like true sons of the Spanish Inquisition, could not be satisfied. Now what have they proved? What have they gained? Where is the good in any of this they have done to an innocent man?

Would these plea-bargaining insects spend even a fraction as much energy in the prosecution of any *real* criminal? The answer is certainly not.

Isn't it a shame that what made Goetz such a prime target for their outrageous ministrations was his sheer innocence? Of course it is, and they should be ashamed. But, depend on it, they are not.

For in New York, only cops and robbers may go armed. The rest must stand to be robbed, shot, stabbed, beaten, killed—you name it. But should they have the temerity to raise even a finger in protest, they must now realize that prosecutors of the current ilk will see to it that they don't earn a living for at least 2½ years and probably longer.

It is something no free people would accept. But New Yorkers are not free. Proof of it is that they retain such meretricious laws on their books.

Yet there is a bright side. What is so appealing is that four established thugs got more than they bargained for when they picked out Bernhard Goetz, a veteran of victimizations who had reached the decision that what had gone down before would never happen again if he could prevent it.

Miraculously, he managed to overcome four—not just one, but four. And no one else in that subway car was injured. Few, if any, of New York's finest could have done as well.

But never forget that this man has been martyred by the very process of that law whose duty it was in the first place to protect him. And when it could not protect him, it prosecuted him for protecting himself. This is worse than shameful. It is madness. Or, to put it another way, it is New York.

SOURCE: Reprinted from *USA Today,* June 18, 1987. Reprinted by permission of the author.

SHOULD
PRIESTS MARRY?

MARTIN RIDGEWAY

I'm told there are hundreds and thousands of priests in this country who want to have wives. Either they've applied for laicization or they're contemplating it or they hope that the Vatican will change the rules and let them marry.

I can see a lonely priest fantasizing about a warm comfortable home and a wife who says, "Is it OK if we have shrimp again tonight?" or "Snuggle up; I'm cold."

I'm sorry, Father, but it doesn't work like that. As you walk through your quiet rooms, you might want to reflect on the language of marriage—the true sounds of a "good" marriage.

"Don't use those. Those are the good scissors."

"You said you'd be home by five."

"Not tonight. I have a headache (or cramps or a cold or depression or toothache or indigestion or swelling or thyroid tiredness or . . .)"

"Don't say 'fixin' to.' "

"Do you really need another drink?"

"I'm having a Tupperware party tomorrow night."

"Take this back to the store for me; tell them I lost the sales-slip."

"Come on, everyone, it's time to watch *Family Feud.*"

"Anyone can put up a swing-set."

"We'd better leave early. I'm worried about the kids (or the car or the baby-sitter or the furnace or nuclear waste or . . .)"

"If you put things in their place, they wouldn't be lost."

"Not in front of the children."

"At least try to talk to my mother."

"How could you forget? Tommy's piano recital is tonight."

"Jimmy says his little-league team needs a coach."

"You didn't get me anything nice last Christmas (or Valentine's Day or birthday or Easter or Thanksgiving or anniversary or Mother's Day or . . .)"

"Be in by 11:30. You know I can't sleep when you're out."

SOURCE: Reprinted by permission of *The National Catholic Reporter*, P.O. Box 491281, Kansas City, MO 64141. From the April 10, 1981, issue.

"The Wilsons feed their cat in the morning." [A line doesn't have to
make sense to express a serious complaint.]

"That dog of yours has ruined the carpet."

"Do you have to see *every* Super-Bowl game?"

Think about it, Father.

In Mark's gospel, the Sadducees ask Jesus about a woman who has
married seven times. They ask whose wife she is in the next life. Jesus
answers that in the hereafter there is no marriage.

That might be why they call it Heaven.

"ENGLISH LEATHER DRIVES ME CRAZY!"

After shave, cologne, toiletries for men.

English Leather.

English Leather. COLOGNE

Courtesy of MEM Company, Inc. Prepared by MacNamara, Clapp & Klein.

SHOULD JOB BE A PERSONAL RELATIONSHIP—OR STRICTLY BUSINESS?

WILLIAM F. DWYER II

The veritable explosion of unjust dismissal lawsuits being brought by former employees against California companies may achieve more than big dollar damages for fired workers. It could prove valuable in human terms as well.

Because my field of law practice is devoted largely to representing victims of wrongful termination of employment, I've seen some of the seamier sides of employer behavior. I've also gained a unique perspective on worker attitudes.

One of the lessons I've learned is that, if more men and women would look at their jobs as a strictly business arrangement with their employer, they likely would be less vulnerable to the trauma of termination. Too many of them are too trusting of their bosses. So much so that, when the ax falls, their lives are wounded in ways resembling the loss of a loved one.

The psychic devastation following a firing is real. At least 90% of my clients are in or have been in post-termination psychotherapy.

Does the hammer have to hit so hard? I don't believe so. However, minimizing the blow means workers must regard their employment relationship for what it really is—legally and economically.

The company you work for is not your family. It's probably not even your friend.

You weren't hired for any reason other than an expectation of hard work. If you still suffer from some delusion that you were employed to add to the makeup of "one big happy family," you're being had. And, to whatever extent your on-the-job performance includes "love of company," you're unjustly enriching your employer.

The office, shop floor, loading dock, truck cab or wherever your work goes on is a center of commerce. It's the agreed-on site for you to perform the tasks that the company considers important enough to cause it to take money from its pocket and put it into yours. But that's all the workplace is. It's no family room, picnic bench or other social site.

One of the first things I insist that my clients abandon is "we" when talking about their former employment. It's necessary as much for their own sense of self as it is to prevent jury confusion down the road. "Those are the folks," I explain, "who brought unemployment to your home. There's no 'we' now."

Psychiatrists and psychologists tell me that the hurt of job dismissal is in direct proportion to the emotional investment a person has made in the employment relationship. It is hardly influenced at all by what amount of money the employee was earning or what job title, big or small, he or she held.

SOURCE: Reprinted from the *Los Angeles Times,* November 24, 1985. Reprinted by permission of the author.

They also point out the probably obvious corollary that those discharged from jobs with employers who were distant and unfeeling, who rarely had a good word for their workers and who frowned on bonuses, almost always recover their sense of self-esteem in short order.

Those fired today are armed with increasing legal protections. The courts of California have cut back significantly on the absolute power of employers to fire at will. Still, these decisions represent after-the-fact remedies.

Hence, my hope is for judicial recognition of a fiduciary relationship by the employer with respect to employees, which means that the employer would be as responsible for his employees as he would be for himself. This concept is already well known to American business: The law imposes fiduciary responsibilities of "scrupulous good faith and candor" on corporate directors in dealing with shareholders, and the principle is also applied to labor unions in representing their members.

Creating such a setting for employer-employee relations would establish an understood legal framework for the job with a clear definition of the duties owed by employers to those who work for them. Replacing sentimental notions about "the boss is my buddy" with legal standards that are unequivocal and enforceable also would enhance and elevate worker status.

Additionally, were the courts to erect such a protective bulwark for American workers, I predict that it would effect a drastic reduction of the court congestion coming from the current wave of wrongful-termination lawsuits.

In the meantime, recalling how corporate chieftains like to proclaim that "the business of business is business," I'd suggest that employees take them at their word. Draw the line between business and pleasure at the office door or factory gate. Should you be fired, you'll feel a lot less loss.

PHENYLALANINE
ASPARTAME
SILICON DIOXIDE
TRIBASIC CALCIUM PHOSPHATE
BENZOSULFIMIDE
CALCIUM SILICATE

PURE 100% NATURAL
SUGAR

WHICH WOULD YOU RATHER PUT ON YOUR KIDS' CEREAL?

The decision is in your hands. But before you make it, here are some things to think about.

SUGAR IS SAFE
Unlike any artificial sweetener, sugar is on the government's FDA GRAS list (Generally Recognized As Safe).

100% NATURAL
Sugar is pure and 100% natural. It contains no mysterious, unnatural ingredients. No man-made chemicals. And no warning labels.

ONLY 16 CALORIES
Surprisingly, real sugar has only 16 calories per teaspoon—16 naturally satisfying calories.

SUGAR TASTES BEST
In a recent taste test, sugar was preferred nearly 3 to 1 over the leading artificial sweetener.

So if you want your kids to have a low calorie sweetener that's 100% natural and perfectly safe, give them real sugar. After all, don't they deserve to have it as good as you did?

100% NATURAL SUGAR.

THERE'S REALLY NO SUBSTITUTE.

The Sugar Association, Inc. 1511 K St. NW, Washington, D.C. 20005. (202) 628-0189

Courtesy of The Sugar Association, Inc.

MARIJUANA AND
COMMON SENSE

NORML

Every American shares a rich, diverse heritage which cultivates a sense of justice that we hold common. The common sense of right and wrong is the moral force behind the laws and the basis of our society. It permeates the Constitution and creates standards by which we claim our government as well as our society is just. One of our strongest beliefs is that *we, the people, have a right to live our lives without undue government interference.* The laws which render marijuana use and cultivation a crime, though perhaps constitutional, are *not* consistent with the sense of justice in America. This pamphlet examines the arguments for criminalizing marijuana use.

Consider this example, and ask yourself if considering this young couple criminals is just:

Jim and Becky Smith are 27 and have a 2 year old daughter, Jennifer. Jim has worked at the local factory for the last three years, ever since he and Becky got married. Becky stays home, takes care of their little girl, and tends their garden which provides a lot of their food. In addition to common fruits and vegetables, they grow hemp, a plant widely used by the American colonists, for their private use.

They cure the flowers of the plant for a variety of uses. Jim's brother is an alcoholic, and Jim doesn't like alcohol and won't permit it in the house. He smokes the flowers of the hemp plant a few evenings a week and on weekends, and they help relieve stress and relax him. Becky smokes them too, but only after she has put Jennifer to bed for the night. She's found that they help alleviate her menstrual cramps, as well as occasional migraines. Once or twice a year, Jim worries that he is smoking too much, and quits for three weeks, because it seems like a healthy thing to do now and then. Becky quit smoking when she thought she was pregnant again, but resumed when she found out she wasn't.

According to the laws of all 50 states, Jim and Becky are criminals simply because they grow marijuana on their own property for their own use. An arrest, or even a urine test, can result in Jim losing his job, going to jail and the family going on welfare or being split up. How can this be justified?

Why do we consider marijuana use a crime?
Because it is a dangerous drug?

No. *No one has ever died from an overdose of marijuana,* or even from its long-term use; it has a lower toxicity than aspirin. The legal drugs *alcohol and tobacco cause over 450,000 deaths a year.*

Because of its ill-effect on the user?

No. Though heavy use of marijuana contributes to lung problems, the moderate use of marijuana by tens of millions of Americans during the last twenty years has failed to produce evidence of dangerous side-effects of marijuana use. Studies have consistently shown that marijuana use *does not* cause brain-damage, genetic problems, psychosis, behavioral abnormalities or other serious life-threatening side-effects.

Because it's addictive?

No. *Marijuana is non-addictive.* In fact, researchers are excited about its potential as a pain killer because it does not produce the physical dependence common with the use of codeine or morphine as a pain killer. Even though compulsive marijuana use does exist, it is not as common as addiction to tobacco (8 out of 10 users).

Because marijuana use leads to hard drug use?

No. Experts now claim that most hard drug abusers start experimenting with drugs by drinking alcohol or smoking tobacco. Only the black-market nature of marijuana sales connects marijuana use to the use of cocaine or heroin. However, over 70 million people have tried marijuana; yet there are only about 5 million regular users of cocaine and only about 500,000 heroin addicts. Clearly, *almost all marijuana users reject the use of dangerous drugs* such as cocaine and heroin.

Because marijuana has no acceptable use?

No. For some people, no drug has any morally acceptable use. For others, no drug has any morally acceptable use except as medicine. Obviously, marijuana is used recreationally by millions and millions of Americans. Marijuana has medical uses as well, uses that have been ignored in the attempts to condemn its recreational use. Marijuana aids in the treatment of glaucoma, in controlling the seizures of multiple sclerosis victims, eases the nausea of chemotherapy, serves as a pain killer for headaches, cramps, and other routine ailments, and has been used as such for thousands of years.

Because law enforcement is the best method of controlling marijuana use?

No. In 1965 there were only about 10 million users of marijuana. In 1985, after twenty years of law enforcement's War on Drugs, there are over 30 million users. Furthermore, law enforcement has failed at keeping marijuana out of your public schools and out of the hands of your kids. In fact, the police and the DEA admit that they will *never eliminate* marijuana from the United States.

Because keeping marijuana illegal is the best way to keep marijuana away from kids?

No. *Kids can get marijuana more easily than alcohol.* The black market has made schools into marijuana marketplaces. Also, the illegality of marijuana makes its use popular to kids as a way to flaunt rebellion. Only a regulated market and the cooperation of marijuana smokers will keep marijuana out of the schools.

Because legalizing marijuana is inconsistent with educating kids about drug abuse?

No. Legalizing marijuana *does not* mean that it is approved by society. Certainly alcohol use, gambling, prostitution, and other morally questionable activities which are legal in some jurisdictions are not socially approved. Tobacco use has been successfully discouraged with honest information, resulting in a 25% decline in use. A tax from legal marijuana sales would generate *over $10 billion annually* to fund real, effective education campaigns, now tragically underfunded because of law enforcement budget priorities.

Because it sends a message of disapproval to our youth?

No. It sends a message of *hypocrisy.* Some kids take the anti-marijuana rhetoric as suggesting that they drink alcohol instead. If we want to send a message to our youth, let's sink our money into education rather than punishment. If we want to keep our kids away from drugs, let's spend money on academic and recreational programs to interest them in life without drugs, and keep them too busy to use drugs.

Because we have enough problems with the legal drugs alcohol and tobacco?

No. It is naive to suggest that legalizing marijuana suggests introducing it to our culture. *Marijuana is already here.* Reforming the marijuana laws is merely recognizing reality. For a long time people thought the way to treat alcoholism was to pretend it didn't exist. Acknowledgement that it was a pervasive problem led to helping to solve it. Keeping marijuana illegal is a cop-out that allows us to pretend we've dealt with a problem we're actually ignoring.

Because fighting marijuana use helps fight crime?

No. Actually, using our police to chase after marijuana smokers *detracts* from their ability to fight violent crime. *We are arresting 50 people every hour for marijuana offenses.* In an age where over half of violent crimes such as murder, rape and robbery go unsolved, do we really want our police to waste their time chasing after marijuana smokers, who otherwise are law-abiding citizens?

NORML'S VIEW

The proponents of criminalizing marijuana users have lots of excuses as to why marijuana use should be against the law, but none of them stand up to examination. They claim the issue is marijuana, good or bad? Actually, the issue is the marijuana laws, what do they accomplish? The answer is this—*they alienate people from society and cultivate disrespect for authority and fail to prevent marijuana use.*

Why is marijuana use a crime? If we can tolerate different nationalities, different religions, different ideas, and different values in a freedom-loving America, why can't we tolerate those people who grow different plants in their backyard? In a freedom-loving America, how can we justify making the Jim and Becky Smiths among us criminals?

By David Seavey, USA TODAY

SOURCE: Reprinted from *USA Today,* March 17, 1987. Courtesy of David Seavey and *USA Today.*

DON'T
EXECUTE CHILDREN

TANYA COKE

The United States virtually alone among the nations of the world punishes children by death.

Only seven states in this country have prohibited capital punishment for offenders who were under age 18 at the time of their crime. The other 30 states which retain the death penalty have either a lower age limit, or no limit at all.

In the past decade, the United States has executed three juveniles and put 32 others on death row.

We are the only western democracy to insist upon death for juvenile offenders, and our laws on this point are harsher than those of nations with abominable human rights records. Countries that use capital punishment frequently, like the Soviet Union and South Africa, refrain from executing children.

The near worldwide repudiation of the death penalty for teenagers is even codified in law. Just last month, a tribunal of the Inter-American Commission on Human Rights ruled that the United States violated international standards in allowing the execution of two teen-agers in 1986—James Roach in South Carolina and Jay Pinkerton in Texas.

Most people in this country, even strong proponents of capital punishment for adults, agree that children shouldn't be held to the same standards. A recent poll showed that while 75 percent of Georgia citizens approve of the death penalty for murder, only 26 percent would sanction its use for juvenile offenders.

In February, the U.S. Supreme Court agreed to review the appeal of William Wayne Thompson, an Oklahoma boy sentenced to die for a murder committed when he was 15.

Why should juveniles escape the death penalty for crimes we might deem worthy of death for an adult?

Juvenile offenders are qualitatively different from adult criminals in moral, emotional and intellectual development. This fact is widely reflected in our society's treatment of minors; in the creation of a separate juvenile justice system and in the heightened legal protection we afford young people, who we presume lack the necessary responsibility to drink alcohol, drive a car, or enter into legal contracts.

The special frailties of the young—in particular their diminished capacity for moral judgment—makes the imposition of society's most severe penalty an affront to the "human dignity" protected by our constitutional ban against excessively cruel punishment.

Proponents of capital punishment frequently cite its deterrent effect on potential criminals. This remains a common myth, although decades of

SOURCE: Reprinted from the *Mobile Register,* April 30, 1987. Reprinted by permission of the author.

social science inquiry have produced no credible evidence that supports that contention.

Victor Streib, an expert on juvenile execution and a lawyer for Wayne Thompson in the Supreme Court, has argued that the deterrence theory is especially weak as applied to very young people.

He suggests that the prospect of a lengthy prison term—no telephone, no cars, no Saturday nights out—has more deterrent value for an adolescent than does the shadowy notion of death.

Another common justification for capital punishment is that it removes from society dangerous people who cannot be rehabilitated. While many older, hardened criminals may be unresponsive to reform, young people possess a remarkable ability to leave their criminal behavior behind within a few short years.

Can we really sanction the extermination of children like Wayne Thompson—some of them first time offenders—to whom no rehabilitative efforts have been extended?

All these arguments find force in the declining rate of juvenile executions over the past century. With only 3 percent of death row represented by juveniles today, we are close to making this reprehensive practice a relic of the past.

Last month, Indiana raised its minimum age for death sentencing from 10 to 16, and last week Maryland abolished capital punishment for people under 18.

Yet this is a debate that should take place on the national level. The Supreme Court must determine what is cruel and unusual punishment according to "evolving standards of decency" and place children beyond the reach of the electric chair.

PENALIZING BAD TASTE
RISKS RIGHTS OF ALL

Is the Rev. Jerry Falwell an incestuous drunk? Of course not. Nobody believes that.

But if a satirist in a mock advertisement depicts him as one, should the publisher be punished by a court—even though nobody would possibly believe it? Of course not.

Then why did a federal court jury in Roanoke, Va., give Falwell a $200,000 judgment when a mock ad depicted him in just that ridiculous way? Quite simply, because the satirist was Larry Flynt, the self-proclaimed "Duke of Raunch" and publisher of *Hustler* magazine.

Falwell sued Flynt for $45 million, claiming he had been libeled when his seamy magazine published the fake ad. The jurors rejected Falwell's libel claim because no one, they said, would believe such an outrageous ad. But, in an effort to flail Flynt, they awarded Falwell the money for "emotional distress." That's like finding a defendant not guilty, then throwing him in the slammer anyway.

Falwell, in fact, was so "distressed" that he reproduced the ad and distributed a censored version to raise more than $700,000 from his followers.

It would be tragic for the Supreme Court, which just agreed to review this case, to let the lower court's ruling stand. Humor at the expense of public figures would no longer invigorate the public dialogue.

Such a ruling would endanger cartoons by Garry Trudeau satirizing the White House or columns by Art Buchwald satirizing the CIA. Johnny Carson could no longer stick pins in society at large. And David Seavey, whose cartoons appear on this page, might as well put away his pen and ink.

If the court said it was all right to sue for hurt feelings, angry public figures could get around libel laws that require them to prove that comments or cartoons were malicious and false. They could even win suits when the truth made them uncomfortable.

The Supreme Court has traditionally held that exaggerated commentary is protected. It should uphold that tradition.

Falwell and Flynt are just the personalities in the case now before the court. It's the legal principle at stake—free speech—that makes their dispute important.

Free speech is not some special privilege for commentators, cartoonists, or comedians. The First Amendment makes no distinction between preacher or publisher, solid citizen or sleaze-bag.

Granted, when Larry Flynt wraps himself in the First Amendment, it may need an airing out afterward. But the same right that protects what Falwell says from the pulpit protects what Flynt said about him.

Sure, Flynt's ad outraged many of us. Satire often outrages its targets and their friends. But as the jury said in this case, even offensive satire is not libelous.

If Larry Flynt violates the law, punish him. But don't risk muzzling all satirists by picking the pocket of the publisher of a sleazy magazine.

When you single out one piece of ridiculous satire, you threaten all free expression.

Before you do crack, do this.

ORGAN DONOR AUTHORIZATION

Pursuant to the Uniform Anatomical Gift Act,
I hereby give, effective upon my death:
A _____ Any needed organ or parts
B _____ Parts or organs listed _____

_____

_____

Signature of Donor: _____

Date: _____

Hey, it's no big deal. It's a simple legal form, that's all.
Take a minute. Fill it out. Sign it. Carry it with you. It's the least you can do.
Then no one can say you didn't do anything worthwhile with your life.

Partnership for a Drug-Free America, N.Y., NY 10017

Courtesy of Keye, Donna, Pearlstein.

REPEAL THE
SON-OF-SAM LAW

ARTHUR EISENBURG

In the mid-1970s a serial killer called "Son of Sam" was terrorizing New York. Provoked by the prospect that even after his arrest, the killer might receive substantial profits from the book, movie and television rights to his story, the New York legislature enacted what has come to be called the "Son of Sam" law.

The law requires that any profits that a convicted person obtains from a published portrayal or an aired account of the crime be turned over to the New York Crime Victims Board. The board must then hold the money for five years to compensate any victims of the crime.

The law appeals to an understandable impulse: Criminals— particularly those guilty of heinous crimes—should not be permitted to profit from their conduct.

Upon closer consideration, however, the virtues of the statute are a good deal more problematical. For at bottom, the Son of Sam law is seriously out of step with the values and principles underlying our First Amendment tradition.

At the heart of the First Amendment is the notion that public debate should be encouraged and that discussion of issues should be as robust and diverse as possible. To that end, the First Amendment insists that government must remain neutral with respect to the expressive activity of its citizens.

This First Amendment command of government neutrality forbids a state from penalizing public expression because of the subject matter or the unpopularity of the speaker. As the Supreme Court observed in a 1972 case: "There is an equality of status in the field of ideas, and government must afford all points of view an equal opportunity to be heard."

The Son of Sam law ignores entirely this important First Amendment principle. At its core, the law singles out certain subject matter for adverse treatment. The statute reaches only books or movies about criminal events taking place in New York and it further focuses its penalties upon convicted persons who seek to present their version of those events. In so doing, the law fails to afford all points of view an equal opportunity to be heard.

Objections to the law rest not merely on principle but upon practical realities. In "Wise Guy," author Nicholas Pileggi presents fascinating and valuable insights into the criminal underworld. To obtain much of the material, Pileggi interviewed mobster Henry Hill and apparently paid him for otherwise inaccessible information. Without the payment, the information would probably not have been provided. New York is now threatening to ask Pileggi to retrieve the money paid to Hill. Should it

SOURCE: Reprinted from the *Mobile Register*, April 8, 1987. Reprinted by permission of the author.

successfully follow through on its threat, it is less likely that inside stories like "Wise Guy" would be published in the future.

The constitutional deficiencies inherent in the statute cannot be justified upon the claim that the law is designed merely to compensate crime victims. If New York were genuinely interested in providing complete restitution for victims, it would not limit its law to the proceeds of books, movies and television shows, but would make all of the criminal's assets available to the crime victims.

The fact that New York has not done this suggests that some other interest better explains the basis for the Son of Sam law—a desire to punish the criminal. Those who drafted the Son of Sam law felt, simply, that it was unseemly to permit David Berkowitz to profit from his crime. So understood, the statute really rests not on the goal of restitution but upon a desire for retribution.

The question remains as to whether retribution is a sufficient justification for burdening First Amendment activity in the way that the Son of Sam law does. It is no response to the burdens imposed by the law to suggest that the statute does not prohibit a convicted person from writing about the crime but merely bars the receipt of money for such writings. The inadequacy of this response is demonstrated by a landmark Supreme Court decision arising in Louisiana in the 1930s. At that time, Gov. Huey Long attempted to impose a tax on newspapers that were critical of him. The newspapers challenged the tax claiming it abridged their First Amendment rights.

Long argued that the Louisiana tax did not prevent the newspapers from writing about politics in Louisiana or even from criticizing the governor—it simply made the newspapers less profitable. In striking down the Louisiana law, the Supreme Court recognized that free expression can be seriously burdened by restricting the financial component of First Amendment enterprise.

The retributive nature of the Son of Sam law is no more justified. It penalizes certain persons in a way that is likely to dissuade them from presenting their viewpoints. In so doing, it discourages rather than encourages robust and diverse discussion. And it violates the state's obligation to afford all points of view an equal opportunity to be heard.

PHONE-IN POLL: SHOULD EVERY
AMERICAN BE TESTED FOR AIDS?

LEONARD KATZ

Should AIDS testing be extended to cover every American?

Yes, says Rep. Dan Burton (R.-Ind.), who points out that the overwhelming majority of AIDS victims don't even know they have the virus and will continue to infect others unless they're made aware of their situation. Rep. Burton has introduced a bill that would require every American to be tested annually for AIDS. He also recently presided over a Congressional hearing on AIDS.

No, says Rep. William Dannemeyer (R.-Calif.), who believes that testing everyone is not only unnecessary at this time, but far too costly.

Rep. Dannemeyer is a member of the House Subcommittee on Health and the Environment, which considers AIDS legislation.

The *Enquirer* takes no sides in the debate. The two experts outline their positions below.

NO: It's Unnecessary, Far Too Costly and Violates Freedoms

Dear *Enquirer* reader:

It's simply unnecessary to test every American for AIDS at this time. It is an extreme measure that would cost untold billions of dollars.

We currently don't have the medical facilities to test every person. The spectacle of 240-million-plus Americans being tested boggles the mind.

First, we should determine the true extent of the AIDS epidemic by testing these groups:

- Immigrants. It is certainly no burden on those seeking to immigrate here to be tested. And it's not asking too much to require them to pay the $5 cost of the test.
- Prisoners, especially convicted prostitutes and intravenous drug users. This is an extremely high-risk group that must be tested.
- Applicants for marriage licenses. These couples have to be tested for venereal diseases anyway. They can easily be tested for AIDS at the same time.
- Patients aged 15 to 49 who are admitted to hospitals. This is the age group where most of the AIDS victims are found.

Once we begin testing these groups we'll be able to get a handle on the extent of the AIDS epidemic—exactly how widespread it has become. What's more, we'll be able to do it without spending billions of dollars and creating social havoc.

If government decreed everyone must be tested for AIDS, it would cause much resentment when the public knows that lesser measures could be taken initially. Most Americans, I feel, would support these lesser measures.

It is imperative that we get busy now taking these more moderate steps—before the AIDS epidemic gets out of control and forces more extreme measures upon us.

—Rep. William Dannemeyer (R.-Calif.)

YES: Most AIDS Carriers Don't Even Know They Have It

Dear *Enquirer* reader:

It is vitally important that we begin testing everyone for AIDS.

More than a year ago, the U.S. Public Health Service estimated 1.5 million Americans were infected with the AIDS virus—and experts have told me that the number has been doubling every 8 to 14 months.

Other authorities on AIDS estimate we have at least three million AIDS carriers in the U.S.—and many researchers believe it's closer to four million.

Experts tell me at least 98 percent of those infected with the AIDS virus don't even know they are. It can remain in incubation up to seven years—and some scientists believe it can lie hidden for up to 30 years.

During this incubation, the AIDS carrier can transmit the disease to others. Condoms may reduce the risk, but they don't eliminate it.

Testing costs less than $5 per person—which means the annual cost for testing the entire U.S. population would be about $1.2 billion.

Compare this figure to the enormous cost of providing health care for the 300,000 Americans who will have contracted full-blown AIDS by 1991: According to a Rand Corporation study, the cost per patient will average more than $100,000. We will have spent a staggering $30 billion to $40 billion treating AIDS victims by 1991!

Dr. C. Everett Koop, U.S. Surgeon General, says a vaccine for AIDS probably won't be discovered until the year 2000, if then. Meanwhile, we don't know exactly how many have the virus, where it's spreading most rapidly and all the ways it is being transmitted.

We need to start mass testing now so we can get all the facts and develop a battle plan to combat this growing epidemic. Test results should be kept confidential. But the uninfected must be protected—and remember, we're all at risk.

—Rep. Dan Burton (R.-Ind.)

TO PHONE IN YOUR VOTE

Do you think all Americans should be tested for AIDS?

YES 900-220-2711

NO 900-220-2722

If you normally dial "1" before placing a long-distance call, then dial "1" before calling one of the "900" numbers. After dialing the number, wait until you hear a recorded message saying that the call is completed, then hang up. Your vote will be recorded automatically.

And don't worry about getting a busy signal. The "900" line can handle up to 350,000 calls an hour. The polls will be open 24 hours a day from Monday, July 13 through Monday, July 20.

The only cost to you for a call will be 50 cents on your monthly phone bill.

We will carry the results of the poll in our issue on sale July 28. So make your voice heard—should all Americans be tested for AIDS?

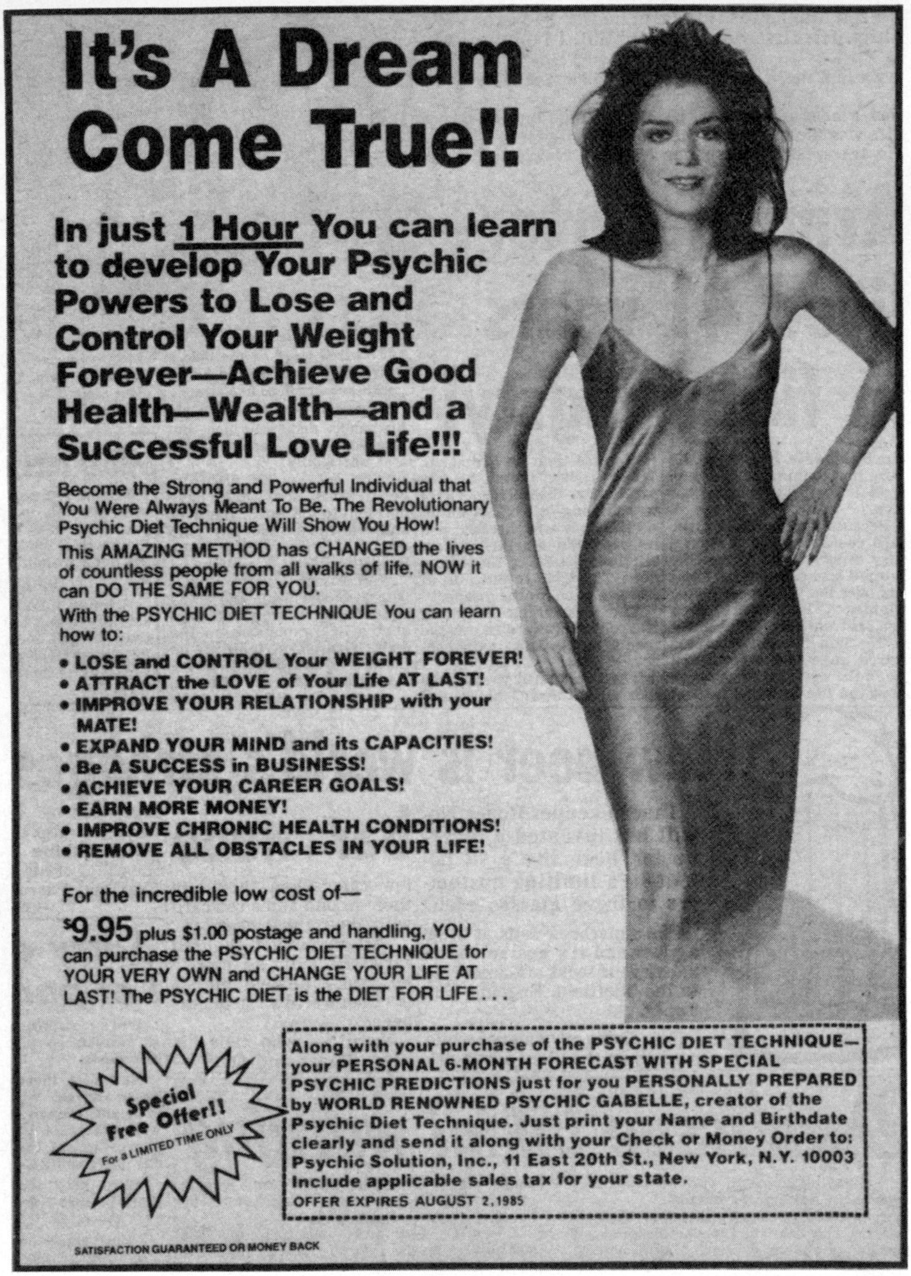

Courtesy of Psychic Solution, Inc.

ANOTHER
BUREAUCRACY

ALEXANDER B. TROWBRIDGE

American business and labor are battling over workplace safety issues again, just as they have for the past hundred years. But the arguments today are uniquely "20th Century."

Currently, debate revolves around how to ensure safety from toxic chemicals—a serious issue that should promote an atmosphere of cooperation, not confrontation. Unfortunately, that's not the case.

Labor claims hundreds of thousands of workers are dying each year as a result of exposure to hazardous substances in the workplace. Industry calls those figures inflated and inflammatory, but recognizes there is a problem. We're addressing it. Companies are willing to do even more.

We agree that American workers should be trained and educated to minimize risks of toxic exposures.

But how best to handle the effort? Organized labor, backed by Sen. Howard Metzenbaum, D-Ohio, and Rep. Joseph Gaydos, D-Pa., support legislation known as the "High Risk Occupational Disease Notification Act of 1987."

It emphasizes after-the-fact notification of exposure to hazardous workplace substances, rather than prevention. It also steps back 20 years to the days when the panacea for all problems was creating a new government agency.

And that's exactly what it would do—create a new multimillion-dollar federal agency, a "Risk Assessment Board" within the Department of Health and Human Services.

The occupational disease bill's sponsors apparently believe that this seven-member board would be more skilled and able than the thousands of employees now working for the Occupational Safety and Health Administration. They are wrong. OSHA was founded in 1970 for the very purpose of protecting worker safety and health. And many other agencies buttress OSHA's protective efforts.

Has the agency been slow to act in some cases, as labor claims? You certainly wouldn't know it from the statistics associated with the Hazard Communication Standard, the most comprehensive chemical safety program ever instituted. The standard, which went into effect only one year ago, requires employers to notify and train workers about the hazards they work with. And OSHA is enforcing it. Already 22,369 violations have been cited by OSHA as industry attempts to grapple with the standard's extensive requirements.

In addition to creating a superfluous new bureaucracy and adding billions of dollars to the cost of doing business, what would the proposed occupational disease legislation do to make workers healthier? Not much.

SOURCE: Reprinted by permission of the National Association of Manufacturers. Reprinted from the *Mobile Register*, August 12, 1987.

The bills require notification of not only current but also former workers who the board believes may be at risk of developing a disease.

Industry isn't opposed to notification. But this kind goes too far. Unwarranted notices are likely to cause panic among employees. Health or life insurance may become impossible to get once notification occurs. And finally, employers are bound to be sued by healthy employees, despite employers' full compliance with the law.

We're not just crying wolf. A pilot notification program conducted in 1980 by the National Institute on Occupational Safety and Health resulted in more than $335 million in lawsuits filed against just one company—with only 849 employees! The company's stock plummeted and it eventually went bankrupt.

If you take that example and extrapolate it to today's workforce, we could end up with as much as $8.6 trillion in lawsuits under the proposed legislation. Do we want American businesses in the courtroom defending notified workers' unwarranted claims for "stress"? Think of what such action could do to our ability to be competitive!

A few companies, fearing that an even worse bill might pass, have endorsed this approach. But the vast majority of the business community, small and large, agree that the Metzenbaum-Gaydos labor bill adds needless burdens and few benefits.

There must be a better way to ensure our workers' health and safety. And there is! Reps. Jim Jeffords, R-Vt., and Paul Henry, R-Mich., have embraced a preventive approach that makes sense. By expanding existing OSHA regulations, their bill emphasizes training and educating workers to prevent hazardous exposures before they occur.

It would require employees to be notified of a hazard if there has been a government study that shows those employees are at risk. And it would mandate a study to determine the impact of this notification on the courts and the workers' compensation system, before haphazardly creating a new, costly program.

The Henry-Jeffords bill requires industry to spend its money on prevention. That's why we support it. The Metzenbaum-Gaydos bill wastes money on new agencies and after-the-exposure notification. That's why we oppose it.

NFL OWNERS
HAVE RIGHTS, TOO

BOB ROESLER

George Young calls it "the Jaguar, second-car strike." The players, Young says, already drive a Porsche and have Jeeps or Broncos for leisure tooling about.

Now they need money for that second car, so they're walking the picket line.

Young, vice president and general manager of the Giants, was being facetious. But he's no clown. He once taught political science and holds a master's degree from Johns Hopkins.

He is right. The union is talking about unfettered free agency, but most players, in my view, are more interested in money issues.

That's fine. Every working stiff deserves as much as he can get from his boss.

Which brings me to my point of view.

If it is reasonable for Brian Bosworth to negotiate an $11 million contract and Jim Kelly, Joe Montana, Bernie Kosar, Dan Marino, Herschel Walker to have $1 million-plus base salaries and Bo Jackson can sign for a $1.4 million bonus, shouldn't an owner expect a fair profit?

Often when speaking to a player, he will say, what the hell, Team A made $2 million. For heaven's sake! Does the union believe it is a sin for a team to make money, but the sky's the limit on player salaries?

Yes, I've heard all the rhetoric: "We are the game."

I've covered all four NFL strikes and listened to all that malarky. Some owners plead poverty, which is a bunch of baloney. And the players shout, "No freedom, no football."

No freedom, hah! The Boz is an unchained wage slave. Bo Jackson should have been given $2.8 million to have fun between baseball seasons? Sorry, Gene Upshaw. Sorry, Ed Garvey. I can't buy that pile of buffalo whiskers.

The more I listen to Upshaw, the more I find myself much more sympathetic toward the owners.

Please understand, I'd rather have a root beer with Billy Kilmer, Elo Grooms, Danny Abramowicz, Manny Zanders or Derland Moore than share a bottle of Chateau Lafite-Rothschild with most NFL owners.

Still, I believe an owner has a right to protect his investment and enjoy a profit. Isn't that the American way, too?

Let's look at the finances, as best an outsider can. In 1986 the average total revenue for each club was between $25 million-$30 million. That is a ballpark figure. But I had that figure triple-sourced and believe it to be accurate.

Out of that came $17 million for what management calls "player-related costs," for bonuses, salaries, pensions and other benefits."

SOURCE: Reprinted by permission from the *New Orleans Times-Picayune*, September 25, 1987.

When all other expenses were paid, operations, travel, nonplayer salaries, etc., owners averaged between $1 and $2 million in profits.

A half-dozen or so teams finished in the red. One owner, who asked not to be identified, said he "barely, barely got into the black" in 1986 after losing "multiple millions" in years immediately after the last strike. The USFL's brief appearance also sent salaries soaring.

An investment specialist told me that corporations like Procter & Gamble and DuPont won't make investments unless there is a possibility of 15 or 18 percent profits. NFL owners do well to get 2 percent return on their investment.

Owners, I'm told, are offering a pension proposal that seems fair. A five-year veteran would receive $4,730 per month when he reaches 60. The union said no, make it at age 40.

Which brings up another irritating point. Upshaw and his officers bemoan the fact that the average career of a player is only three-plus years. Management says, toss out those who don't last beyond their rookie year and the athlete's lifespan is 6.7 years.

Whatever it is, I can't understand the union. They act as if once a player's football days are over, he is helpless to work in the outside world. Are you and I to believe that pro football should provide financial security when an ex-player reaches 30? And pension him handsomely until he dies 45 years later?

There is another bothersome NFLPA point. They talk about free agency and how, under present rules, there has been virtually no movement. They claim that the compensation clause keeps teams from bidding for players whose contracts have expired.

The lack of movement, the union says, prevents players from making bigger bucks. They point to baseball, where players are making megabucks for moving about. What isn't mentioned is that baseball is spending itself into the poorhouse. And that's no bull.

Did you know that 27 percent of salaries being paid in baseball right now go to players no longer in the game? That's guaranteed money given stars who have fizzled.

That's great for the athlete, but dangerous for the owners and the sport's financial stability.

Another thing, how badly would a prolonged strike hurt owners such as Billy Sullivan, Joe Robbie and Tom Benson? Sullivan, financially strapped in Foxboro, could lose his Patriots. Robbie is opening his new stadium and needs to keep the cash flowing in Miami.

So does Benson, who paid John Mecom too much for the team, but had to or they would now be the Jacksonville Saints.

Yes, owners are not without blame. But ask people on the street and you'll find about 80 percent of them blame the players.

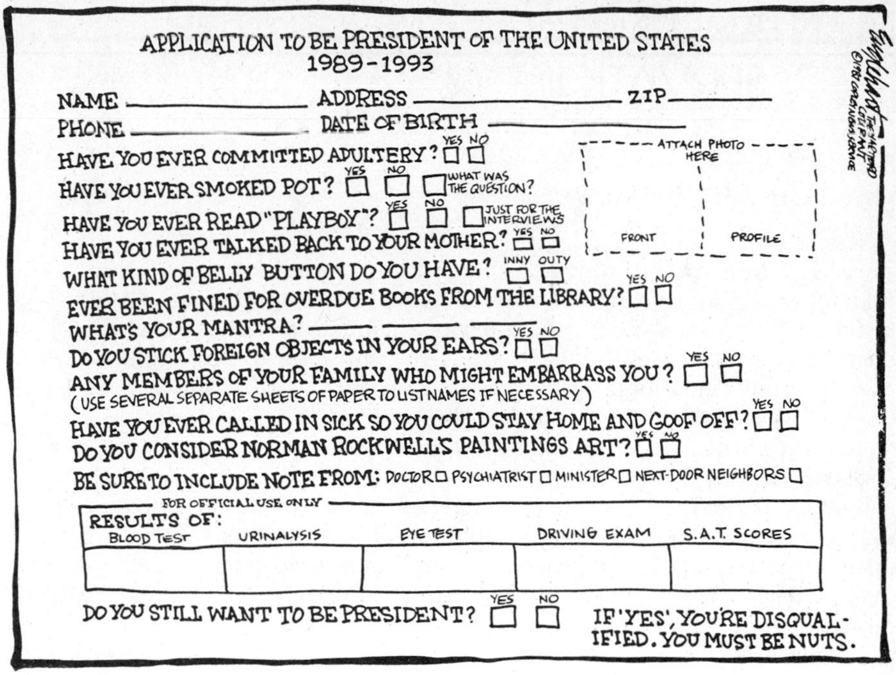

Courtesy of Bob Englehart and Copley News Service.

MAN AND NATURE—
A PRESERVATION

R. JOHNSON
Vegetarian Liberation Organization

There is a force in this universe that guides us into a realm of true understanding and begifts us with a viable realization of peace and beauty. Within its domain, there exists an innate sense of unity that deepens the correlation between ourselves and nature. The Human race—we must not forget—was placed into this creation much after its origin and set into a world filled with potential self-sufficiency.

The kindness of NATURE has gently protected and nourished our ancestry as well as ourselves. Modern man has realized many ideals in achieving a consistency of self-sufficiency and has learned a reliance on synthetic options which protects our natural environment in turn. It is essential in these days of progress to maintain a closely guarded watch over Mother Nature. She has cared greatly for each of our lives and has offered sweet EDEN without a need to destroy.

From fluorocarbons to plutonium, we have invaded the essential rights of nature. We have violated a sacred trust by prostituting the fundamental elements that keep our very existence intact. An overwhelming majority disapprove of these absurdities yet they do not dissuade the invasion on our simple freedom to survive.

We are animals—an intricate fiber in this cradle of existence. With great deserve we have accepted the intellect of a freeing race; the sensitivity of Appreciators of life; the skill of leadership among our animal brethren; and the gentle ability to always live in harmony. There is NO NEED—essential or convenient—to prey upon *any* life in order to satisfy our own insufficiencies.

The abuse of animals should not be permitted or tolerated. In any form, this is a violation of our own rights. Too often "justification" is nurtured by inane rationalizations viewing experimentation in laboratory settings as something positive and beneficial. This thought is a FARCE . . .A BOGUS ATTEMPT TO COMPLY WITH APATHY. . .DO NOT SURRENDER UNTO IT! Speak against the malconceived notions that allow this abuse to continue. Respect Mama Nature and love her as faithfully as she has loved you. Touch her with the hand of kindness and she will touch you with her warm sun and loving rain.

SOURCE: Reprinted by permission of the author.

A SMOKE-FREE
SOCIETY

REP. THOMAS A. LUKEN

The time has come for Congress to declare an objective of a smoke-free society. We will not achieve that goal until the tobacco companies are held legally responsible for their misdeeds.

When a deceased smoker's family sues a tobacco company for wrongful death, they encounter a legal shield of immunity protecting the cigarette company. Congress created that protective armor for the tobacco industry when it passed the Federal Cigarette Labeling and Advertising Act in 1965. Under that law the courts have said that a tobacco company can issue blatantly false and deceptive advertising, and then be absolved of liability by placing a warning label on the cigarette package.

Yet no other industry—not even "smokeless tobacco" products such as snuff and chewing tobacco—enjoys such a shield.

If cigarette advertisements are required to comply with the same standards for truthfulness as other industries (as provided in my bill, the Cigarette Testing and Liability Act of 1988, H. R. 4543), then, and only then, will they be held responsible for false claims in advertising.

Cigarettes are the most dangerous product sold in the United States. The Surgeon General of the United States says that 320,000 Americans die each year from smoking. By comparison, only about 4,000 Americans die each year from cocaine and heroin. In addition to causing these 320,000 deaths each year, smoking-related diseases, according to the United States Office of Technology Assessment, cost $65 billion in extra medical costs and loss of productivity each year.

My bill is supported by the American Medical Association, the American Heart Association, the American Cancer Society, the American Lung Association, Consumers Union, and the Washington Business Group on Health (whose members include more than 200 of the country's largest companies).

The absurdity of the current situation for cigarette advertisements is illustrated by the recent trial in New Jersey where a federal jury awarded Antonio Cipollone $400,000 in damages because of his wife's death in 1984. Rose Cipollone began smoking Liggett & Myers' cigarettes in 1941. In 1968 she switched to a Philip Morris brand. In 1974 she began smoking a Lorillard brand. The jury found that her death from lung cancer in 1984 was caused by smoking. However, while the jury found Liggett & Myers was responsible for her death, Philip Morris and Lorillard were held not responsible because she didn't smoke their cigarettes before 1966.

My bill would also make it clear that state and local governments can use their traditional power to protect the health of their citizens by regulating cigarettes in the same way they regulate other products. The

SOURCE: Reprinted from the *Mobile Register*, June 29, 1988. Reprinted by permission of author.

need for such granting of authority to the states was highlighted when witnesses at a recent hearing told us that cigarette companies have warned local governments that they cannot pass laws prohibiting the distribution of free cigarette samples. Many state and local governments desire to ban free cigarette samples as a means of preventing juveniles from obtaining these harmful products in this manner. We also heard testimony that the cigarette companies told the Maine legislature that under federal law Maine could not restrict advertising of cigarettes in connection with children's skiing events.

If my bill does not pass, it will be a testament to the wealth and power of the tobacco industry. In 1985, the last year for which figures are available, the cigarette industry earned profits of $3.45 billion. In 1986 the cigarette industry spent $2.4 billion advertising and promoting cigarettes. The tobacco companies are reported to have spent $50 million just in defending the New Jersey lawsuit involving Mrs. Cipollone.

Yet, in our system of government the voters are more powerful. I urge you to let your congressman and senators know whether you think the tobacco companies should be held responsible when smokers die after they have been lulled into a false sense of security as a result of false and deceptive cigarette advertising.

PART THREE

EIGHT RULES FOR GOOD WRITING

What matters is that we get done
what we have to do and get said what
we have to say.
—*Donald J. Lloyd*

The following pages will show you how to write clear, straightforward prose. This is the language you would use in explaining a situation or arguing an issue. It expresses itself in a direct, informal style.

There are other styles of writing. For an inaugural address or a theological essay, you would want a more formal, balanced presentation. For an emotional appeal or an angry condemnation, you may want a more colloquial style. But such occasions are rare. The informal style recommended here will serve you in almost all writing situations. You can use it to propose marriage, explain entropy, or plead not guilty.

The eight rules that follow should make you a better writer. They offer material you need to know, and they omit areas you don't need to worry about. The intent is practical—not to tell you about "good writing," but to show you how to do it.

These rules will be sufficient for most people on most writing occasions. The weak student who cannot recognize a sentence and does not know that a period goes at the end of it will need additional help; so will the refined writer who seeks a singular style. Nevertheless, the rules can help most people become fluent, correct, and effective writers.

RULE 1

Find a Subject You Can Work With

Choosing a subject is one of the hardest parts of writing, and perhaps the most important. In many writing situations, of course, you do not have to choose a topic. You want to write the power company protesting the latest rate hike. You have to send a thank-you letter to your aunt. Your boss asks you to prepare a marketing report. In these cases the subject is there, and you have to tell a particular audience about it.

Still, there are occasions when you select a topic for an essay or speech, and there are times when you might be given a general subject ("The American Dream" or "Tomorrow's Promise") but can approach it in a number of ways. You need to recognize the problems in making a choice.

To produce a good essay, you need a topic that will interest your audience, that lends itself to detail, and that can be covered in a prescribed number of words. (The point here will be clearer if you recall the last dull sermon you heard.)

If you were assigned to write a 500-word theme for a general audience (think of the people you see around you in class or at a movie), how good would these topics be?

1. "Death Awaits All Men"   Unless you are going to write of something unusual—an exploding sun, the bloody prophecies of Revelation, or the mathematics of entropy—this will be a boring subject. When you write of "all men," you tend to say what everyone knows.

2. "My Brother, the Practical Joker"   This topic concerns an individual rather than all men. The experience, however, is pretty close to that of all men. Most people have met practical jokers. Unless your brother's jokes are particularly brilliant or outrageous, you would do better with a different subject.

3. "I Am Sure I Have Pierced Ears"   This subject does not lend itself to detail. What can you write after the first sentence? Why should anyone be interested?

Remember that everything you write—every essay, every paragraph, every sentence—has to answer the question "Who cares?"

4. *"The Sun Also Rises*—Hemingway's Masterpiece" This topic is interesting and rich with detail, but it is more suitable to a 300-page book than a 500-word theme. If you wish to write on a novel, you must restrict yourself to one feature of it. Here you could limit yourself to one character ("Robert Cohn—the Outsider") or to one fairly defined theme ("Fishing in Spain—a Symbolic Quest"). Remember that, almost invariably, you will choose a subject that's too broad rather than one that's too narrow.

5. "Hank Aaron Was a Better Hitter Than Babe Ruth" This could be a good choice. The subject would interest many readers. It provides a lot of detail—comparison of number of times at bat, number of hits, quality of opposing pitchers, the kinds of baseballs used, sizes of stadiums, and so on. If you keep the focus on batting and avoid discussions of fielding, base running, and personality, the theme can be finished in 500 words.

Another element that makes this a good subject is that it presents a minority opinion. This always adds interest. "Cleanliness Is Important" is a vague truism, but "Cleanliness Is Dangerous" could make a fascinating theme.

6. "How to Clean a Bassoon" This subject lends itself to detail; it can be covered in 500 words; and it is beyond the experience of "all men." But it would have little appeal for most readers.

Of course, if you're a knowledgeable and creative writer (like Tom Wolfe), you can make any subject interesting. And you can imagine particular readers (like your mother) who would respond to any topic you chose. But these exceptions don't change the situation for you. You need a subject that will keep the interest of a fairly general audience.

Probably, you should write on the subjects you know most about and are most interested in. What do you think about? What do you and your friends talk about every day? This is what you'll write best about.

EXERCISES

Which of these subjects would be more likely to produce an acceptable 500-word theme? Why?

1. The Virtue of Thrift
2. Space Travel Will Have a Drastic Effect on Contemporary Art
3. A Sure Way to Pick Winners at the Dog Track
4. The Importance of a College Education
5. Tennis Balls
6. My Brother Collects Green Stamps
7. Dogs Are Better Than Cats
8. Drag Racing Cars Perform Mathematically Impossible Feats
9. Robert Redford
10. Aspirin, Bufferin, Anacin—Somebody's Lying
11. The World Is Ending: Prophecy, Weaponry, and Ecology
12. My Family's Vacation at the Gulf

RULE 2

Get Your Facts

An interesting theme has to be specific. No one can write a compelling essay on entropy or Hank Aaron or space-age architecture or much else without seeking out a body of factual information. Writing involves research.

Unless you are writing from personal experience, you will probably want to build your theme around people you can quote and facts you can bring forward. You obtain such material from a number of sources.

VISIT THE LIBRARY

Large stores of information can be unearthed by using the card catalog and the *Reader's Guide.* The card catalog, which may be computerized, lists author, title, and subject for every book in the library. The *Reader's Guide,* under subject headings, lists magazine articles printed over the years. (You can find the magazines in the periodicals section or on microfilm.)

This list illustrates some of the titles available to you and the kinds of information they contain.

Acronyms and Initialisms Dictionary
   (What is the NAFGDA?)
American Movies Reference Book
   (Who won the Academy Award as Best Supporting Actor in 1966?)
Bartlett's Familiar Quotations
   (Who said, "A reformer is a guy who rides through the sewer in a glass-bottomed boat"?)
Baseball Encyclopedia
   (Who was the only major league pitcher to pitch two consecutive no-hit games?)
Benet's *Reader's Encyclopedia*
   (Who is the hero of Henry James's *The American?*)

Black's Law Dictionary
   (What is the Miranda rule?)
Book Review Digest
   (When David Garnett's *Shot in the Dark* was published in 1959, how did
   critics react to it?)
College Handbook
   (What is the ratio of male to female students at Loras College?)
Crime in the United States (The FBI Report)
   (How many aggravated assaults were reported in Madison, Wisconsin,
   in 1985?)
Current Biography
   (Name the two daughters of jazzman Chuck Mangione.)
Cyclopedia of Literary Characters
   (Name the Three Musketeers.)
Dictionary of American History
   (Who founded the NAACP? When?)
Dictionary of American Slang
   (What is a "hodad"?)
Dictionary of Classical Mythology
   (Who is Aemonides?)
Dictionary of Foreign Terms
   (What does *ignis fatuus* mean?)
Encyclopedia of the Opera
   (Why couldn't Hoffmann wed his beloved Olympia?)
Facts on File
   (Why was New York Police Chief John Egan sent to prison in 1974?)
Famous First Facts
   (Who received the first kidney transplant?)
Funk's *Word Origins and Their Romantic Stories*
   (What is the source of the word *tantalize*?)
Gallup Poll
   (In 1977, what percentage of Americans believed that homosexuality
   is a condition some people are born with?)
Gray's Anatomy
   (If you strain the muscles of your thenar eminence, where do you
   hurt?)
Guinness Book of World Records
   (How long was the world's longest hot dog?)
International Who's Who
   (Who is Gaetano Cortesi?)
Interpreter's Bible
   (What did Jesus mean when he said it is easier for a camel to go
   through the eye of a needle than for a rich man to enter the kingdom
   of God?)
McGraw-Hill Encyclopedia of Science and Technology
   (What are the characteristics of synthetic graphite?)
Menke's *Encyclopedia of Sport*
   (What golfer and what score won the U.S. Open in 1963?)

Mirkin's *When Did It Happen?*
   (Name two famous composers born on May 7.)
The Murderers' Who's Who
   (How did an earlobe figure in the "death" of murderer Charles Henry
   Schwartz?)
Oxford Companion to Music
   (What is the Impressionist School of music?)
Oxford English Dictionary
   (When was the word *fair* first used to mean "average"?)
Prager Encyclopedia of Art
   (What is the real name of the painting usually called *Whistler's Mother*?)
Rock Encyclopedia
   (Who was the lead singer in the original Jeff Beck Group?)
Statistical Abstract of the United States
   (How many American women used poison to commit suicide in 1976?)
Telephone Directory (any large city)
   (If you want tickets to a Chicago White Sox game, where should you
   write? What 800 number can you call?)
The Way Things Work
   (Why doesn't the ink leak out of your ballpoint pen?)
Webster's Biographical Dictionary
   (What is Mary McCauley's better-known name? Why is she famous?)
Webster's Dictionary of Proper Names
   (When and what was the Chicken War?)
Webster's Geographical Dictionary
   (In what country and state is Black River Falls?)
Who's Who in American Women
   (What is Linda Ronstadt's birthday?)
World Almanac
   (Name the junior senator from Oregon. What is the capacity of the
   Notre Dame stadium?)
World Encyclopedia of the Comics
   (What was Blondie's maiden name?)

Also, make particular use of the *New York Times Index.* This gives you
references to names mentioned in that information-packed newspaper. Many
libraries have microfilm collections of the *Times* dating back to the 1890s.
Learn to thread the microfilm projector, and you can have a fine time reading
how Red Grange scored four touchdowns in ten minutes or how Neil Arm-
strong walked on the moon.

You will need all these sources to provide facts for your essays. And don't
be afraid to ask for help in the library. Most librarians are nice people.

USE YOUR TELEPHONE

Libraries employ reference people who spend a good part of every day answering questions over the phone. If you need to know Babe Ruth's batting
average in 1928, you can either find the answer in a baseball almanac or phone

your local reference librarian, who will look up the information and call you back.

You can phone others too. If you need to know whether there is an apostrophe in "Diners Club," call an elegant restaurant and ask the cashier. If you have a brief legal question ("What would it cost to change my name?"), phone a lawyer. If you need to know the current price for wastepaper, call a junkyard. For specific information, don't be afraid to call a priest or banker or news reporter or sheriff or insurance agent. Most of these people are willing to help you, and many will be happy to.

When you need to, don't hesitate to call long-distance. Suppose you have to write to "Leslie Johnson" and don't know if the person is male or female. Suppose you're writing to a personnel manager and don't know the manager's name. In such cases, call long-distance and get the information you need. These calls are relatively cheap.

It helps to have a WATS line or to know someone who has access to a WATS line. Think about this when you're making new friends.

WRITE FOR FACTS YOU NEED

Many sources are available to you. U.S. government agencies will send you documents on a range of subjects. Organizations with a message will send you stacks of literature. (Both the American Cancer Society and the Tobacco Institute have dozens of pamphlets on smoking and health.) You can base your writing on materials from Common Cause, the National Rifle Association, the Confraternity of Christian Doctrine, the Non-Sectarian Committee for Life, the Moral Majority, the National Organization for Women, People for the American Way, and similar groups. (When the National Rifle Association was asked to send material that might appear in this book, they responded with a letter that weighed 3½ pounds.)

Two sources deserve special mention. If you want the script of a particular news program, say, *60 Minutes,* write and the network will send you a copy. For anything related to new laws, politics, or government programs, write your senators or representative. You will *always* get an answer from a member of Congress.

If you make the effort, you will find plenty of information to give meaning and interest to your argument.

Warning: Get your facts right. Factual errors in your writing are just like spelling and punctuation errors. They make you look ignorant or careless. In persuasive writing, they are fatal.

EXERCISES

Use your library and other sources to locate the following information.

1. What was the front-page headline in the *New York Times* on the day you were born?

2. What is the source of these lines?
   a. "Watchman, what of the night?"
   b. "When in doubt, punt."
3. What causes blue babies?
4. Name the individuals who won more than one Academy Award, Cy Young Award, and Heisman Trophy.
5. What day of the week was June 16, 1904? Why is that day important in English literature?
6. What was the famous crime involving Winnie Ruth Judd?
7. What does *in gremio legis* mean?
8. Why didn't Hoffmann wed his beloved Olympia?
9. Name six performers who appeared in the movie *George Washington Slept Here.*
10. What is meant by "filial regression," "blood-packing," "sophomania," and "lycanthropy"?
11. Identify as many of these as you can:
    Sir Andrew Aguecheek
    Asiatic Annie
    Allan Paul Bakke
    Melvin Belli
    Suzette Charles
    Denton Cooley
    Pete and Frank Gusenberg
    Nile Kinnick
    Nathan F. Leopold, Jr.
    Greg Louganis
    Captain Midnight
    Donald T. Regan
    Django Reinhardt
    Christopher Robin
    Broadway Danny Rose
    Daley Thompson
    Tommy Tittlemouse
    Uriah the Hittite
    Johnny Vander Meer
    Sigourney Weaver
    John A. Zaccaro
    Pinchas Zukerman

ALTERNATE EXERCISES

Use your library and other sources to locate the following information.

1. What were two of the leading sports stories in the *New York Times* on the day you were born?

2. What is the source of these lines?
   a. "Hold the fort, I am coming."
   b. "I begin to smell a rat."
3. Name the victims of Jack the Ripper.
4. Give ten words that rhyme with "aggle."
5. In *Cavalleria Rusticana,* who kills Turiddu and why?
6. Give the complete major league batting record of Ernest William Rudolph.
7. How many aggravated assaults were reported in Milwaukee, Wisconsin, in 1985?
8. Give the source of the words *buxom, cravat, sabotage,* and *vermouth.*
9. What movie stars played *The Duke of West Point* and *The Duchess of Idaho?*
10. Distinguish between *Chapter Two,* Leo II, *Walden Two,* and helium II.
11. Identify as many of these as you can.

> Kathy Boudin
> William H. Bonney
> Reginald Bunthorne
> Hilda Doolittle
> Morgan Fairchild
> Doctor Fell
> Louis Farrakhan
> Uri Geller
> Bruno Hauptmann
> James Huberty
> Meadowlark Lemon
> Ed "Stranger" Lewis
> Marian McPartland
> Mercutio
> Professor Moriarty
> Linus Pauling
> Sneaky Pete
> Raina Petkoff
> Baron Scarpia
> Frank Sinkwich
> Uncas
> Frank Urban Zoeller

RULE 3

Limit Your Topic to Manageable Size

Most writing is subject to space and time limitations. You are preparing a magazine advertisement or a campaign document (one page). You are writing an editorial or a letter to the editor (under 1000 words). You are preparing a sermon or an after-dinner speech (20 minutes or less). Rarely will you have an opportunity that will permit, or an audience that will tolerate, a discussion of all aspects of an issue.

Therefore, you must limit your topic. Do not, for example, write about "Dieting." Even "Crash Dieting" is too broad a subject. But you can argue that "Crash Dieting Is Dangerous." Similarly, do not speculate about "America's Unjust Drug Laws"; write "Alabama's Marijuana Laws Violate the Fifth Amendment."

Narrowing a topic is particularly important when you write argument. A vague and rambling essay is never persuasive.

Don't write an "about" theme—that is, a general theme about fishing, about communism, about heart disease, or about love and death. These aren't helped by bland titles like "The Joys of Fishing" or "The Truth about Communism." Such unfocused subjects lend themselves to vague generalizations. They produce themes that lack unity, coherence, and interest.

Your essay is probably unfocused if it discusses unnamed or hypothetical people, such as "students," "Cora Crazy," "Tom J.," or "a doctor in Florida." When you find yourself writing "some people" or "in life," you can be sure you're in trouble.

You probably shouldn't write about your most serious and profound feelings. You can have a wonderful love and dedication for your father, your spouse, your baby, or your dog. You can have a warm and genuine commitment to God or to democracy. But when you write such things on paper, they turn into clichés. The way you love your baby is the way other people love their babies. It's something everyone already knows about. So it's dull.

Jesus was too good a teacher simply to tell us to love our neighbor. He focused his message. He talked of the Good Samaritan, the lost sheep, and the Prodigal Son.

A carefully focused theme demands specific detail. You will need these facts if you want to keep your reader awake.

EXERCISES

Limit each of these topics; that is, isolate parts that you can discuss in a 500-word theme.

1. Improving American Education
2. LSD—A Blessing or a Curse?
3. The Assassination of John Lennon
4. Women in Politics
5. Jim and Tammy Bakker
6. God in Everyday Life
7. Traffic Signs
8. Travel Is Educational
9. Current Slang
10. Extrasensory Perception
11. Situation Ethics
12. Animals Can Talk
13. Cocaine

RULE 4

Organize Your Material

Most essays—and indeed most reports and business letters—are made up of an *introduction,* a *body,* and a *conclusion.* The introduction says, "I am going to write about X." The body discusses X in some organized way. And the conclusion says, "That's what I have to say about X." Good writers keep this pattern from being too obvious, but this is the pattern they use.

THE INTRODUCTION

The purpose of the introduction is to catch the reader's attention, to declare your subject, and sometimes to outline the direction of your essay.

The best way to get the reader's interest is to announce your subject and get on with it. You can, of course, try a witty opening ("If my brother had two more IQ points, he would be a tree") or a dramatic one ("I know who killed Jimmy Hoffa"); these might work for you. If you are not confident about such lines, however, it is best to rely on a straightforward opening.

Just say it. Write, "America can't afford nuclear power" or *"Dallas* has all the characteristics of a morality play." Then get on proving your point.

Although you may not seek a dramatic opening line, you should try to avoid sentences that turn off your reader. If you begin your essay by saying, "Time is the auction block of the world" or "My brother collects Green Stamps," it probably doesn't make much difference what you write afterward. Nobody will be reading it.

The line in your opening paragraph that announces the main idea or purpose of your theme is called the *thesis statement.* You may include another sentence with it, giving a general outline the essay will follow.

Most topics can be divided into parts. Your essay praising Joe DiMaggio might discuss his fielding, base running, and hitting. Your argument against abortion might describe the growth of the fetus month by month. Your

265

analysis of a physical or social problem (lung cancer, skyjacking, etc.) might first describe the effect, then indicate some probable causes.

See how these introductions announce the outline of the essay:

> There can be no doubt that extrasensory perception exists. How else can one explain the results of the Spranches-Malone experiment conducted at UCLA in 1975?
> [The theme will discuss the experiment.]

> Legal abortion is necessary. Otherwise we will be back with vast numbers of women getting amateur surgery in bloody abortion mills.
> [The theme will discuss earlier years: (1) vast numbers of women and (2) bloody surgery.]

> The only way to stop inflation is to raise taxes and impose wage and price controls, but I don't think the president has the courage to support these measures.
> [The theme will cover (1) anti-inflation measures—a tax raise and wage and price controls—and (2) presidential courage.]

Keep your introductions short.

THE BODY

The introduction and conclusion are little more than a frame surrounding what you have to say. The paragraphs of the body *are* your essay.

Each paragraph presents a unit of your message. This does not mean that each division of your topic, as announced in the introduction, must be covered in one paragraph. In the anti-inflation theme just introduced, your discussion of wage and price controls might take two, three, or six paragraphs.

Just as the introduction has a thesis statement announcing what the whole theme is about, so most paragraphs have *topic sentences* telling what they will cover. Usually this is the first sentence. Because they show exactly what the rest of the paragraph will discuss, these are effective topic sentences:

> These gun laws haven't reduced the crime in Cleveland.
> Why did the price of electricity go up in July?
> Consider what the human fetus can do in the third month.
> Secretary Shultz was equally unsuccessful with the Italians.

Your paragraph should not bring in material beyond the scope of the topic sentence. In the paragraph about gun laws in Cleveland, for example, you should not discuss other crime-fighting measures in Cleveland; you should not mention crime in Detroit.

Topic sentences are effective in linking paragraphs. In the examples given, the references to *"these* gun laws" and to Secretary Shultz's being *"equally* unsuccessful" show a relation to material in previous paragraphs. Words like *therefore, however, such, second,* and *similarly* have the same effect.

Within each paragraph, try to give the sentences the same grammatical subject. (In the paragraph on Secretary Shultz, the subject of most of the sentences should be "he" or "Shultz" or "the Secretary.") If you vary the kinds of sentences, as in the following example, the practice should not seem monotonous.

> A variation popular with *sensational writers* is to make an extravagant claim and then point to conclusive evidence—which happens to be unavailable. *They* argue that superbeings from outer space built Stonehenge and that President Warren G. Harding was murdered by his wife; then *they* regret that evidence is lost in the past. *They* talk confidently about bigfoot, Atlantis, and the Loch Ness Monster—and then lament that proof remains out of reach. *They* insist that UFOs are extraterrestrial spaceships and that a massive conspiracy led to the attempted assassinations of President Reagan and Pope John Paul II—then *they* protest that government officials and law enforcement agencies are withholding crucial evidence.

Remember that the grammatical subject is not necessarily the first word of a sentence. It may follow an introductory phrase ("After the dance, *he* . . .") or clause ("When Kathy remembered the accident, *she* . . .").

In some paragraphs, keeping the same subject will prevent you from saying what you want. Or it can make your writing seem stilted and artificial. In such cases, don't do it.

Here's an important point. *Avoid long paragraphs.* Part of writing well is making someone else want to read your work, and people are turned off when they face long, block, single-spaced paragraphs. (Think how you feel beginning a chapter in your sociology textbook.) Make use of short paragraphs, headings, blank space between sections, indented material, and similar devices to make your ideas easy to read. *Write with white space.* (Notice how material is laid out on these pages.)

When in doubt about whether to begin a new paragraph, always begin the paragraph.

THE CONCLUSION

The last paragraph of your essay echoes the introduction. It summarizes and generalizes about the subject discussed.

Unless your paper is long or particularly complicated, you do not need to restate the structural outline. ("In this theme, I have discussed first the language of Mark's gospel, then its historical qualities, and finally its theology.") Instead, just give a sentence or two expressing the main point. Here are some acceptable concluding paragraphs:

> Mark's gospel is more like a sermon than a biography. It is a work of profound faith and impressive artistry.

> No one favors abortion. But we have to admit that, in many cases, it is the only humane alternative.

The Spranches-Malone experiment proves conclusively that ESP exists. Now we have to figure out what we can do with it.

Keep your conclusions short.

EXERCISE

Discuss the strengths and weaknesses of this essay. Consider the thesis statement, the topic sentences, transitions between paragraphs, keeping the same subject within a paragraph, unity of a paragraph, and so on.

POETRY

All my life I have hated poetry. I hated it in high school, in grade school, and in the sophomore poetry course I've just completed here at South Alabama. Why we serious students have to study jingled nonsense, I will never know.

I live in Reedsburg, a community of farmers, merchants, and practical people. Nevertheless, the Reedsburg Grade School subjected me to all sorts of frivolous and impractical poetry. From the first grade on, my class endured semester after semester of cute rhyme. We read teddy-bear poems from *Winnie the Pooh.* We read Mother Goose rhymes about Simple Simon, and Robert Louis Stevenson poems about a "friendly cow all red and white." We read jingles telling us to drink our milk. I always wonder why the poets didn't just *say* things instead of chanting and jingling them. It was silly.

I had some poetry in Reedsburg High School too. However, I escaped much of it by signing up for speech classes. In speech, I studied more sensible subjects. I learned to think on my feet. I learned to make a talk interesting by referring to the audience and adding humor. Most important, I learned to say things directly, without all the cute ornament of poetry.

The sophomore poetry class I've just finished at South Alabama has only made me dislike poems more. Mr. Remington, my instructor, was incompetent. The way he read them, all poems sounded just alike. When he wasn't mumbling about Shelley, we were taking impossible tests on Keats and nightingales. Either it was assumed we knew everything about epics or he was talking down to the class as though we had never heard of metaphor. The day before the final exam, he didn't even show up for class. The whole quarter was a waste of time.

In fact, all the poetry discussions I've had from grade school up to now have been a waste of time. I just don't like poetry.

RULE 5

Make Your Writing Interesting

Remember that no one *has* to read your writing. And if people have to hear your speech, they don't have to pay attention. The burden is on you to make your subject interesting.

This is not a huge task. If you have a topic you think is important, and if you present it with clarity and specific detail, your reader or listener will be interested.

Generally, you maintain interest by avoiding certain practices that deaden language.

TRUISMS

Do not say what everyone knows. Don't be like actress Brooke Shields, who told a congressional subcommittee, "Smoking can kill you. And if you've been killed, you've lost a very important part of your life."

Your readers will not be thrilled to hear that third-degree burns are painful or that the president of the United States bears great responsibilities. Don't write, "Every great man has moments of profound sorrow, but Thomas Eaton's life was genuinely tragic." Write, "Thomas Eaton's life was tragic."

CLICHÉS

Some phrases have lost meaning through overuse. Your writing will lose emphasis and interest if you use tired phrases like these:

    acid test
    and . . . was no exception
    at this point in time
    at your earliest convenience
    beginner's luck

bite the bullet
bottom line
constructive criticism
could care less
the cutting edge
down to the wire
few and far between
first and foremost
in a very real sense
an in-depth study
is invaluable
last but not least
let's face it
meaningful relationship
needs no introduction
nitty-gritty
pure and simple
on the other hand
share this idea with you
shot in the arm
slowly but surely
sneaking suspicion
snow job
state of the art
status quo
touch base with
uncanny ability
user-friendly
white elephant
viable alternative

Watch out for emerging clichés—words that were once new and colorful but are now becoming overused. There's a danger in writing about an "awesome" blonde, a "Type-A" personality, or a "Catch-22" situation. The language is losing force even as we speak.

A good rule: If you suspect a particular phrase is a cliché, it is. Avoid it.

Remember that avoiding a cliché can produce a rich substitution. A CBS sports announcer once described a Green Bay quarterback as (not "cool as a cucumber" but) "cool as the other side of the pillow."

GENERALIZED LANGUAGE

The point cannot be overemphasized: *To be interesting, you must be specific.* Let's call this "the Ginger principle." (You'll see why in a minute.)

Write of real things. Use proper names, words that begin with capital letters. (Don't say "lunch"; say "a Big Mac.") Use real numbers. (Don't say "a lot"; say "725.") Give specific places, dates, and quotations. You can, for example, refer to a person in a number of ways:

an athlete
a ball player
a baseball player
an infielder
a third baseman
a Philadelphia third baseman
Mike Schmidt

Always choose the most specific word that serves the purposes of your essay. Good writing uses proper names.

Generally, your ideas will be more interesting if you avoid the words *good, bad,* and forms of *to be.*

Substituted words are almost always more meaningful. Instead of "good," write "even-tempered," "inexpensive," "compassionate," or "crisp." Instead of "bad," write "moldy," "pretentious," "degenerate," or "unfair."

Similarly, try to avoid forms of the verb *to be*—that is, the words *is, are, was, were, am,* and *been.* Much of the time, you will have to use these words, but substitutions are invariably more effective. For example, "Sue Walker *was* injured" becomes "Sue Walker smashed two bones in her right foot." And "The weather *was* horrible" becomes "Eight inches of snow fell on Buffalo yesterday." (Some scholars have designated the English language without *to be* forms as "E-prime.")

To see the degree of interest that specific detail can give a sentence, compare Irving Berlin's lyric "I'll be loving you always" with George Kaufman's suggested emendation, "I'll be loving you Thursday."

The best way to win interest is to force a lot of real names and numbers into your prose. Don't write, "His cousin drove me to a nearby woods, and we sat drinking beer and listening to music until very late." Write, "Ginger drove me over to Johnson's Woods, and we sat in her new Toronado till four in the morning. We drank three six-packs of Coors and listened to her Frank Zappa tapes." Look at the "Ginger" in those sentences. This kind of writing doesn't just tell you of an event, it shows it to you.

Another good rule: *Don't write about nobody.* Look at this infirm passage: "The American public is tired of football. People are bored by all the hype. Every time you turn on your TV set, you see another ad for the Super Bowl." Here, the words "public," "people," and "you" refer to nobody in particular. They express a dull generalization. Write of real people—yourself, Henry Kissinger, or your brother. Write, "Every time *I* turn on my TV set, *I* see another ad for the Super Bowl."

This doesn't mean you can't generalize. It means that when you want to talk about the generation gap, you begin "I can't talk to my mother."

INFLATED LANGUAGE

Except in rare cases, you will want your writing to be clear. To do this, keep your language as simple and direct as possible. When addressing a general audience, try to avoid these forms:

> Foreign words—*bête noir, ne plus ultra, coup d'état*
> Learned words—*penultimate, symbiotic, alumna*
> Poetic words—*repine, oft, betimes*
> Technical words—*input, societal, spousal units*
> Odd singular and plural forms—*datum, stadia, syllabi*
> Literary allusions—*Lot's wife, protean, the sword of Damocles*
> Current in-words—*parameter, viable, ambience*

Such words are more acceptable if you are writing for an educated or specialized audience. But a really fine writer wouldn't use them there either.

Reading William F. Buckley's column in your newspaper can be a useful exercise. You, like almost everyone else, will stop reading early on, probably at his first reference to "biblical irredentism."

Write with everyday words, words you would say. Don't use "in view of the above" or "for the above reasons"; write "consequently" or "for these reasons." Try not to use "the addressee," "the executrix," "the former," or "the latter"; write "Robin Carpenter" (or "she" or "her"). Never refer to yourself as "the writer" (or "we"); say "I."

The next time you hear a dull lecture or sermon, don't tune it out. Ask yourself why it is dull. It is probably dull because it is a collection of truisms, clichés, and vague or inflated phrases. You can learn from such examples.

EXERCISES

Rewrite these sentences. Make them more likely to sustain the interest of a general audience.

1. This insult was the last straw. I decided to leave Marcia, and I spent the next few hours preparing for the trip.
2. The Book of Jonah illustrates the ludicrous intractability of a particular mind-set.
3. Scott Daniel was a fine basketball player. I believe he was the best to play in the league in the last 20 years. He was really fine.
4. Vis-à-vis our tête-à-tête: I must say the rendezvous filled me with ennui.
5. We will never know everything about the atom, but some of the recent discoveries have been fascinating.
6. Driving the L.A. freeway is like crossing the river Styx.
7. In the following weeks at school, I worked frantically. Every day I became busier and busier.
8. As we entered the restaurant, Wade stated that the chicken there was good but the service was bad.
9. Anyone can suffer with a rotten tooth or a sprained thumb, but the man with kidney stones endures a superexcruciating kind of pain.
10. In the final analysis, there are few rugged individualists in this day

and age who are really down to earth in expressing nothing but the truth about the seamy side of life. Perhaps in the near future . . .

11. Salespeople should cultivate a charismatic emphasis to facilitate contractual negotiations on an interpersonal basis.
12. Graduate school can be a procrustean bed.
13. Sorting on the part of mendicants should be interdicted.

Make Your Writing Emphatic

Sometimes unnecessary words or particular word forms detract from the point you want to make. These recommendations should help you emphasize the important ideas in your writing.

AVOID WORDINESS

Unnecessary words may confuse, bore, or antagonize your reader. Say what you have to say as briefly as possible. Too often writers use a series of words where one word will do.

> *am of the opinion that* = believe
> *due to the fact that* = because
> *the man with the dark complexion* = the dark man
> *people who are concerned only with themselves* = selfish people
> *I disagree with the conclusion offered by Professor Lally* = I disagree with Professor Lally

Certain pat phrases have extra words built into them: "end result," "component parts," "advance planning," "large sized," and so on. Omit the extra word.

Some introductory forms can usually be dispensed with:

Needless to say . . .
Let me say that . . .
It is important to recognize the fact that . . .

And commonly one or more words appear where none is necessary.

> Molly *really* is a *very* beautiful girl.
> *Personally,* I agree with him.
> I asked whether *or not* the twins looked alike.

274

I dislike his personality *and his temperament.*
There were several people at the party *who* saw the fight.

Don't worry about wordiness when you're putting together the first draft of your essay; just get down what you have to say. It's in rewriting that you can change "And I think it is necessary to add that Tom wasn't there" to the more forceful phrase "Tom wasn't there."

WRITE IN THE ACTIVE VOICE

In sentences written in the active voice, the grammatical subject is the acting agent. ("*The Brezinsky Commission* has attacked public apathy.") In sentences written in the passive voice, the subject receives the action of the verb. (*"Public apathy* has been attacked by the Brezinsky Commission.")

You can use the passive voice in sentences where the acting agent is obvious or irrelevant ("The president was reelected") or where you want to deliver bad news and avoid personal involvement ("The decision is to buy our supplies from a different source"; "Your contract will not be renewed next year").

The passive voice, however, is generally a bad thing. It doesn't sound natural and seems wordy and evasive. Where you may want particular emphasis, it can produce a mushy effect: "Home runs were hit by both pitchers during the game."

Often, using the active voice means beginning your sentence (or beginning the main clause of your sentence) with acting agents: *we, she, Jim Phillips,* or *the Brezinsky Commission.* This gives force and directness to your prose. Try to avoid forms that keep you from doing this. Here are some examples:

My intention is . . .
It was soon evident that . . .
There were . . .
. . . was seen
. . . could be heard
The assumption was that . . .

If you are writing a personal essay, begin most sentences (or main clauses) with *I.*

Think of the passive voice as you do a visit to the dentist. It's necessary sometimes, but you want to avoid it whenever you can.

EXPRESS YOUR MAIN IDEA IN THE
SUBJECT-VERB OF YOUR SENTENCE

Make the subject-verb unit of your sentence express your main thought. Put less important information in modifying phrases and clauses.

Don't express your main thought as a modifying phrase ("Harold Lord slipped in the outfield, *thus breaking his arm"*) or as a *that* clause ("I learned *that*

Aunt Rita had been arrested for arson"). Give your point subject-verb emphasis: "Harold Lord slipped in the outfield and broke his arm"; "Aunt Rita was arrested for arson."

DO NOT WASTE THE ENDS OF YOUR SENTENCES

Because the end of a sentence is the last thing a reader sees, it is a position of emphasis. Don't use it to express minor thoughts or casual information. Don't write, "Both candidates will speak here in July, if we can believe the reports." This is correct only if you want to stress the doubtfulness of the reports. Don't write, "Pray for the repose of the soul of John Bowler, who died last week in Cleveland." Your reader will wonder what he was doing in Cleveland. Notice how emphasis trails away in a sentence like this:

> The B-1 bomber, a brainchild of the U.S. Air Force and Rockwell International, is trying a comeback as one of America's leading defense weapons after President Carter, in June 1977, put a stop to the plans to complete the project.

For particular emphasis, write your thought in subject-verb form (see previous section) and give the unit an end-of-the-sentence position. Don't write, "The union reluctantly approved the contract." Write, "The union approved the contract, but they didn't want to do it."

Because the beginning of a sentence also conveys a degree of emphasis, you should not waste that position either. Try to put words like "however," "therefore," and "nevertheless" in the middle of sentences. ("The mail carrier, however, arrived at five o'clock.") Don't do this if it makes your sentence sound awkward.

KEEP YOUR SENTENCES RELATIVELY SHORT

To avoid a monotonous style, you should build your essay with sentences of different kinds and lengths. But using short or relatively short sentences will help you avoid difficulties.

When sentences go beyond 15 or 20 words, punctuation—which can be a problem—becomes complicated; meaning gets diffuse; their pronouns are separated from the words they refer to; and the reader or listener finds it difficult to see the continuity and may lose interest. Short sentences are better.

When you finish a sentence of reasonable length, fight the temptation to extend it by adding a unit beginning "which" or "when" or "because" or "according to" or some other "-ing" form. Put that additional material in a new sentence.

If you're typing, try to end your sentence within two lines of type. Only rarely should it go beyond three lines.

EXERCISES

What changes would make the meaning of these sentences more emphatic?

1. I was born in the city of Chicago, Illinois.
2. Trapped in a drab life with a dull husband, Hedda Gabler shoots herself, partly because she is threatened by Judge Brack.
3. The eagle suddenly loosed its grip, allowing me to escape.
4. Though I had more than several reasons to dislike and distrust Libby MacDuffee before the accident, I found still more when she tried to take me to court to pay for the hospital costs and when she claimed I had had three martinis at the Red Oak Bar an hour (or at the most two hours) before the wreck.
5. Reviewing the past history, we found that the team was weak on basic fundamentals and that the average age of the players was 17 years old.
6. Nevertheless, I must refuse your kind offer.
7. His hope was that he could conquer Paris by June.
8. Although Jeannine feared flying, she took the 9:02 flight from Milwaukee, being already two days late for the convention.
9. This book concerns itself with language intended to deceive.
10. It is greatly feared by the crowd that an honest decision would not come from the referee.

RULE 7

Avoid Language That Draws Attention to Itself

You want your audience to follow your ideas, to follow the argument you're developing. Don't break their attention by using odd words or phrases that catch their eye. Try to avoid these distracting forms.

SEXIST LANGUAGE

If you want to persuade your audience, you can't use words that offend them. And today, many people—of both sexes—are turned off by terms they consider offensive to women. They don't like masculine forms of words used in references that can apply to either men or women. Here are some examples:

chair*man*
spokes*man*
man kind
man power
all *men* are created equal
everyone did *his* best
a doctor earns *his* money
separate the *men* from the *boys*
take it like a *man*

Don't use this kind of language.

Find synonyms. Instead of "chairman," "spokesman," and "manpower," write "chair," "advocate," and "work force." Instead of "mankind" and "all men," write "humanity" or "all people." When you come to "a doctor earns his money," go plural—"doctors earn their money." Rewriting "separate the men from the boys" and "take it like a man" can call for some creativity. Try "separate the winners from the losers" and "shape up."

Avoid "his or her" whenever you can; it always sounds artificial.

REPETITION

Repeating a word for emphasis can be effective ("government of the *people*, by the *people*, and for the *people*"), but often it distracts attention. Avoid repetition of sentence forms ("I went to see the accident. Fifteen people were there. Each told a different story."); of particular words ("Going to school is not going to be easy. If the going gets tough . . ."); and even of sounds ("The black boxer was bloody, beaten, and battered.")

Don't write three adjectives in a row. ("Suzanne is a lovely, energetic, red-haired girl.") This becomes a habit.

Time magazine once wrote of a New York police officer with problems. It said, "The people he works for have cases to break, headlines to make, careers at stake." *Time* can write that way occasionally, but you shouldn't.

DANGLING AND MISPLACED MODIFIERS

Make it clear what words your adjectives and adverbs are modifying. You do this by putting modifiers close to the words they refer to. Avoid examples like these:

When nine years old, my grandmother took me to the circus.

He was reported drowned *by the Coast Guard.*

I *only* shot two deer.

By knowing what you want to say, your essay will progress more easily.

Notice that these sentences are clear enough; in context, your reader would know what they mean. But such awkward and even humorous lines draw attention to themselves and away from your meaning.

ELABORATE FIGURES OF SPEECH

A mixed metaphor often produces irrelevant laughter. ("You're the salt of the earth and the light of the world, but you've thrown in the towel.") Even a meaningful figure of speech can be distracting. You could write, "Reagan steered the ship of state over treacherous seas; he was a star-crossed president." Such a sentence, however, stops your readers. Instead of following the rest of your ideas, they pause to interpret the metaphor.

You will, of course, want to use figures of speech in your prose. But don't let them obscure your meaning by being too dramatic:

Auto sales got a big *shot in the arm* in March from the *price slashes.*

Or pointless:

Lee Bailey wore a suit *the color of a thousand-dollar bill.*

Or redundant:

At the wedding, the champagne *flowed like wine.*

Or strange:

When God fights your battles, He *does it in spades.*

Keep your metaphors relatively simple.

FAULTY PARALLELISM

You should express coordinate ideas in similar form. You do this mainly to avoid awkward and distracting sentences. Clearly, "I was *alone, uncertain,* and *possessed of a considerable degree of fear"* is less emphatic than "I was *alone, uncertain,* and *afraid."* Consider these examples:

The teachers were burdened with *large classes, poor textbooks,* and *the necessity to cope with an incompetent principal.*
I love *seeing my daughter* and *to hear her voice.*
For a settlement, I will accept *a new stove* or *having my old stove repaired.*

Some sentences cannot be made parallel. You cannot change "Ted was tall, charming, and wore a blue hat" to "Ted was tall, charming, and blue-hatted." In such cases, write the first units so your reader doesn't expect the final one to be parallel. Write, "Ted was tall and charming; he always wore a blue hat."

AWKWARD CONSTRUCTIONS

Try to give your sentences the sound of talk, of natural speech. Don't break the continuity with intrusive passages.

I promised to, *if the expected raise came through,* take her to the Grand Hotel.
Her brother, *if we can believe local historians (and who can),* was a senator.

Any time your subject is six words away from your verb, you're probably in trouble.

Avoid noun clusters. Business and technical writers sometimes seek a kind of forceful compression and talk of a "once-in-a-lifetime, million-dollar career-decision dilemma." In doing so, they produce sentences a person has to read twice to understand. It is better to write in a natural speaking voice.

Don't seek a poetic style by inverting word order. Don't write, "Quiet was the night" or "The reason for suicide, we shall never know."

Keep it natural. Where it sounds all right, don't be afraid to begin a sentence with a conjunction or to end it with a preposition. ("And suddenly I realized where the money had come from.") And don't let some dated

English textbook persuade you to say, "This is we." You *know* how that sounds.

ABRUPT CHANGES IN TONE

Your tone is your personal voice, your way of saying things. This will vary with your audience and your subject. You talk one way to an intimate friend and another way to a visiting archbishop. You would use a formal style when writing a letter of application, and you might use colloquial—or even coarse—language in describing your fraternity house.

It is important to keep your tone appropriate and consistent. Don't jar your reader by describing a United Nations charter provision as a "crapheaded experiment." And don't call your fraternity dining room "a haven of calculated insouciance."

If your tone is light enough to permit contractions ("can't," "wouldn't"), use them right from the beginning of your essay. Don't begin to use them in the middle of a relatively formal paper.

Remember that any time your reader is more impressed by your writing than by your meaning, you have failed. No one can improve on the advice lexicographer Samuel Johnson gave in the eighteenth century. He said, "Read over your composition, and where ever you meet with a passage which you think is particularly fine, strike it out."

EXERCISES

Correct weaknesses in these sentences.

1. Saberhagen was pitching beautifully until the seventh inning, and then the fireworks fell in.
2. When reading late at night, the book should be held under a strong light.
3. Juan Perón's rise to power was a slow one. There were many pit stops.
4. We traveled for six days, and the car broke down. We hitchhiked to Laredo, and I took a job gardening. I had the car towed into town, but no one there could fix it.
5. I'm sorry about the story, Laurie. It's as bad as your messy essay. I warned you frequently to rewrite your work.
6. Mrs. L. Williamson earned her Ph.D studying DNA at M.I.T.
7. Cancer hit my family with full force this year, sending two of my aunts to the Mayo Clinic.
8. Professor Dendinger is giving a lecture tonight on student unrest in the faculty lounge.
9. Pamela was pretty, energetic, and carried a file of history notes.

10. The movie producers saw *Heaven's Gate* and immediately removed it from circulation. They could smell the handwriting on the wall.
11. Every engineer must get his work in on time.
12. Roman Catholics tend to be uptight about premarital sex. Baptists are more laid back.
13. When you go to the doctor, it costs you an arm and a leg.

RULE 8

Avoid Mechanical Errors

To write effectively, you need to know a number of elementary rules of usage. But there are some you don't have to know. An important truth is expressed in this story:

> A man went to his doctor and described his ailment. Clinching his right fist tightly, he complained, "It hurts me when I go like that." The doctor prescribed the remedy. He said, "Don't go like that."

The story tells you many things about writing: how to punctuate long and involved sentences, where to put apostrophes in unusual constructions, the way to use quotation marks within quotation marks, and how to spell "infrastructure." The advice: "Don't go like that."

The following rules on punctuation, abbreviation, number, and spelling should take you through most writing situations.

PUNCTUATION

Use Commas to Make Your Sentences Easier to Read

Textbooks routinely tell you to put a comma before the conjunction in a compound sentence ("Pam is a good student, but she cannot learn economics"); after introductory clauses ("When I went home, I saw my brother's car"); and before the *and* in elements in a series ("I bought a suit, three ties, and a sweater"). The problem is that many professional writers do not punctuate like this. Hence you may be confused.

A good rule to follow is this: Always use commas in these constructions *when the sentences are long.*

> Arthur had traveled 57 miles through the desert to meet the prince, and he knew that nothing in the world could make him turn back now.

283

When I saw that the young soldier was holding a gun on Martha and me, I became most obedient.

Suddenly Henry saw that the parable applied to him, that he must change his life, and that the time to start was now.

Similarly, you should always insert commas in these constructions *when there is a danger of misreading.* See the possible confusion in these sentences.

The fox ate three chickens and the rooster ran away.

When they finished eating cigarettes were distributed to the soldiers.

They stopped looking for Irene became tired.

If you use normal word order (a "talking" voice) and keep your sentences relatively short, you should have little difficulty with commas.

Use a Semicolon to Show That Two Independent Clauses Are Closely Related

Sometimes you want to indicate the particularly close relationship between two statements. Here you merge the statements into one sentence and connect them with a semicolon.

Her brother has been sick for years; now he is going to die.

To know her is to love her; to love her is a mistake.

This construction often occurs when the second statement contains "however," "therefore," "consequently," or "nevertheless."

The 747 was two hours late getting into O'Hare; consequently, he missed his connection to Reno.

Billy wanted to propose during final-exam week; he saw, however, that this would cause problems.

You can also use semicolons to separate the halves of a compound sentence or the units in a series when the separated passages have commas within them.

My boss, Patrick Henderson, was there; but before I could talk to him, he fell and broke his arm.

Among those present were Dr. Williams, an English professor; Mr. Rainey, head of the Presbyterian meeting; and Mrs. Milliken, president of the PTA.

If you have problems punctuating such long sentences, don't write them. It is possible to write effectively and never use a semicolon.

Use a Colon to Introduce a Unit

You use a colon to introduce something: an announcement, a clarification, or a formal series.

In May, the professor made his decision: he would leave the university.

The difference between fathers and sons used to be a simple one: fathers earned the money and sons spent it.

Molly excelled in active sports: tennis, swimming, badminton, and gymnastics.

When a complicated sentence follows a colon, the first word may be capitalized—especially if the sentence is long. ("In May, the professor made his decision: He would leave the university, move to Cleveland, and take a position with the Pater Academy.")

In general, you shouldn't use a colon except after a complete statement. Don't write, "Her favorites were: Andy Williams, Tim Conway, and Brack Weaver." Write, "These were her favorites: Andy Williams, Tim Conway, and Brack Weaver" or "Her favorites were Andy Williams, Tim Conway, and Brack Weaver."

It is permissible to use a colon after "the following." ("He did it for the following reasons: . . .") But when you can avoid it, don't write "the following" at all. It's not something you would *say*. (Write, "He did it for several reasons: . . ." or "He did it for these reasons: . . .")

Use an Exclamation Mark to Show Emphasis

Because adding an exclamation mark is an easy way to gain emphasis, you may be tempted to overuse it. Try to reserve it for "Wow!" or "Fire!" or some comparable outcry.

Never use two or more exclamation marks to seek additional emphasis. Never!

Use a Question Mark After a Direct Question

You will, of course, put a question mark after a question. But be sure it is a direct question.

What can they do in 12 minutes?

He asked, "Did you see Sylvia there?"

Don't use a question mark after an indirect question or after a question form that is really a polite command.

She asked if I knew the way to school.

Will you please hand in your blue books now.

Try not to use question marks to express uncertainty or irony.

John Wilcox was born in 1657(?) and died in 1760.

Those amateurs(?) made a very good living playing tennis.

These are weak constructions. Say instead that Wilcox was born "about 1657"; criticize "those so-called amateurs."

Use Hyphens to Form Compound Adjectives and to Divide Words at the End of a Line

Use a hyphen to join a compound adjective when it *precedes* a noun. You can write "the theory was out of date," or you can call it "an out-of-date theory." In such examples, the hyphens make your meaning clearer:

> a Monday-morning quarterback
> a dog-in-the-manger attitude
> a long-term investment
> germ-free research
> a 40-pound weight

Remember there is a crucial difference between "an Oriental-art expert" and "an Oriental art-expert."

Hyphens are particularly necessary to make sense of the noun clusters that occur in technical writing. An engineer may refer to "polyethylene coated milk carton stock smoothness test results." What does that mean? It becomes clearer with hyphens: "Polyethylene-coated milk-carton-stock smoothness-test results." But it is always best to keep the hyphens and rewrite the phrase: "The results of smoothness-tests conducted on polyethylene-coated milk-carton stock."

Use a hyphen to divide a word at the end of a line. But remember that you must divide the word between syllables ("when-ever," "in-tern," "pho-bia"). You should not divide a word so that only one letter appears on a line ("a-bout," "phobi-a"); and you should never separate a one-syllable word ("doubt," "called," "proved").

If you don't know where to divide a word, consult your dictionary. If you don't have a dictionary at hand, don't divide the word. Write it all on the next line (that's how the word processor does it).

Use Parentheses to Tuck in Extra Material

Parentheses are useful. They let you include additional information without breaking the continuity of your message. As these examples show, you can tuck in dates, examples, clarifications, and whatever else you want.

> Nicholas wrote *Corners of Adequacy* (1981) to answer charges made against his father.

> Dylan Thomas (1914–1953) was a Welsh poet and an alcoholic.

> Some foreign words (*Gemütlichkeit,* for example) can't be easily translated into English.

> His wife (he married about a year ago) was barely five feet tall.

Don't misuse parentheses. Don't use them to set off material that is necessary in the sentence.

> "Nice" (in the old sense of "discriminating") is seldom used any more.

And don't use parentheses so often that they call attention to themselves. If you use too many in your sentence (i.e., more than two or three), you can lose (or antagonize) your reader (especially if he or she is concerned about writing style).

Use a Dash Where You Need It

Like commas and parentheses, dashes can be used to set off an element. If you want to set off an idea that is closely related to your sentence, use commas. ("My father, who always loved fruit, died eating an orange.") To set off a unit that is less closely related, use dashes (or parentheses). ("My father—he would have been 39 next month—died eating an orange.")

Indeed, a dash—used in moderation—is acceptable punctuation in many circumstances.

Don't bet on Red Devil—he's a loser.

He thought about the situation for weeks—never able to get it all together.

It became clear that only one man could be the murderer—Dr. Dorrill.

The dash is a handy mark of punctuation. Just don't overuse it.

APOSTROPHES, QUOTATION MARKS, ITALICS, AND CAPITAL LETTERS

Use Apostrophes to Show Possession, to Indicate an Omission, and to Form Unusual Plurals

As a general rule, you show possession by adding 's to any singular or plural noun that does not end in *s*.

the dog's collar
the woman's hand
Michelle's trumpet
the men's boots

For nouns ending in *s,* you add either an 's or simply a final apostrophe. Punctuate it the way you say it; add the 's where you pronounce the extra syllable.

the girls' room
the Clardys' house
James's reign
the Harris's car

(In describing the Hiss-Chambers case, most commentators write of *Chambers'* accusations and *Hiss's* response.)

Sometimes you can avoid problems by not using apostrophes at all. The sentence "Being ready for auditors' inspection is part of the company's policy" can also be written "Being ready for auditor inspection is part of company policy."

In more complicated cases, it is better to avoid the issue. Don't speculate on how to punctuate "Charles and Bobs television," "Jesus parables," or "the last three months pay." Write "the television Charles and Bob bought last June," "the parables of Jesus," and "pay for the last three months."

You also use apostrophes to replace omitted letters or numbers in contractions ("I've," "couldn't," "the class of '45") and to form unusual plurals.

A formal essay is not full of and's.
Today Ph.D.'s can't get jobs.
I got one A and four C's.

Usage is changing here. Many respectable authors no longer use apostrophes in these constructions. They write of "Ph.D.s" and "Cs" and "4s."

If you wonder whether you need an apostrophe with proper names (like "Veterans Administration") or brand names (like "French's mustard"), there is no rule to help you. The correct form is whatever the organizations use. In a difficult case, you may have to consult magazines, advertisements, or letterheads; phone for information; or even drive to your shopping center.

You need to include brand names in your writing because such details give color and interest to your prose. But the names do bring apostrophe problems, especially if you're trying to champion "Miller" beer over "Stroh's" and "Coors." This following list gives some of the more common trade names and shows how complicated apostrophes can be.

Benson & Hedges cigarettes
Betty Crocker cake mix
Bride's magazine
Brooks Brothers clothes
Campbell's soup
Consumers' Research magazine
Diners Club
Dole pineapple
Elmer's glue
Folgers Coffee
Haagen-Dazs ice cream
Hertz rent-a-car
Hunt's ketchup
Jergen's lotion
Johnson wax
Kellogg's cereal
Ladies' Home Journal
L'eggs pantyhose
Levi's jeans
L'Oréal hair products

McDonald's hamburgers
Myers's rum
Oscar Mayer meats
O'Shaughnessys' whiskey
Parents magazine
Parsons' ammonia
Phillips 66 gasoline
Phillips' milk of magnesia
Planters peanuts
Pond's cold cream
Popeyes chicken
Reader's Digest
Sears
Stroh Light beer
Wards
Wilson sporting goods
Woolworth's
Wrigley's gum

Nobody knows all these forms. The difference between a good and a bad writer is that a good writer takes the trouble to check out such things.

Use Quotation Marks to Enclose the Exact Words of a Source, Titles of Short Works, a Word Used as a Word, and (Sometimes) Words Used in an Odd or Ironic Sense

Use quotation marks to enclose material taken directly from a book or person.

> In 1955, Aaron Mitchell wrote that the failure of democracy would derive from the "continuing derision of the mob."

> Reynolds said, "There is no reason to suspect murder."

But don't use quotation marks for a paraphrased statement.

> Reynolds said that there was no reason to suspect murder.

Put quotation marks around titles of shorter works: magazine articles, short stories, poems, artworks, and songs.

"A Rose for Emily"
Frost's "Mending Wall"
Picasso's "Three Musicians"
"White Christmas"

Titles of longer works are put in italics.

Use quotation marks to indicate you are using a word as a word rather than as a meaning.

I can never spell "surgeon."
"Cellar door" has a pleasant sound.

The usage here varies. Many writers use italics in such instances.

Finally, use quotation marks to show the odd or ironic use of a word.

> The Prime Minister lifted the first volume of the Encyclopaedia Britannica from his desk and "clobbered" his secretary.

> These "teachers" are a disgrace.

Try not to use quotation marks this way. When you can, just write the words.

Where do you put end punctuation when you are quoting? The rules are uncomplicated. Put periods and commas inside quotation marks—*always.* Put semicolons and colons outside. And put question marks and exclamation marks inside if they are part of the quotation; otherwise, put them outside. These examples show the pattern:

> "When you come," Nick said, "bring your boat."

> Molly had said, "I'll never forget you"; however, she forgot me in two weeks.

> Rebecca asked, "How long has this been going on?"

> Who wrote "the uncertain glory of an April day"?

> All I can say is "Wow!"

> I did too say "Monday"!

To show a quotation within a quotation, use single quotes.

> Jack complained, "I can never remember who wrote 'to be or not to be.' "

A better suggestion: Reconstruct your sentence so you don't have to put quotes within quotes.

> Jack said he could never remember who wrote "to be or not to be."

Use Italics for Titles of Longer Works, for Foreign Words, and (If You Have to) for Emphasis

You indicate *italic* type by underlining.

Use italics to mark titles of longer works: books, magazines, newspapers, TV shows, movies, plays, operas, and long poems, as well as the names of ships and airplanes. Consider these examples:

> Walker Percy's *Love in the Ruins*
> *Psychology Today*
> the *Washington Post*
> *Family Ties*
> *Star Wars*
> *General Hospital*
> *Carmen*

Paradise Lost
the *Titanic*
the space shuttle *Columbia*

Do not use italics or quotation marks for the Bible—or books of the Bible—or for famous documents like the Declaration of Independence or the Magna Charta.

A useful rule: Whenever you are in doubt whether to use quotation marks or italics to indicate a title, use italics.

Use italics for foreign words. But remember that many foreign words have now become part of the English language and do not need italics.

He was permitted to graduate *in absentia.*

Do not use clichés.

Kathy has a certain *élan,* but she acts like a prima donna.

What should you do about foreign words that have almost become English ("a priori," "coup d'état," "non sequitur")? When in doubt, don't italicize them.

Finally, you can use italics to give some word a special emphasis.

That's *precisely* the reason I am here.

Virginia didn't just act like a princess; she *was* a princess.

It is best not to use italics for emphasis, but sometimes you will want to.

Use Capital Letters with the Names of Specific Persons, Places, and Things

Knowing when to use a capital letter is not always easy, but the main rules are clear enough.

Capitalize the names of *people,* as well as their titles and words derived from their names; *places,* including countries (and national groups), states, counties, cities, and defined areas; *time units* like days of the week, months, and holidays; *religious entities; organizations,* their abbreviations and brand names; *historical events and documents; titles* of books, magazines, plays, poems, stories, movies, television shows, musical compositions, and art objects; and *structures* like buildings, monuments, airplanes, and ships. These examples show common usage:

Denise Cannon
Captain Kirk
Addison's disease
Shakespearean sonnet
Holland
General Motors
G.M.
Ovaltine

the Battle of Hastings
the Gettysburg Address
the Dutch
Europeans
the Riviera
California
Monroe County
Black River Falls
Tuesday
February
Memorial Day
God
Methodist
the Pope
the Archbishop of Canterbury
Genesis
the Magna Charta
Fear of Flying
Room 280
Epilogue
Newsweek
The Importance of Being Earnest
"The Killers"
"Mending Wall"
All My Children
"Margaritaville"
Beethoven's *Seventh*
the Empire State Building
the Washington Monument
the *Spirit of St. Louis*
the *Titanic*

You should have little problem with such examples.

Some words are capitalized in one context and not in another. They are capitalized when they name or relate to a specific entity. These instances show the distinction:

I knew Major Jones.
   He rose to the rank of major.

I saw Mother there.
   I will see my mother there.

I support the Democratic candidate.
   I believe in the democratic system.

I attend Spring Hill Baptist Church.
   We drove by a church.

I love the South.
We flew south.

This is the Sewanee River.
We swam in the river.

Turn to Chapter One.
Read the next chapter.

Any word is capitalized, of course, when it begins a sentence or when it begins a line of poetry.

Do not capitalize words like "spring" or "freshman."

Finally, there are the words that cause problems. Here the usage varies with educated writers, and you may have to make your own decision. Here are some guidelines.

A.M. or *a.m.* Either form is correct. Just be consistent.

Coke or *coke.* When a product is vastly popular, its trade name may become the name of the product itself and thus lose its capital letter. This has happened to "ping pong," "thermos bottle," "kleenex," and "band-aid." It is now happening to "Xerox" and "Musak." Right now, it is probably best to write "Coke" when you specifically mean Coca-Cola, and "coke" when you mean any other soft drink.

Roman numerals or *roman numerals.* Sometimes a national reference becomes part of a common word and no longer conveys a sense of nationality; it may then lose its capital letter. You wouldn't capitalize "dutch treat," "french fries," or "turkish towel." Some words, however, are still changing. At present, you can write either "Roman numeral" or "roman numeral."

Psychology or *psychology.* You should always use capital letters with specific courses ("Psychology 201") and lowercase letters with the area in general ("I used psychology to convince my mother"). Capital letters, however, are sometimes used to discuss academic courses in a general way. You could write, "The University has strong programs in Psychology and Sociology, but it is weak in Languages."

Black or *black.* This can be a sensitive area, and there is no firm convention to guide you. A decade ago, the word was routinely capitalized. Thereafter, many people capitalized it when referring specifically to race ("the Black heritage") but not when merely offering description ("the black boxer"). Currently, following the usage of noted black leaders, most writers no longer capitalize "black." But *Ebony* magazine still does. To help you decide, judge the likely response of your reader before you choose to capitalize (or not capitalize) "black." No usage is correct if it offends someone you don't want to offend.

Truth or *truth.* From time to time you will be tempted to capitalize a word to show special emphasis ("Tom and Laura used to be Close Friends") or to show irony ("Carl sees himself as a Very Important Person"). You may want to praise a poet or philosopher by stressing her or his "continuing pursuit of Truth." Try to avoid using capital letters this way.

Despite the complexity of some of these examples, most uses of capital letters follow a simple rule. You capitalize proper names—the names of specific persons, places, things, and events.

ABBREVIATIONS

Because your writing should be an extension of the way you talk, you would do well not to write abbreviations at all. You say words, not abbreviations. Clearly, you'd sound unusual talking like this:

We'll be there the second week in Feb.

In Madison, Wis., I worked for the Rogers Express Co.

This is the St., but I don't know the No.

However, many abbreviations *are* words. You would sound odd saying this:

I have to hurry to my Reserve Officers Training Corps class.

At two post meridiem, she drove her car into the Young Women's Christian Association parking lot.

The rule is to follow your own voice. Write the word where you say the word and the abbreviation where you say the abbreviation. Thus you can write either "television" or "TV," either "CIA" or "Central Intelligence Agency." Probably you would never write "Blvd.," "MSS.," "e.g.," "anno Domini," or "University of California at Los Angeles."

There are a few exceptions to this rule. Standard usage dictates that "Mr.," "Dr.," "Mrs.," "Rev.," and comparable abbreviations can be used before proper names. Similarly, it permits you to write "etc." instead of "et cetera." In general, however, you should not use abbreviations that are not also words (and use "etc." sparingly).

A common practice—especially in technical reports—is to write a complex term and then put the abbreviation after it in parentheses: "ethylenediaminetetraacetic acid (EDTA)." Once you do this, you can use the abbreviation throughout your document.

You use periods after most abbreviations "B.C.," "p.m.," "M.D."). Some abbreviations, however, are so much a part of the language that they have become words themselves. You don't need to punctuate these acronyms:

UNESCO
YMCA
UCLA
FBI
NBC-TV

If you have doubt in such cases, you probably don't need to use the periods.

In writing addresses, use the U.S. Postal Service abbreviations for the states. Over half of them are simply the first two letters of a one-word state name ("CA" for California) or the first letter of each word in a two-word name ("NY" for New York). Routinely, these are written without periods.

The following are the only states for which the USPO abbreviation is not the first two letters:

AK—Alaska
AZ—Arizona
CT—Connecticut
GA—Georgia
HI—Hawaii
IA—Iowa
KS—Kansas
KY—Kentucky
LA—Louisiana
ME—Maine
MD—Maryland
MN—Minnesota
MS—Mississippi
MO—Missouri
MT—Montana
NB—Nebraska
NV—Nevada
PA—Pennsylvania
TN—Tennessee
TX—Texas
VT—Vermont
VA—Virginia

You would do well to memorize this list. If you routinely use these abbreviations (instead of "Wisc." or "Ala." for example), your writing will look more professional.

NUMBERS

The question is whether to write out a number in words ("three hundred and sixty") or to use numerals ("360"). The usage varies.

A good general rule is to write out numbers when they are small (say, ten or under) and when there are only a few of them in your essay.

There were seven people in the plane, but only two of them were injured.

On all other occasions, use numerals.

You should always use numerals in dates, addresses, percentages, units of measurement, page numbers, and hours followed by "a.m." or "p.m." Use these forms:

December 15, 1976
15 December 1976
639 Azalea Road
16 percent
4.2 minutes
page 37
8:20 a.m.
14,987 students

When writing large numbers, remember that numerals look bigger than words. If you want to justify America's national debt, put it down as "$1.7 trillion." If you want to protest it, write "$1,700,000,000,000.00." When you want your readers to think a number is large, rub their nose in zeros.

If you have more than several numbers to express, use numerals throughout. But don't begin a sentence with a number.

SPELLING

The one best way to improve your spelling is to read extensively.

The best short-term way is to keep a dictionary at hand and to look up words you are in doubt about. You should have doubts when you face plainly difficult words, commonly misspelled words, and words you have had trouble with before.

You should never misspell "rhododendron," "bourgeoisie," "alumnae," and "hieroglyphic." You know these are difficult words; you should consult your dictionary and spell them right. (If you don't have a dictionary, consider using another word.)

Here are the most commonly misspelled words in English. Look over the list. If any one of the words looks unusual to you, circle it. Then try to memorize the correct spelling.

absence	apparent
accept	appreciate
accommodate	Arctic
achievement	athletic
acquainted	attendance
addressed	believe
advice	benefited
advise	Britain
AFFECT–EFFECT	bureau
aggravate	calendar
all right	capital
allusion	capitol
A LOT	category
amateur	cemetery
analyze	changeable
angle	choose
apology	colonel

committee

comparative

compliment

conceive

conscience

contemptible

cooperate

courteous

deceive

desert

dessert

dictionary

difference

dormitories

eighth

embarrass

environment

especially

exaggerate

excellence

existence

existential

fascinate

February

forehead

foreign

fourth

government

grammar

handkerchief

humorous

influence

initiate

intellectual

irrelevant

ITS–IT'S

let's

library

LOOSE–LOSE

mathematics

misspelled

ninth

occasion

occurrence

omitted

pamphlet

parallel

perform

permanence

personnel

persuade

playwright

politician

preferred

prejudice

PRINCIPAL–PRINCIPLE

pronunciation

prophecy–prophesy

psychology

questionnaire

RECEIVE

recommend

resemblance

reservoir

restaurant

rhythm

seize

sense

SEPARATE

sincerely

sophomore

stationery

subtle

syllable

temperament

tendency

than–then

THEIR–THERE

TO–TOO

truly

until

usually

Wednesday

were–where

whether

writing

Pay particular attention to the capitalized words on this list. They are the ones that cause the most trouble.

Finally, make your own list. Keep track of words you have misspelled on your essays or on early drafts of your papers. Learn these words. There is no excuse for misspelling "separate" twice.

EXERCISES

Punctuate these sentences. Insert commas, semicolons, colons, exclamation marks, question marks, periods, hyphens, and dashes where needed.

1. When the outfielder caught the second hand baseball he saw that the hide was torn
2. Charles Lackey the famous actor died on stage last week
3. He never complained he knew it would do no good
4. The nun asked me if I knew the way to Elm Street
5. During the summer I spent at least eleven thousand dollars on eighteenth century furniture
6. The price and I can't tell you how pleased I am to say it is only $4800.00
7. After six weeks of trying my brother finally learned to play hearts
8. The boy who won first prize a silver cup was our neighbor's son
9. I think *The Iceman Cometh* is the best American play written in this century and I absolutely refuse to teach it to this know nothing class
10. Would you kindly pay this bill by the first of the month
11. The wife got the stereo the television and the Thunderbird but the husband got to keep the dog
12. They insisted on waiting for Rex had never been there before
13. Then he wrote *Getting There from Here* 1955 a play about Nazi oppression
14. He studied seven year old children with personality problems

In these sentences, add apostrophes, quotation marks, italics, and capital letters when they are needed. Remove them where they are unnecessary.

15. My lawyer asked if I read georges mail. I said never in a million years.
16. My Mother loved to read the *Bible,* especially the story of Moses's flight from Egypt.
17. It became an idée fix: he was sure he could find a word to rhyme with jeffersonian.
18. Kate said my favorite song is Bette Davis Eyes.
19. They worked hard on it, but the boys buick was still a wreck.
20. I prefer Yeats poem that celebrates Ulysses courage.
21. His first poem winter dreams was published in the Atlantic Monthly.
22. The Professor asked In what year did Coleridge write Christobel?
23. No wonder he gets straight Cs in mathematics. His 7s all look like 1s.
24. The details of the coup d'état were published in last sundays New York Times.
25. The best song in hello dolly is hello dolly.

Correct any errors in abbreviation, numbers, and spelling that you find in these sentences.

26. The suspect lived at 901 West Blvd. for 6 months. He burglerized a jewelry store, taking stones valued at ten thousand three hundred and fifty dollars. He was indited and convicted, and his new adress is Rockway Prison, Temple City, Mich.
27. 15 percent of the students at the Massachusetts Institute of Technology do not plan to work in the U.S. Most want to get their doctor of philosophy degree, emigrate to Canada, and make fifty-five thousand a year working for the aircraft industry.
28. Your education already has cost me thirty-six hundred dollars. By the time you get you're M.A. in math, I'll be bankrup.
29. Citizens of Washington, District of columbia, love Pres. Reagan. 10,000 of them attended his speech praising the C.I.A. and it's dedicated Personell.
30. We watched TV from eleven ante meridiem until after midnight. No more than ten % of the shows, however, were worth watching.
31. It's an odd occurence. Whenever we hire new personell, they expect to recieve top wages.

FINAL
REMINDERS

"It's not creative unless it sells."
—Al Hampel

The eight rules for good writing should help to make you an effective writer. You may be further helped by these general recommendations.

CREDIT YOUR SOURCES

In general writing, you do not need formal scholarly documentation. But often you will want to specify your sources. Don't use footnotes for this; few people read them. Put information about your sources in your text. Any of these forms is acceptable.

> According to Genie Hamner (*Bald Windows Revisited,* 1985), man has endured . . .

> In *Bald Windows Revisited* (1985), Genie Hamner argues . . .

> In her article "Decision Making in Washington Transportation Systems" (*Fortune,* June 1977), Kathleen Kelly describes . . .

> According to *Time* (February 15, 1984), President Reagan has . . .

This kind of informal documentation need not be elaborate. But it is good to give your readers enough information to enable them to refer to the sources you used.

USE YOUR SPEAKING VOICE

Try to get your talking voice in your writing. You would never say, "This radio needed repair from the date of purchase"; you would say, "This radio hasn't worked since I bought it." In talking, you tend to use short sentences, plain words, active voice, and specific details. You don't worry about beginning a sentence with "and" or "but." You don't use words like "shall" or "secondly" or "societal." You rarely say words in a series, and you'd never say, "My reasons were the following" or "Quiet was the night."

Try to avoid long sentences full of paired or parallel constructions. Look at this example. (Italics and parentheses are added to show the pattern.)

Children need generous amounts of *affection, guidance,* and *discipline* in order to develop into *intellectually* and *emotionally* mature adults. Children (who feel *rejected* or *unloved*) or (who are given *inconsistent* or *ineffective* discipline) tend to develop *serious* and *long-lasting* psychic disorders, such as *schizophrenia, alcoholism, drug addiction,* and *psychopathic personality.*

This is *written* language; nobody talks like that. Don't write this kind of social science prose.

Trust your ear. What sounds like good spoken language—at a level suited to your subject and your audience—will be good writing. In this book, you have been advised to keep the same grammatical subject throughout a paragraph, to tuck words like "however" and "therefore" in the middle of sentences, and to avoid "there is" and "there are" forms. Whenever you think this advice would make your writing sound awkward, don't follow it.

A reminder about the importance of simple language appeared in a recent document addressed to practicing attorneys. It said, "When you begin your final summation to the jury, imagine that you're talking to 12 garbagemen who just stepped off the truck."

GET HELP FROM FRIENDS

In all likelihood, you will never be asked to write an essay or letter that someone else will read and judge immediately. Impromptu themes may be assigned in college classes, but in the outer world you will always have time for reflection and revision. As part of your revision, have a friend, spouse, teacher, secretary, or colleague read through your essay for clarity and correctness.

Correctness in matters of punctuation, italics, number, idiom, and spelling is important. A misspelled "their" or "it's" can make a well-informed paper seem illiterate. An omitted comma can make an important sentence almost unreadable. A "not" that is typed "now" can cause big trouble.

Proofread your work carefully. Authors report sad examples where "a bead" became "a bear"; "a political ideal" became "a political deal"; and "therapist" became "the rapist." A document from Senator Bill Bradley's office in 1984 assured readers that, under his tax plan, a family with a $15,000-a-year income would pay $16,000 in federal tax.

Of course, you should resort to a dictionary or an English handbook when you have difficulties. But serious errors may exist where you don't recognize a problem. If a particular piece of writing is important to you, ask a knowledgeable friend to look it over.

MAKE IT NEAT

Imagine you're applying for an executive position and are well qualified. Then you come to the interview chewing gum and wearing an old Batman sweatshirt. You're not going to get the job.

Similarly, if you write a first-rate letter of application and send it off in sloppy form (with bad handwriting, cross-outs, irregular margins, and on paper ripped from a spiral notebook), you won't get the job. If you send a messy manuscript to an editor, forget it. Major publishing houses and magazines now receive so many submissions that they immediately dismiss those that are sloppily presented.

This is a reasonable response. The form in which you send out your material says something important about you and about your attitude toward your reader and your subject matter. Make it look good.

Neatness counts.

REMEMBER YOUR AUDIENCE

Keep in mind the kind of audience you are writing for. It makes a difference.

There is a danger in assuming that your reader knows what you know. This can lead you to commit what Edgar Dale calls the "COIK fallacy" and to write casually about Ken Maynard or Riverside Drive or real time because these terms are clear and meaningful to you. They are *Clear Only If Known*.

Addressing an educated audience, you can use words like "arcane" and "protean." Speaking to Southerners, you might venture "tump" or "cattywampus." Writing to a specialized group (scholars or athletes or priests), you can refer to Romantic poetry, a trap play, or John 3:16. But don't use such terms with a general audience; they won't understand you. Don't say, "They can look it up." They won't.

A problem arises when you are forced to use an obscure term. Here, along with the word, you should include an explanation of what it means. But you don't want to sound preachy or condescending. ("I suppose I have to explain to you that a 'shard' is a piece of pottery.") In such instances, you have to give the explanation in an indirect way. See how necessary clarification is included in these sentences:

> As spokesmen for the Jewish establishment, the *Scribes* and *Pharisees* were immediately hostile to the message of Jesus.

> The *trap play* worked perfectly: The linebacker charged through the space we left open and was blocked out of the play.

> No one ever understood what motivated Lizzie Borden. She remains an *enigma*.

The burden is always on you to make sure your reader understands your message.

Writing school assignments, you may have to violate many of the rules in this book. Your sociology teacher may assign a term paper and ask for 25 pages of text and dozens of footnotes. Your education professor may ask for a 200-page dissertation full of technical jargon. When teachers want that, give it to them. But remember that, in the outside world, it's always better to keep things clear, short, and talky.

Remember that some audiences are sensitive in particular areas. Writing to a black reader, be careful about using words like "negro" and "boy." Don't tell Polish jokes in Milwaukee. Addressing women's groups, try not to say "chair*man*" or "spokes*man*" or to insist that "a surgeon really earns *his* money." Don't address a letter to *"Miss* Gloria Steinem" or to *"Ms.* Phyllis Schlafly."

Finally, recognize that some audiences cannot be reasoned with at all. When someone begins inquiring about your position on abortion or gun control, find a way to change the subject. Ask, "Did you see the Dolphins play last Sunday?"

REMEMBER YOUR PURPOSE

The motto of one New York advertising agency is "It's not creative unless it sells." There is a lot of truth in that. Keep in mind the purpose of your writing. (Remember what you're trying to "sell.")

The eight rules of good writing just given are based on the assumption that you want to communicate information, to make an argument in a clear, forthright manner. But this is not always the case.

Sometimes it's best to say nothing. Recent history provides examples of a number of individuals who spoke out forthrightly when they shouldn't have. When the Democratic national headquarters at the Watergate was burglarized, Republican officials denied involvement before anyone had accused them of anything. When pro-life and pro-choice delegates conflicted at the 1980 Democratic convention, President Carter volunteered a middle-of-the-road statement on abortion. Addressing stockholders of Bendix, Inc., the board chairman announced that the young lady working as vice president for strategic services had won the job on her merits, not because of her personal involvement with him. In each case, silence would have been a more effective argument.

President Reagan learned this lesson well. After a few early (and conflicting) statements about the Iran/contra affair, he resolutely kept quiet. He avoided reporters' questions and held few press conferences. Only when the congressional committees had finished their investigations did he comment on the outcome.

Any time you are involved in an adversarial situation—that is, when you are responding to police officers, lawyers, newspaper and television reporters, relatives who enjoy lawsuits, an ex-spouse, or an insurance adjustor—don't be too quick to frame an argument, volunteer information, or write clever letters. They may return to haunt you.

In argument, it is always a mistake to lie. But there are times when truth won't do you much good. Always consider the virtues of silence.

There are also situations where you will want to express yourself indirectly. You might want to spare the sensibilities of your reader ("By the time he was twenty, Dudley had demonstrated a range of sexual abnormalities"). You might want to discredit an enemy ("The initial response to his book seems to be fairly favorable") or to veil a threat ("If you pay this bill promptly, your credit rating will remain excellent"). Such situations are not uncommon.

Suppose, for example, you are obliged—in a school or business situation—to write on a subject you know little about. Now your purpose is to conceal your deficiency. You want to fill up a page, to sound fairly learned, and to avoid any specific assertion that could demonstrate your ignorance.

So you reverse many of the rules in this book. You will add "which" clauses and sprinkle modifiers (like "truly," "more or less," and "on the other hand") to ensure that no sentence has fewer than 25 words. You will write of *quintessential* issues and suggest that *procrustean* tactics are the *ne plus ultra* of folly. (This will obfuscate your message.) You will avoid proper names by using the passive voice ("a decision has been made that" or "word was received that"). You will write of vague entities like "business leaders," "the former," and "fair play." These can be described as "adequate" or "unfortunate"; but if you want to avoid even this minimal level of judgment, you can call them "impressive," "notable," "meaningful," or "significant." (These words don't mean good or bad or much of anything.)

Write all this in small print (either in cramped handwriting or typed with 12 letters to an inch) and put it in long block paragraphs. The final work will be meaningless and unreadable, but in particular situations—where you can't or don't want to communicate directly—this may be exactly the kind of writing you want.

Most of the time, however, you write to say something specific. You want to persuade your audience that marijuana should not be legalized, that gas rationing is essential, or that Sacco and Vanzetti were guilty. You want to describe your new boat. You want someone to give you a job, to buy mutual funds, or to settle that insurance claim in your favor. In such cases, the eight rules for good writing will help you get the effect you want.

Anything that thwarts the purpose of your writing (misspelling, wordiness, errors of fact, or even direct and meaningful statements) should be avoided. And anything that furthers your cause with a particular audience (even such features as expensive paper, folksy language, neat typing, and footnotes) should probably be used.

Good writing may not always win you the final effect you want—that job, that insurance adjustment, that sale. But it will do all that language can do to achieve that end.

BE SMART

Here is an important question: How many of these topics do you need to know about to be a persuasive writer?

alcohol and baldness
Antarctica
Apollo 13

biorhythms
the causes of homosexuality
competition in China
creationism in court
Freudian psychology
friendly fire
a googolplex
Halley's comet
the Patty Hearst trial
Lyndon Johnson
modern cryptography
monkeys and sign language
the power lunch
Rubik's Cube
Duke Snider
The Tales of Hoffmann
true believers
ufologists
zen tennis

The answer, of course, is all of them. Nothing is irrelevant in persuasion.

Remember that every book you read, every movie you attend, every town you visit, every TV show you see, and every relative and bartender you talk to is giving you material you can use in writing.

The lessons in this book will be useful. But you also have to read a lot of books, talk to all kinds of people, and stay alert if you want to be a first-rate persuader. It's a worthy goal.

Go for it.

APPENDIXES

EXERCISES FOR REVIEW

How valid are these arguments? Identify examples of induction, deduction, expert testimony, semantic argument, analogy, argument in a circle, post hoc, begging the question, argumentum ad hominem, extension, the either-or fallacy, and statistical manipulation.

1. "Crisco'll do you proud every time."—Loretta Lynn

2. Of course you favor federal aid to education. You're a teacher. You stand to profit on the deal.

3. "Our cheese is like a good love affair."—Rondele

4. A Tampax poll found that 22 percent of the respondents thought menstrual pain is psychological.

5. "Each ring is Solid 14 Karat Gold; the Stone is guaranteed to be a Genuine 17-faceted, .25 pt. Diamond, anchored in a Solid Sterling Silver setting."—Ad for a ring costing $9.95

6. Asking Britain to desert Northern Ireland is like asking the United States to give up Texas.

7. "Seven out of ten Americans cheat on their income tax."—Professor R. Van Dyke Ellington III

8. I never knew an Auburn football player who could read or write beyond the eighth-grade level.

9. In March 1987, Peter Holm filed an alimony suit against actress Joan Collins, giving a breakdown of his estimated $960,000-a-year expenses.

10. *Poll Question:* Should the United States continue providing support to people in Central America who are fighting for their independence from Soviet-backed Marxists? Yes _____ No _____

11. One Pass: "The fastest way to touch down almost anywhere in the world free."—John Elway

12. It takes 400,000,000 years to make a bourbon as good as Old Grand-dad.

13. We should not ban laetrile just because it didn't prove effective in laboratory tests. Pretty soon, they'll want to ban holy water.

14. In 1985, Ann Landers polled her female readers. She asked, "Would you be content to be held close and treated tenderly, and forget about 'the act'?" Over 90,000 women wrote in, and nearly three-quarters of them said "Yes." I guess that proves something.

15. "There is no proof that sugar confectionary gives rise to dental cavities."—*Association Internationale des Fabricants de Confiserie*

16. I don't believe drugs, alcohol, and gambling are addicting habits. Pretty soon they'll claim that Billy Cannon had a counterfeiting sickness and Jesse James had a train-robbing sickness.

17. Why not a 45-mph speed limit? Wouldn't that save more lives?

18. Over 60,000 doctors recommend Preparation H, according to a survey of doctors who recommend OTC products.

19. Snickers—"The official snack food of the 23rd Olympiad."

20. *The Husband* (a novel by Sol Stein): "The dilemma of countervailing demands on the sensual man of good will . . . rich and true . . . modulated with a respectful reserve . . . handled with hardly a false note."—*New York Times*

21. "For every rape that is reported, from 9 to 23 are not."—Southwest Radio Church

22. "When the fish-pond that was a meadow shall be mowed.
Sagittarius being in the ascendant,
Plagues, famines, death by the military hand,
The century approaches renewal."
(Prophecy of Nostradamus)

23. What did you do to deserve Beefeater?

24. If your name is Makay, Malloy, or Murray, beware of drink. According to John Gary, director of the Council for Alcoholism in Glasgow, Scotland, people whose last names begin with the letter "M" may be eight times more prone to alcoholism than others.

25. *Miss MacIntosh, My Darling* by Marguerite Young: "What we behold is a mammoth epic, a massive fable, a picaresque journey, a Faustian quest, and a work of stunning magnitude and beauty . . . some of the richest, most expressive, most original and exhaustively revealing passages of prose that this writer has experienced in a long time."—William Goyen, *New York Times*

26. We scientists working on astrological data expect to be criticized. We know that Newton and Einstein were ridiculed in the past.

27. All this effort to register and confiscate handguns will not help us fight crime. Violence rises from the souls of men.

28. It's not safe to walk on the streets of New York City. I'm glad I live in Cleveland.

29. "Ever wonder why kids instinctively go for soft drinks in bottles?"—Glass Container Manufacturers Institute

30. *Miss MacIntosh, My Darling* by Marguerite Young: "In fact, this is an outrageously bad book, written by an author with very little of interest to say and very little skill in saying it . . . wholly unreadable."—*Time*

31. "Thank You for Not Speaking in Tongues"—a placard distributed by the Tobacco Institute.

32. If you smoke, please try Carlton.

33. "Smaller-chested women can't make it."—Donna Rice

34. A clever magician can always perform tricks, but a genuine psychic can sometimes produce paranormal effects and sometimes not. Uri Geller produced no effects at all when he appeared on the *Tonight Show*. He is a true psychic.

35. On a typical television poll, an early-evening newscaster poses a yes or no question, asking viewers to phone one number to vote "yes" and another to vote "no." Then a late-evening newscaster reports the results—for example, that 72 percent oppose socialized medicine.

36. If secular humanism is a religion, what isn't?

37. What I want to know is who masterminded the plot to impeach Richard Nixon.

38. How about a law to compel anybody publically lobbying against abortion to have a baby, or two or three, or else go to jail. Same thing.

39. "One Out of Two Marriages Has Serious Sex Problems"—*National Enquirer* headline.

40. Dial. The most effective deodorant soap you can buy.

41. Do you approve of pornographic and obscene classroom textbooks being used under the guise of sex education? Yes _____ No _____

42. I disagree with Abby Van Buren when she says no woman should be forced to have a baby she doesn't want. A lot of people have parents they don't like, but we don't let them go around murdering their fathers and mothers.

43. "Will $1 million be enough to solve your problems for the moment?"—Poll question from an ad offering "Your Golden Astral Number"

44. Athletics teach our young people how to play the game of life.

45. Naval ROTC should be abolished. I'm learning nothing from it.

46. Read *One in Twenty* by Bryan Magee—an adult, plainly written study of male and female homosexuality.

47. Burt Reynolds told the truth when he declared, "I'm not suffering from AIDS." That's the conclusion of Charles McQuiston, who used the truth-detecting Psychological Stress Evaluator (PSE) to analyze Burt's answers to probing questions from Rona Barrett on *Entertainment Tonight* (8/16/85).

48. Everyone knows that America's greatest threat is not from foreign powers, but from within.

49. We can't get family counseling from a priest. What does he know of marriage?

50. Homosexuality is no illness. It is a widespread practice, like vegetarianism. The homosexual has a sexual preference for members of the same sex; a vegetarian has an alimentary preference for noncarnivorous foods. In neither case is there any impairment of function or any disease.

51. All I say is that a baby shouldn't have to suffer for a mother's convenience.

52. "You wouldn't sweep dust under the rug—so don't put clean food in a dirty oven!"—Easy-Off Oven Cleaner

53. Gordon's—Largest selling gin in England, America, the world.

54. To All Citizens and Taxpayers. QUESTION: "Do you favor our city and county governments devoting more of our present tax money to police protection?" Yes _____ No _____

55. "A good club soda is like a good woman: it won't quit on you."—Canada Dry

56. How can you deny the power of the moon's influence? The oceans have tides; women have periods; and emergency rooms are full on moonlit nights.

57. Did Pennzoil have a binding contract with Getty Oil that was violated by the Texaco takeover? "Pennzoil relied on written documents signed by holders of a majority of Getty stock."—Terry Hemeyer, Vice President of Public Affairs, Pennzoil. "The fact is, no one ever—to this date—has been able to produce a contract or any written document containing the signature of any representative of

Getty Oil Company agreeing to an arrangement with Pennzoil."—a Texaco statement

58. I can't decide which Supreme Cutlery setting to buy. I'm choosing between Ron de Vu, Bamboo, Arctic, Marchese, Colonnade, Ionic, and Snowflake.

59. *Playboy* estimated that, among news reporters and editors working on the Bakker and Hart sex scandals, the number who were faithful to their wives was 0.00001 percent.

60. "Cougar is like nobody else's car."

61. Ford LTD—"700% Quieter."

62. A new study interviewed more than 500 men and women who had recently suffered cardiac crises and compared them to over 500 healthy men and women. Out of the sick group, over half said they were nonreligious. But in the healthy group, only one in five were nonreligious. This proves religious men and women suffer significantly fewer heart attacks than people who don't believe in God or go to church regularly.

63. A Polish household is suffering the pranks of a poltergeist. It throws furniture and lamps around the rooms and is ruining the family silverware. As evidence of the truth of this story, a tabloid published the picture of a young girl holding a fork that was bent in the middle.

64. "When Nazi atrocities took place, Kurt Waldheim was 100 miles away—or at law school, or recovering from a foot injury. Or he was merely an Army translator, a desk jockey who knew nothing, heard nothing, saw nothing. That's how Waldheim has presented his wartime experience."—*Newsweek*

65. "In recent years there has been a growing insistence on the part of many people that the Church re-think its classical position on homosexuality and homosexual relationships. Theologians, philosophers, psychologists and pastors of many denominations, including the Catholic Church, are beginning to believe and state openly that, under certain conditions, a homosexual can express her/his sexuality (including genital sex) in a way that does not necessarily separate him/her from either the Christian community or the love of God which includes (for some) full participation of the Eucharist by the reception of Holy Communion."—DIGNITY/USA

66. I have found an interesting pattern in U.S. history that tells me we're due for a war. The WWI soldier fathered a son in 1918; that boy was 23 in 1941, just the right age to fight a war. The WWII soldier had a son in 1945; the child was 20 years old in 1965, just right to fight at the start of the Vietnam War. The Korean War soldier had a child in

1951; the boy was 18 in 1969 when the Vietnam War was at its height. You see the pattern? Now consider a child fathered in the middle of the Vietnam War; he's 19 today. And he's ready.

67. "Why is it that Joe Biden is the first in his family ever to go to a university? . . . Is it because our fathers and mothers were not bright? Those same people who read poetry and wrote poetry and taught me how to sing verse? Is it because they didn't work hard? My ancestors who worked in the coal mines of northeast Pennsylvania and would come up after twelve hours and play football for four hours?"—Senator Biden at the Iowa State Fair, August 23, 1987

68. Dialogue overheard at a school board meeting:

    WIFE: I see that David Millar, who used to be the Marlboro man on television, just died of emphysema.

    HUSBAND: How old was he?

    WIFE: Eighty-one. Some people never learn.

SUBJECTS FOR ARGUMENTATIVE ESSAYS

abortion
Abscam
absurd drama
Academy Awards
acid rain
ACT tests
acupuncture
adoption
adoption by unmarried people
Afghanistan
aging population
aging process
AIDS
AIDS testing
airline accidents
air-traffic controllers
alcoholism
Alice in Wonderland
alimony
All My Children
Alzheimer's disease
ambassador to the Vatican
American vs. foreign cars
amnesty
animal research
anorexia
Antichrist
antitrust laws
aphrodisiacs
arthritis cures
assassinations
astrology
athletes' salaries
Atlantis
automobile as status symbol

Baby Faye
bad teachers
the Bakke discrimination case
Jim and Tammy Bakker
balance of payments
baldness cures
the Baldus Study
banning cigarette ads
banning textbooks
the new baseball and old records
battered wives
bending spoons with mind power
Bermuda Triangle
the Bible
Senator Joseph Biden's plagiarism
the big bang theory
Bigfoot
bikini bathing suits
bilingual education
biofeedback
biorhythms
Larry Bird vs. Magic Johnson
birth control
birth order
black power
body building
Ivan Boesky
bombing abortion clinics
Robert Bork
bottled water
boxing
Boy George
brainwashing
Break of Dawn, the garbage tugboat
breast enlargement

William F. Buckley, Jr.
bulimia
busing

Cabbage Patch dolls
cabinet appointments
cable TV
Cambodia
cancer cures
capital punishment
capital punishment for minors
carbon dating
Joanna Carson's alimony
Johnny Carson
Catholic schools
Edgar Cayce
celibacy for priests
censorship
chain letters
Challenger explosion
chemotherapy
Chernobyl
child abuse
childhood obesity
child pornography
child support
children of divorce
chiropractors
Christmas
the Chyrsler bailout
CIA
cigarette ads
cigarette smoke and the nonsmoker
circumcision
circumstantial evidence
civil rights for immigrants
civil rights for men
civil rights for women
cloning
coaches' salaries
cocaine
cohabitation
Coke vs. Pepsi
college football #1
color analysis
colorization of black-and-white
    movies

comic books
communist threat
competency tests for teachers
computer games
computer revolution
condoms
the Condon Report
consenting adults
conspiracy theories
corporate raiders
correct English
cosmetic surgery
Cosmopolitan
crack
creationism
credit cards
credit unions
cryonics
Cuba
cults
cultural illiteracy
cybernetics

Dale Carnegie courses
date rape
dating services
day-care centers
daylight saving time
Dear Abby
death wish
declining educational standards
Deep Throat
defense attorneys
the defense budget
deficit spending
John DeLorean
the designated hitter
designer-label clothes
dialects
dieting
diet pills
Dirty Harry
dirty jokes
disarmament
divorce
Jeane Dixon
docudramas

dog racing
dousing
the draft
Michael Dukakis
Dungeons and Dragons

Easter Island
ecology
ecumenism
effects of a full moon
Electoral College
electronic surveillance
El Salvador
Elvis
endangered species
energy sources
English classes
English teachers
entrapment
entropy
ERA
escort services
ESP
euthanasia
evolution
exorcism

faith healing
Falkland Islands
Jerry Falwell
family life
father-daughter relationships
Fatima
fear of flying
fear of public speaking
federal aid to cities
Geraldine Ferraro
the fetus
high-fiber diets
fire walking
the First Amendment
fluoridation
Larry Flynt
Jane Fonda
food stamps
football
foreign aid

foreign languages
four-letter words
Michael J. Fox
freeway shoot-outs
frozen embryos
Freud
Friday the 13th
Friday the 13th

the G spot
gambling
Uri Geller
genetic engineering
ghosts
Glasnost
glossolalia
concepts of God
Bernhard Goetz
gold standard
good manners
good taste
Dwight Gooden
Mikhail Gorbachev
grade inflation
grammar
Grenada invasion
gun control

hackers
Jessica Hahn
Halley's comet
handwriting analysis
Gary Hart
health foods
health insurance
Patty Hearst
heaven
hell
heredity
herpes
heterosexuality
high school dropouts
the Hillside Strangler
John Hinckley
homes for the elderly
homosexuality
homosexual teachers

Lee Iacocca
illegal aliens
income tax
infant formula
inflation
insanity plea
insecticide manufacturing
insider trading
instinct
intensive-care nurses
interest rates
International Paper strikes
interracial marriages
intuition
IQ tests
Iran-Iraq war
Iran/contra investigation
Ireland
Islamic fundamentalism
Israeli wars
the IUD

Jack the Ripper
Japanese technology
Japanese trade competition
jargon
Jesus
jogging
junk food
the Jupiter Effect
"Just say no"

KAL Flight 007
Erica Kane
Senator Edward Kennedy
Kennedy assassination
Kennedy family
Ayatollah Khomeini
killer bees
Korea
Ku Klux Klan

labor unions
laetrile
Lake Wobegon
The Last Temptation of Christ
latchkey children

leash laws
legal insanity
John Lennon
lesbians
Jerry Lee Lewis
libel laws
Libya
lie detectors
life in space
life-support machinery
literature classes
living alone
lobbyists
Loch Ness monster
lockouts
Lourdes miracles
love
lucky numbers

Mafia
man as animal
Manhattan Project
marijuana fields
marijuana laws
Dan Marino vs. Dan Fouts
marriage
McCarren-Walter immigration law
medical costs
medical school quotas
Medjugorje
Ed Meese
menopause
the Mexican debt
military secrets
miniskirts
minoxidil
miracles
Miss America pageants
the missing link
Miss Manners
modern architecture
modern art
modernism in the churches
Marilyn Monroe's death
Moonies
modern morality
personal morality of candidates

Moral Majority
mother-daughter relationships
Mothers Against Drunk Driving
movie critics
mud wrestling
Muslims
mutual funds

names
names of automobiles
national debt
National Enquirer
National Security Council
NATO
natural law
Nazi party
NCAA Proposition #48
NCAA rules for football
negative ions
neutron bomb
the new Coke
new morality
NFL strike
Nicaragua
1984
Noah's Ark
No-Doz
noise pollution
non-English-speaking American
    citizens
no pass–no play
Colonel Oliver North
Nostradamus
NRA
nuclear power
nuclear waste
nudism
numerology

offtrack betting
oil prices
one-night stands
one-parent families
OPEC
opera
organ transplants
orthodontists

overachievers
overweight people
ozone depletion

palimony
Panama Canal
papal infallibility
paranoia
parent-child relationships
paroles and pardons
PATCO
patriotism
People for the American Way
perpetual motion
Persian Gulf escort missions
PG-13 movies
phobias
teaching phonetics
memorizing pi to 100 places
T. Boone Pickens
pit bulls
pitchers carrying emory boards
placebos
plagiarism
Platoon
plausible deniability
Playboy
PLO
PMS
Admiral Poindexter
Poland
Polish jokes
political action committees
political appointments
polling
pollution
poltergeists
polyunsaturates
the Pope's visit to America
population problems
pornography
posing for a centerfold
POSSLQ
postage rates
the power lunch
prayer in public school
preservation of historic buildings

presidents elected in years ending
  in "0"
Princess Di
prison reform
prisoners' rights
privacy-invading reporters
private schools
prophets
prostitution
psychic surgery
psychoanalysis
psychobiology
psychokinesis
psychometry
PTL
public radio
public smoking laws
the public's right to know
public television
punk rock
purgatory
pyramid power

quack doctors
Dan Quayle's military record
Karen Quinlan

race and capital punishment
racial superiority
raunch radio
readers vs. nonreaders
Reaganomics
Reagan the communicator
recruiting top athletes
redshirting freshmen athletes
reincarnation
required courses in college
résumés
retarded children
retirement age
Book of Revelation
reverse discrimination
rights of the accused
rights of the victim
right to bear arms
right-to-work laws
ritual

Joan Rivers
rock music
Rolex watches—real and imitation
Roman Catholicism
romantic love
Rosenberg trial
royal jelly
Rubik's cube
running as a religious experience

saccharin
Sacco-Vanzetti
sadism
safe sex
salt as a health threat
Santa Claus
Satan worship
mandatory seat belt laws
secular humanism
selling college degrees
sensitivity sessions
sentencing criminals
sex and politics
sex-change operations
sex education
sex in advertising
sexism in language
sexual equality
sexual harassment
Shakespeare
shock treatments
shoplifting
the Shroud of Turin
Sikhs
single parents
666
skyjacking
slander
sleeping pills
smoking and health
soap operas
social science classes
Social Security
solar power
Solidarity
Son of Sam
Son-of-Sam laws

South Africa
Southern Methodist University
    football
space creatures
space program
speed limits
speed reading
spelling reform
standard English
U.S.S. Stark incident
Star Wars weaponry
state lotteries
states' rights
Statue of Liberty
statute of limitations
statutory rape
steroids
Stonehenge
strikes
student illiteracy
student rights
subway crime
sugar
suicide
summer movies
Super Bowl
superconductivity
Supreme Court
surfers
surrogate mothers
Jimmy Swaggart
swingers

tabloid advertisements
tabloids
a talisman
talking animals
tarot cards
tax reform
tax relief for private schools
tax shelters
teacher strikes
teenage pregnancies
teen suicides
telephone company breakup
telephone rates
televangelism

television commercials
television game shows
television ratings
television watching
term papers for sale
territoriality
terrorism
test-tube babies
Texaco vs. Pennzoil
third parties
Third World
Third World loans
Three Mile Island
salvaging the *Titanic*
tithing
the tobacco industry
the top 40
Toshiba
the Tower Report
toxic wastes
tranquilizers
transactional analysis
translating the Bible
translation
trickle-down economics
Trilateral Commission
true believers
Ted Turner

UFOs
unauthorized biographies
unemployment compensation
unions
United Nations
unlisted phone numbers
U.S. companies leaving South
    Africa
U.S. savings bonds
USSR
utopias

vampires
Vatican II
VCRs
vegetarianism
Velikovsky
veterans' rights

the vice presidency
victimless crimes
Vietnam
vigilante justice
apparitions of the Virgin Mary
virginity
vitamin C
vitamin E
vocabulary
Klaus von Bülow
Erich von Däniken
vote fraud

Kurt Waldheim
want-ad dating
Watergate
weaponry
weddings
weight lifting
welfare
Dr. Ruth Westheimer
General Westmoreland

whiskey ads
Vanna White
white-collar crime
wife swapping
wilderness preservation
witchcraft
woman's role
women candidates
worker protection laws
workers' compensation
professional wrestling

brand X
X-rated movies

yoga
yuppies

zero-zero missile option
Zionism
zombies
zoning laws

GOOD WORDS, BAD WORDS, AND PERSUASIVE WORDS

GOOD WORDS

In these lists, the word on the left may be perfectly correct on a particular occasion. Most of the time, however, the word on the right is clearer, more direct, and less clichéd. Write with these everyday words.

achieve	do, make
advise	tell
and/or	and, or
approximately	about
attempt	try
benefit	help
commence	start, begin
conclude	end, stop
contribute	give
deem	think
demonstrate	prove, show
depart	leave
desire	want
disclose	tell, show
discontinue	stop
due to the fact that	because
e.g.	for example
enumerate	count
exhibit	show
expertise	skill, ability
the fact that	(omit)
failed to	didn't
finalize	complete, finish
for a period of	for
the following	these
Gentlemen:	Dear Mr. Clark:
has the ability to	can

herein	here
i.e.	that is
in addition	besides, too
in order to	to
in regard to	about
in the event that	if
in the near future	soon, Wednesday
invaluable	valuable
it is noted that	(omit)
last but not least	last, finally
the latter	(repeat the noun)
locate	find
the majority	most
the month of	(omit)
my intention is	I will
notify	let me know
not later than	by
not only . . . but also	and
numerous	many, two dozen
observe	see
obtain	get
parameters	limits
perform	do
personnel	people, Molly and Steve
possess	own, have
prepared	ready
prioritize	rank
prior to	before
probability	chance
provided that	if
purchase	buy
regarding	about
relative to	about
remainder	rest
remuneration	pay, payment, $50
request	ask
secondly	second
shall	will
similar to	like
state	say
state-of-the-art	latest
submit	give, send
sufficient	enough
terminate	end, stop
therefore	so
touch base with	talk to
transmit	send

truly	(omit)
until such time as	until
utilize	use
very	(omit)
viable	practical, workable
whenever	when
whether or not	whether
with reference to	about
with the exception of	except
the writer	I, me

BAD WORDS

These words will weaken any argument you try to write. They make you seem vague, illiterate, clichéd, angry, insensitive, and pretentious. Avoid them.

the above	keratectomy
am of the opinion that	logistical
and . . . was no exception	mesdames
asinine	mode
bastard	Mr./Ms.
bimonthly	N.B.
cognizant	Negro
crap	nitty-gritty
datum	per
Dear Sir:	peruse
down through the ages	Polack
enclosed please find	quintessential
falsa lectio	Sear's
first and foremost	separate
goddam	shall
his or her	societal
his hope was that	some people
history teaches us	stated
idiotic	syndrome
ignorant	thirdly
in lieu of	Tom J.
in life	To Whom It May Concern
in relation to	truly
in view of the fact that	viz.
let's face it	

PERSUASIVE WORDS

After you have made your best case, you can enhance it by using some of the favorite words of professional persuaders. These ten are particularly useful.

Claim—This is a word to apply to your adversary. You *say* (*insist, prove*) vitamin C cures a cold; he *claims* it does not.

Clearly—You can use this to begin any sentence: "Clearly, John Hinckley was framed."

Colonel—People with titles love to hear them. Use them often. Work *Colonel* (or *Mayor* or *Doctor*) into every fourth sentence.

Fair—This, of course, describes your position. Because it cannot be specifically defined, *fair* (like *positive, realistic, just,* and *reasonable*) is a key word in politics and commerce.

Integrity—Write of "personal integrity," "family integrity," "professional integrity," "instructional integrity," etc. The terms mean pretty much what you want them to mean.

Mature—This sounds like a compliment, but you can use the word to suggest your opponent is old and his ideas are obsolete. Other double-edged words are *young, sensitive, free-spirited, witty,* and *intellectual.*

Notable—This is an important word when you have to evaluate something and don't want to call it either good or bad. *Notable* (like *meaningful* and *significant*) means almost nothing.

Relatively—This is a useful qualifying word. You can talk of "a relatively short time" or a "relatively inexpensive product." This can mean anything.

Superficial—Because your opponent's argument cannot treat every conceivable detail involved in the issue, you can always dismiss it as *superficial.* Another good adjective is *unrealistic.*

Unfortunate—This is the perfect word when you have to say something negative and don't want to assign blame. You can speak of "an unfortunate decision," "an unfortunate incident," or "an unfortunate choice of words."

These persuasive words won't win an argument for you unless you have your facts, authorities, and statistics in order. But they can help.

WRITING A BUSINESS LETTER

Probably the main form in which you will write argumentative prose is the business letter. You'll want to convince someone you deserve a job or a raise. You'll want to make a sale or get a larger insurance adjustment. You'll want to pacify someone who has written an angry letter to you.

Business letters take a fairly standard form.

Read the two letters on the following pages. Both are effective examples of business writing.

Now consider the seven parts of a business letter as illustrated in these examples.

THE RETURN ADDRESS

Notice that this is omitted if you write on letterhead stationery. Always use the two-letter U.S. Postal Service abbreviations to indicate the state (see page 295). And always include the ZIP Code, in its five- or nine-digit form.

THE DATE

Either of the two forms shown is acceptable. Just be consistent.

INSIDE ADDRESS

If your letter is at all important, send it to someone by name.

On pedestrian matters, you can address "Subscription Office" or "Catalog Department," but never address anyone simply as "Personnel Manager," "Chairman," "Publisher," or "President." If you make careful use of your library and your telephone, you can get the name of the person you want to write to.

If you raise the question, you will probably find that friends of yours (either through their jobs or their parents) have access to a WATS line. This can be immensely useful when you have to write to the personnel manager at Philip Morris or to Mr./Ms. Leslie Rogers.

862 Callaway Drive
Medford, WI 54101
15 December 1986

Mr. George Blazdon, President
Silver Shadow Pen Company
1515 Vermont Street
New York, NY 10009

Dear Mr. Blazdon:

Last year I was given one of your Silver Shadow pens (Model 364A) for an anniversary present. I love its looks, but I'm having trouble with it. I wonder if you can help me.

After a few months, the point no longer came out when I twisted the pen. I had kept all the original papers and followed the warranty instructions. I sent the pen to your Atlanta office, and they fixed it and returned it.

At the same time, because I can't seem to find refills locally, I sent for half a dozen red-ink refills. You sent them, along with a bill for $18. This seemed pretty steep to me, but I had no choice if I wanted to use the pen, so I paid it.

Now the pen is broken again. When I twist it, the point doesn't come up. I phoned your Atlanta office to see if the pen was under warranty. They said it wasn't, but that they'd be able to fix it for $10.75.

I'm not sure I should have to pay this amount. Either the pen was defective in the first place or repaired poorly in the second place. Should I have to pay for your mistakes?

I'm not a consumer crank, Mr. Blazdon, but I don't think this situation is fair. What do you advise me to do?

Sincerely,

Thomas Ridgeway
Thomas Ridgeway

SILVER SHADOW PEN COMPANY
1515 Vermont Street
New York, NY 10009

December 21, 1986

Mr. Thomas Ridgeway
862 Callaway Drive
Medford, WI 54101

Dear Mr. Ridgeway:

Thank you for your letter of December 15. I'm pleased you like our Silver Shadow pen, and I'm sorry it's giving you trouble. I hope this information helps you.

Your pen is indeed out of warranty. You have used it for over a year. I'm sure you understand that we cannot offer a lifetime guarantee with our products.

You can purchase refills for your pen at Redman's Office Supplies in Medford or at Quality Stationery Company (3201 West Lane) when you drive into Milwaukee. The refills do cost $3 each, but these are jumbo-cartridges containing 2½ times as much ink as usual ballpoint refills.

May I offer a compromise, Mr. Ridgeway? You don't want to be without your Silver Shadow pen, and we can't afford dissatisfied customers. I suggest you have the pen repaired in Atlanta and pay the $10.75. Thereafter, if the same problem recurs, send it to me and it will be repaired free of charge.

I hope you have a pleasant holiday.

Sincerely,

George Blazdon
President

GB:itm

THE SALUTATION

Write "Dear Mr. [or *Mrs.* or *Miss* or *Ms.*] Name." This is always followed by a colon. Writing to a friend, you can use "Dear Bill," but this too must be followed by a colon.

Try never to write "Dear Sir," "Dear Madam," "Dear Sir or Madam," or "Gentlemen." These forms, which prevailed some years ago, now seem offensively vague and sexist. If you don't have a name to write to, address a title. You can get by with "Dear Editor" or "Dear Manager." You might try "Dear Red Cross Representative." But it's always best to take that extra time and find a name.

THE BODY OF THE LETTER

Usually a letter has at least three paragraphs, with the first acting as introduction and the last as conclusion.

The first paragraph should be short and should define the issue. Your reader should never have to move on into the second paragraph to know what your letter is about. If you are answering someone, it is a good idea to begin, "Thank you for your letter of July 17." Giving the date lets the reader check the appropriate file and refer to the original message. Saying "thank you" sets a positive tone.

Through the body of your letter, use the forms that mark good writing anywhere. Use short sentences, plain words, active voice, specific detail, and so on. Sound like yourself talking. At all costs, avoid "letterese," the clichés of business writing:

am cognizant of

are in receipt of

as per your request

at your earliest convenience

do not hesitate to

enclosed herewith

thanking you in advance

under separate cover

with reference to

Work particularly hard to avoid the words "advise," "acknowledge," "per," and "transmit."

Keep your language plain. Remember you're not answering a letter. You're answering a person.

It is often effective to repeat the name of the person you're writing to. ("I am genuinely sorry, Mr. Metcalf, but there is no possibility we can give you a loan at this time.") Save this for important sentences.

Never express anger in a business letter. You can feel it, but don't write it.

The concluding paragraph should be short, general, affirmative, and personal. Even if your letter expressed criticism and unhappy truths, finish on as positive a note as you can. ("I'm sorry I have to give you this bad news, Bill. But I know you can handle it.") And even if you've been speaking for your company and using "we" throughout your letter, use an "I" in the conclusion.

THE COMPLIMENTARY CLOSE

A simple "Sincerely" or "Sincerely yours" is probably best. If you're writing a governor or an archbishop (or some other official), use "Respectfully."

THE SIGNATURE

Always type your name beneath your signature. And put your title (if you have one) on the line below that.

If someone else types your letter, the typist indicates the fact by putting the author's initials, then his or her own, on the left margin below the signature.

A final word about the overall appearance of your letter. Keep it on one page if at all possible. Center the writing so that the white space around it seems to frame it. Double-space between paragraphs, and begin a new paragraph often. All this will make your letter more inviting to read.

In general, your business letter will be most effective and persuasive if it is short, informed, natural-sounding, and marked by unrelenting goodwill.

You can learn a good deal from the following document. It was published in the *ABCA Bulletin* under the title "The World's Worst Business Letter: A Candidate."

PROCANE INSURANCE
5111 Lincoln Avenue
Mobile, Al.

Feb. 22nd. '84

Anarda Bonding Co.
1601 Mirrabel St.
Locksley, Ala.

Attn: Mrs. Sally Hall

RE: Truckstop Ranch
Mobile, Alab.
QAP #958-254-8927A

Dear Madam,

Per our telephone conversation this date, please be advised of the fact that we are no longer insurance carrier for the above referenced company. We regret we cannot, pursuant to your request, transmit information in regard to the record of said account in the area of fire-protection viability. Enclosed please find documentation in reference to the referenced account. Be advised that during the month of January and subsequently, the above company and/or its personnel did not honor our requests to forward data describing interface between manpower and fire-protection hardware capability. Again, permit me to remind you that insurance was carried on the subject company only for the period from June 1973 to December 1982. Transition data relative to specific transactions prior to termination date are indeed available. In the event that you can utilize aforementioned documentation (in lieu of requested information), do not hesitate to contact me at your earliest convenience or at any point in time thereafter. Feel free to direct your request to the writer (at the above address), and we shall transmit required data by return mail.

Thanking you in advance, I remain

Very cordially yours,

J.D.R. McMann, Jr.
Thomas D. R. McMann, Jr.
B.S.C.

TDRMc/MH/jp

MAKING A SPEECH

Another form in which you may have to make an argument is the platform speech. You may have to speak before a civic club, a church organization, a union group, or a town meeting to plead a cause. You may want to champion a school tax referendum. You may favor a particular candidate for office. You may want to sell some product or service or idea. You're going to have to stand before an audience and talk.

It is not very difficult to make an effective speech if you're willing to give necessary time to the job.

PREPARING THE SPEECH

Most of the suggestions about good writing apply equally to effective speaking.

In writing your speech, you need to choose a subject that lends itself to detail, get specific facts, narrow the topic, organize the material, and express it in an everyday talking voice. But a speech is different from a written essay in several ways.

Here are rules to remember:

1. *Make Your Organization Clear.* Because your audience has no paragraphs to look at, you have to be more specific in announcing the outline of your talk. You might say, "I have three reasons for opposing the construction of a nuclear power station in Arneson," then follow this with markers "first," "second," "third," and "in conclusion." (This would be mechanically offensive in an essay, but it helps a speech.) You can get the same effect with a time reference ("Every day last week, I thought of a new reason to vote for the school tax") or with an extended metaphor ("If the Patman Bill was a used car, you wouldn't buy it"). Your audience should always have a general idea of how far along your speech is and where it's going.

2. *Make Your Introduction Short and Provocative.* Don't dawdle around. Greet the audience. ("Good morning, gentlemen.") Add a note or two of personal goodwill. ("I'm pleased to be here with you today.") Announce your subject. ("I want to talk to you about our new

turbines.") And make it interesting. ("They're giving us strange problems, and they're costing us money.") Then get on with your talk.

In platform speaking, you have about 30 seconds in which to "catch" your audience. If you don't win them then, you probably won't do it at all.

Don't begin your speech with a joke unless it is particularly related to your topic. The isolated opening joke is now almost a cliché. It suggests the speaker has a frivolous attitude toward the audience and toward the subject. You can, of course, offer any amount of relevant humor as your speech moves on. But don't begin, "Being here today reminds me of the story of the monkey and the artichoke." Spare your audience that.

3. *Refer to the Audience and the Local Scene.* Don't talk *to* an audience, talk *with* an audience. Address them as "ladies and gentlemen" or "gentlemen" or "friends" or "you" or "we" (meaning you and them together). Speak to them courteously and directly. ("Please follow this now; this is important.") Refer to people in attendance. ("Tom here can tell you what happened.") Never let your talk become so abstract and objective that it loses this "you and me" note.

Refer to what is going on around you. Mention other features of the occasion: the preceding speaker, the orchestra, the meal, the awards ceremony, a special guest, whatever. Use immediate objects as illustrative props. ("It's like this saltshaker; if you don't shake it, nothing comes out.") Mention things everyone is concerned with at the moment (Christmas shopping, unusual weather, inflation, a hit movie, an election, the Super Bowl, etc.). These things tie you and your audience together.

4. *Don't Let Your Speech Get Boring.* You know how quickly you lose interest in a sermon on "faith" or a graduation speech on "responsibility." When a book becomes dull, you can skim a few paragraphs and get on to the more compelling material. When a speech gets dull, it just drones on, and you begin counting the bricks in the wall.

In preparing your talk, therefore, it is important to narrow your subject to a richly specific topic. Then talk about real things and use proper names. Say "for instance" and "for example" a lot.

Don't give long lists of names, facts, or statistics. These might be acceptable in an essay, but they're deadly in a speech. Put such material on a chart or a handout sheet; then refer to it.

Always edit your speech to make sure you're not saying the same thing over and over.

Unless you are singularly eloquent, don't let your speech go beyond 20 minutes. And shorter is better.

5. *Keep Your Concluding Remarks Brief.* When you've said what you have to say, quit. Never pad out a speech in order to fill up some artificial time frame.

Have a memorable final line. Don't trail away with a dull sentence. ("That's pretty much what I have to say about those turbines.") Make it more dramatic: "We *can* make these turbines work, but it won't be easy. We have to begin now."

GETTING READY FOR THE EVENT

Besides preparing an effective speech, you can do other things ahead of time to ensure the success of your talk.

1. *Rehearse.* Practice your speech. Give it over and over. Talk to anyone who will listen to you: your spouse, your brother, your golden retriever, anybody. If you plan to use an opaque projector or flip charts or a pointer, practice with these props.

    You might even have a dress rehearsal. Invite over a few friends, ply them with food and drink, and make them listen to your speech. Pay attention to their response.

2. *Make Yourself Look Good.* In a speech, everything counts. The audience is looking at you and making judgments. While a writer is happily invisible, a speaker has to be concerned about appearance. A man might want to buy a new suit; certainly he should have a haircut and shoeshine. A woman should never wear clothes or accessories that draw attention away from her message. For an important occasion, you might want to lose 5 or 10 pounds.

    These things may sound trivial. But they're all part of the total impression you make. They are part of the persuasive process.

3. *Arrange the Setting.* It's important to get to the speaking site at least a half an hour early and look over the scene.

    Make necessary arrangements. Check the lighting. Make sure there is a speaker's stand, and adjust it to the right height. See that the microphone works. Get props and audio-visuals ready. Make sure that you have a blackboard (or a flip chart) if you need one and that there is something to write with. Sometimes you can even arrange the chairs so the audience will sit where you want them.

    None of these things happens by itself. Many speaking problems can be avoided if you take time to check things out.

DELIVERING THE SPEECH

Finally, the moment arrives. It's time to stand up and give that talk. This counsel should help you.

1. *Stand Up Straight.* Never give a speech or deliver a report sitting down. And when you stand, don't slouch in an effort to look supercasual.

    Face the front. Don't make extended references to a blackboard or flip chart and talk with your back to the audience. When pointing to things on a chart, stand directly beside it so you're still facing your listeners.

2. *Control Any Nervousness.* The best way to avoid nervousness is to prepare a first-rate speech and rehearse it a lot. If you're confident you can do a good job, you'll have less reason to be nervous.

Even if you are terribly uncomfortable, don't mention your nervousness to your audience. Unless you are shaking severely or falling down, they won't know you're nervous. It doesn't show.

3. *Sound Natural.* Don't be intimidated by a formal term like "platform speaking." You've been talking to people all your life. Speaking in public isn't that much different.

Always sound like one human being talking to another human being. In a formal speech, you'll want to talk somewhat slower than you usually do and, if you don't have a microphone, you'll have to speak somewhat louder. Nevertheless, keep your tone as conversational as the audience, subject, and occasion will allow.

Don't use any models. Don't try to sound like Dan Rather or Ronald Reagan or Barbara Walters. Sound like yourself.

Never sound (or look) like you're reading a document to the audience.

4. *Speak from Notes or from a Full Text.* Once you have written your speech and rehearsed it and rehearsed it, you can decide whether you want to bring the full text to the speaking event or whether you want to rely on outlined notes. Either way has advantages.

Never memorize your speech; you could black out in the middle of it. Because you want to look like you're "just talking" with the audience, however, you shouldn't keep looking down to card notes or sheets of paper you're holding in your hand.

If you are comfortable speaking extemporaneously, simply put an outline of your speech on the speaker's stand and resort to that when necessary. This allows you to sound conversational and to talk more directly at your audience. (You can also put an outline of your talk on a chart and have it up front for the audience to look at. The lines on the chart are, in fact, your notes.) Not being tied down to the exact words of a written-out text, you're freer to modify your talk so it meets the responses of the audience.

If you need the security of the full text, you must take care that it's written to sound like natural speech and that it doesn't freeze you so you can't change your lines when necessary. With a text, however, you can be sure you're giving your talk exactly as you wrote it.

In general, it is better to speak from notes than from a full text.

5. *Use Whatever Gestures Come Naturally.* As you address your audience, don't simply stand motionless, and don't move in any way that feels artificial to you.

Remember you have many props to occupy your hands. You have

the speaker's stand, your pockets, a pointer, chalk, your glasses, and so on. Feel free to use these.

Be careful of mannerisms that draw attention away from your message. Don't fiddle with a paper clip or with your hair or tie. Don't click your ballpoint pen. Watch out for those collapsible pointers. Almost invariably speakers begin opening and closing them and look like they're playing an accordian.

If you can relax and get involved with what you're saying, whatever gestures come naturally will be fine.

6. *Use Common Sense.* Sometimes all your preparations aren't enough. Before or during your speech, unexpected things happen. Here you have to make commonsense adjustments.

If you are one of a series of speakers and those preceding you have all run overtime, what do you do? If you rise at 5:10 P.M. and have a 15-minute speech to deliver, forget it. Say one or two ingratiating things, then sit down.

If your speaker's stand faces directly forward and all the audience is sitting on one side, turn the stand a few degrees.

If you discover your audience is more conservative or more hostile than you expected, skip over material they are likely to find offensive.

If you are in the middle of your speech and find you are taking longer than you should, paraphrase a long section into a sentence or two. If you find you're going to end sooner than you expected, don't pad. Let the talk end.

If you misspeak, correct yourself. ("Excuse me, I should have said *Henry* Kissinger.") Then go on.

Watch your audience. You can tell when they are with you and following your argument. You can also tell when they start to shift around in their chairs and the glaze comes over their eyes. If you feel you're losing them, you may want to insert a quick, stimulating line ("Now get this; this is important" or "Anyone who doesn't understand this next point is going to lose money"). You may also need to end your speech as soon as possible. An audience always wakes up when it hears, "In conclusion."

If during your speech a water glass tips over or your manuscript falls on the floor, mention the accident ("I'm sorry about that"), then get back to your talk. Don't panic or giggle or make jokes about the event; that just draws attention away from your subject.

These are just a few of the unexpected things that can happen during a speech. When they happen to you, make the necessary adjustments. Use your common sense.

The best way to give a good speech is to have a good speech. When you stand before your audience, all that time you took researching and writing and rehearsing your talk will pay off handsomely.